MEDITERRANEAN SEA

ALGIERS -- Dellys
Rouïba
Bougie
Bizerte
Blida • Bouira Akbou
Djidjelli Philippeville Bone
TUNIS
• Beni Mansour
Duzerville
Médéa
Sétif
Guelma
Aumale
Constantine
Boghari
Tocqueville
Le Khroubs
Souk Sakhiet Sidi Youssef
Ahras Le Kef
Ouenza
Sousse
Batna
• Bou Saâda
Khenchela Tebessa
• El Kantara
M'chounèche Arris
Kasserine
Djelfa • Biskra • Guentis
Sfax
• Messad
Gafsa
Laghouat
Gabès
• Hassi R'mel
TUNISIA
• Touggourt

RIA
• Guerrara
• Ghardaia

. Ouargla
• Hassi Messaoud

• Fort Lallemand

Colea

| 100 | 200 | 300 |
Miles

Edjeleh

THE ALGERIAN PROBLEM

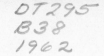

THE ALGERIAN PROBLEM

by

EDWARD BEHR

Prospero:
        ¨Abhorred slave,
Which any print of goodness wilt not take,
Being capable of all ill! I pitied thee,
Took pains to make thee speak, taught thee each hour
One thing or other. . . .

Caliban:
You taught me language; and my profit on't
Is, I know how to curse.

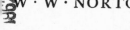

W · W · NORTON & COMPANY · INC · *New York*

CONTENTS

ACKNOWLEDGEMENTS

THE longer a journalist reports on a given situation, the more he becomes convinced that he knows nothing and that his judgements, and reports, are partial, over-simplified and even inane. I first started reporting North African events in 1951, and in 1952 was given my first assignment in Tunisia, then in the throes of nationalist agitation for independence. From then until 1955, as one of Reuter's staff correspondents in Paris, I reported consistently on the changing North African scene. After a brief spell as an international civil servant, I returned to North Africa, for *Time*, in early 1957, and have spent all my time on the North African "beat" since.

As a correspondent I tried—as I have attempted in this book—to strive towards total impartiality. In a subject as complex and as baffling it is inevitable that there should be gaps caused by insufficient knowledge (a foreign correspondent cannot pretend to the leisured certitude of an academic historian) and perhaps by unconscious prejudice. The book may offend some of my numerous French friends in Algeria and in France, as well as my numerous Algerian friends in Algeria and Tunisia. All generalisations are dangerous, and—in this complicated, indeed almost insoluble Algerian problem—I may be charged with the reporter's habitual failings: partiality, over-simplification and superficiality.

All I can say in my defence is that this book was honestly written, and its conclusions honestly arrived at with the reporter's limited and ephemeral baggage of facts and experience. I have drawn heavily, as far as the historical side goes, on the authors listed in the bibliography; my special thanks are due to the valuable advice of my old friends and fellow-reporters of the Algerian scene: to the Royal Institute of International Affairs, for permission to use material I wrote in "Foreign Affairs"; to Stan Karnow, of *Time*; to Thomas Brady, of the *New York Times*; to Jean Daniel, of *l'Express*; to Serge Bromberger and Jean-François Chauvel, of *Le Figaro*; to Guy Sitbon, of *Le Monde*; to Robert Soulé and Henri de Turenne, of *France-Soir*; and to countless others,

Acknowledgements

including the long-suffering French officials of the French Government's "*Délégation Générale en Algérie*"; last but not least, I should like to thank the editors of *Time* and *Life* who, by granting me a completely free hand to report the North African situation, enabled me to write this book.

INTRODUCTION

ONE summer's day in 1957, a rebel band of some 250 men broke through the Algerian frontier defences from Tunisia and lay up on the hills adjoining the old Roman town of Tébessa. They were spotted and surrounded. After an unsuccessful attempt to break through a strong paratrooper and Foreign Legion cordon, they fought it out to the death: one French lieutenant described how, in the final assault (in which eight paratroopers, including an officer, were killed) some of the rebels rose from their hiding-places and, their ammunition gone, smashed their rifles against the rocky hillside. Only eight rebels survived.

"Psychological warfare" was already the order of the day, and after the battle, the unit's Psychological Warfare Officer, a French air force captain, decided to parade the captives through the streets of Tébessa, "to show them" as he put it "that we won". The prisoners were sat on stools in open army trucks, with recorded military music blaring, and the grisly procession wound its way through the Roman ruins and the narrow streets of Tébessa, to the disgust of the few French and foreign journalists present. The Moslems of Tébessa reacted in a way which must have infuriated the Psychological Warfare expert: they behaved as though the hideous procession before them was a figment of the imagination. They neither looked at it nor deliberately away from it. Sipping mint tea at café tables, haggling over small purchases in squalid shops, they carried on as though nothing unusual was happening. The ignored French troops escorting the prisoners felt, and looked, foolish.

The instinctive reaction of the inhabitants of Tébessa goes far to explain why Algeria, conquered and colonised successively by the Phoenicians, the Romans, the Arabs, the Spaniards, the Turks and the French, has constantly eluded its conquerors. "If they [the Berbers] have adapted themselves to the material domination of alien peoples whose outward characteristics they submitted to rapidly but superficially," wrote Professor Charles-André Julien,[1] "they kept themselves free from any alien moral imprint." Through an elusive compound of pride, clannishness and passivity, both Arabs and Berbers of North Africa, and particularly of Algeria, have consistently behaved, under stress, in sturdy nonconformist fashion: forcibly converted to Islam, they incorporated in their new religion many of the animist features of their pre-Islamic faith, to the dismay of orthodox Islamic religious leaders; in constant rebellion against centralised Roman, and later Turkish, rule, they fought bureaucracy and orthodoxy with equal tenacity. Specifically Algerian non-conformist sects, such as the Kharijites (later known as the Mozabites) came into being partly because they satisfied a deep puritanical need amongst a desperately poor, excessively clannish people, partly because theirs was their only way of protesting against a remote, alien and corrupt government. Although it is perfectly true that the concept of an "Algerian nation" did not exist until after 1945, this does not mean that the inhabitants of Algeria were the docile tributaries of their more advanced, more organised Phoenician, Roman, Spanish, Turkish or French colonisers. They were often on the brink of rebellion, even though their very clannishness and inter-clan rivalry made them rather vulnerable opponents. Their history, since the beginning of recorded time, has been an intermittent struggle against the successive waves of foreigners who settled on the Barbary coast.

[1] *L'Afrique du Nord en Marche.*

CHAPTER ONE

THE FRENCH CONQUEST

CAPTURED from Spain by Barbarossa and placed under Turkish suzerainty in the sixteenth century, the hillside port of "El-Djezaïr" (later known as Algiers) grew into a noisy, prosperous motley anthill of Arabs, Berbers, Turkish merchants, half-breeds, Negroes, Jewish merchants and moneylenders, Sicilian adventurers and a changing population of Christian slaves. Miguel Cervantès lived in bondage there for five years. Turkish authority was represented by the Dey, the Turkish Sultan's representative, and his Janissaries were supposed to control the territory from the Moroccan to the Tunisian borders. In fact, real Turkish authority hardly existed: in typical Berber fashion, mountain and desert tribes and brotherhoods lived by their own laws and customs, and attempts to tame them provoked insurrection. Between 1815 and 1825, the Dey's army was constantly at war with Flissa, Titteri, Derkawa and Babor tribesmen, as well as waging intermittent war with Tunisia and trying to defeat the Moroccan-aided desert Tijaniya and Aïn Mahdi sects.

At regular intervals, throughout the eighteenth century, various maritime European powers, declaring themselves fed up with Algerian piracy—the city's most lucrative activity—considered going to war. But in the end, Europe found it was cheaper to pay protection. It was not until late in the 1820s that France seriously considered Algiers as a possible trans-Mediterranean prize, and her excuse for an invasion expedition grew out of a complicated commercial tangle.

During the French Revolution and after Napoleon's rise to power, the French had bought cereals from the Dey of Algiers, and even borrowed money from him to pay for wheat purchases. Eventually, however, Algiers' wheat commerce had passed into the hands of two Jewish merchants from Leghorn, Joseph Bacri and Neftali Busnach, who had built up a commercial empire that spread from Marseilles to Alexandria, even controlling the financial life of the Dey himself: Talleyrand, while he was Minister of Foreign Affairs for Napoleon, was an invaluable (and presumably suitably rewarded) ally. "I could count on nothing," wrote Jacob Bacri, the partner's agent in Paris to his brother in 1803, "if I did not have the lame one in my hand."

As the years passed, France's debt to Bacri and Busnach increased, and knowing France could not pay, they did not press for reimbursement. By the time France was ready to repay its debts—after scaling down the figure considerably—Bacri and Busnach had themselves fallen on bad days, and themselves owed money to the current Dey of Algiers, Khodja Husein, who insisted on direct and immediate settlement by France. He wrote to Paris and pestered the French Consul in Algiers, Pierre Deval, but got nowhere. Perhaps Talleyrand's influence was still strong, for Bacri and Busnach did receive some payment, while all the Dey got was a note from the French Government protesting against the piratical habits of Algiers' seamen. On April 29, 1827, Deval called to present his compliments to the Dey on the occasion of a Moslem feast. Husein asked him point-blank why he had not received his money. "My Government will not reply, it is useless to write," Deval answered. Husein flew into a rage, hitting Deval repeatedly with his ivory, peacock-feather flywhisk, and shouting: "You are a wicked, faithless, idol-worshipping rascal."

It was three days before Deval sat down to report that he had been insulted, and it took France three years to avenge the fly-whisk incident. There was no popular enthusiasm in France for an Algiers expedition. France was in the throes of a reaction against military glory—the logical result of Napoleon's conquests, which had bled the country white in manpower and ended in disaster. Most Frenchmen felt that France should concentrate on winning back the regions lost at the Congress of Vienna, and the deputy Hippolyte Passy summed up their feelings in the National Assembly: "I would gladly," he said, "exchange Algiers for the most wretched hole on the Rhine." But Charles X's régime was weak, unpopular, its people unhappy; and it was not the first, nor the last Government to seek an outlet in some "foreign adventure". As Charles X's Defence Minister, the Comte de Clermont-Tonnerre, wrote to the king, "the turbulent and light-hearted spirit of our Nation needs, from time to time, some unusual circumstance that will occupy its over-ardent imagination." The romantic intellectuals backed anything that smacked of exoticism, and the commercial-minded believed—wrongly, as it turned out—that Algeria would yield oils, silks, cotton, indigo, tobacco, sugar and coffee. In May 1830, a French force of some 35,000 men and 600 ships prepared to sail from Toulon.

Less than three weeks later, Algiers fell, the Dey's Treasury— which more than covered the cost of the expedition—was in French hands, and France's military commander, Marshal Louis de Bourmont, predicted that "the whole kingdom of Algeria will probably surrender within fifteen days, without our having to fire another shot". Bourmont's optimism was symptomatic of French ignorance about Algeria. If Turkish power had been real, continued conquest—after the fall of Algiers—would have been an easy matter. But the tribes of the interior were no more prepared to accept French rule than they had been to submit to Ottoman rule. Three weeks after the capture of Algiers, a French reconnaissance column to Blida, about thirty miles south, was attacked and almost wiped out.

Moslem "holy men" began preaching the "jihad", or Holy War, against the infidel invaders. The July Revolution, which overthrew Charles X, was not known in Algeria until August 11, but led to the return to Algiers of part of the expeditionary force which had captured Bône and Oran and the tricolour flag was run up in Algiers instead of the white fleurs-de-lys. Army elements at first wondered whether Charles X's successor might not order the withdrawal of the French army from Algeria, but from across the Mediterranean came the news that Algiers, at least, would remain in French hands. Meanwhile the French expeditionary force added blunder to blunder; a column to Médéa—in

1831—was forced to retreat back to Algiers; the Janissaries, after putting up a half-hearted fight, had volunteered in a body to serve under French command against the independent-minded tribes of the interior, but the French High Command insisted on shipping them back to Turkey; a docile group of "collaborating" Jewish and Moorish merchants was nominated to local Algiers municipal office, and indulged in gross corruption, under the protection of the French army; a Moorish merchant was installed, also under French protection, as Bey of Titteri and the Arabs and Berbers in the city revolted and forced him to flight; the Duc de Rovigo, Napoleon's former Chief of Police, violated basic Moslem precepts of hospitality by executing two Moslem notables for whose safety he had made himself personally responsible.

Soon the divided, anarchical Moslem tribesmen had found themselves an uncontested leader against the French: in 1832, at Mascara, they united behind Abd-el-Kader, the handsome, intelligent, warlike son of an influential local "marabout". He was barely twenty-five, but had made the pilgrimage to Mecca, and his first proclamation to his followers contained a breath of modern nationalist spirit. He assumed leadership, he said, as "the means of uniting the great body of Moslems, of preventing dissensions among them, of according general security to all dwellers in the land, of checking all acts of lawlessness on the part of the disorderly against the well-disposed, and of driving back and overcoming the enemy who has invaded our country . . ."

Abd-el-Kader had definite plans for organising Algeria, and by 1833, with roughly two-thirds of the country under his control, he tried to create a kind of federal government based on tribal equality, with regular troops, assisted by locally enrolled militiamen. He set up Khalifaliks (provinces) with a hierarchy of officials to collect taxes, dispense justice and stock granaries for the Emir's armies. He failed because Algerian tribesmen were willing enough to fight a jihad against the French, but were no more willing to submit to Abd-el-Kader's organised, centralised government than they had been to previous Turkish and Roman rulers. No gifted Moslem subordinate emerged to remove some of the administrative burdens from Abd-el-Kader's own shoulders, and he failed, though through no fault of his own, in his pledge to end lawlessness. Algeria's tribal structure had not broken down sufficiently to sustain a feeling of national homogeneity. Independence, to most Algerians, meant a return to the former loose-knit or rival clannish communities, not the creation of a modern state.

Abd-el-Kader's inability to achieve national unity was matched by French indecision over Algeria. Eventually a working committee, the "Commission d'Alger" decided not only against withdrawal from Algiers but in favour of a moderate extension of the conquest, though at the least possible cost, together with the establishment of an increased joint civilian and military staff to administer the country.

At the same time the French Government was eager to end the war, and believed that a deal could be made with Abd-el-Kader, whereby the latter would recognise the sovereignty of France in Africa in return for French protection. A peace treaty was signed, on February 26, 1834, which gave satisfaction to both parties mainly because it was discovered, after signature, that substantial differences existed between the French and Arabic texts. Abd-el-Kader used French offers to start peace talks as an additional means of increasing his prestige with the Algerians. After the cease-fire—which was to last little more than a year—he used his ambiguous position as a nominal French vassal to consolidate his power still further and to increase his personal fortune through a virtual commercial monopoly. By June 1835, Abd-el-Kader was once more at war with France, and the de Broglie Cabinet sent to Algeria the first in a long line of "energetic" French generals, Count Bernard Clauzel, who proceeded to act on his own initiative, obtaining post-facto approval from Paris. Clauzel embarked on a succession of punitive columns to Mascara and Tlemcen, which succeeded only in antagonising the Moslem population against the French army. Clauzel's reports to his Government wildly exaggerated the importance of his operations, but they found an enthusiastic supporter in Thiers, who came to power in February 1836. Thiers obtained Parliament's consent for an increased war effort in Algeria, and a recognition of the principle of "total occupation". But Thiers fell in September and the new Molé Government, while incapable of deciding to make peace, did not want to commit any more troops to Algeria. It turned a deaf ear to Clauzel's appeals for an expeditionary force of 30,000 fighting men, hoping he would resign of his own accord. Instead, Clauzel marched on Constantine with insufficient troops and was thoroughly defeated: his column encountered snowstorms and nearly froze to death; the supply system broke down and troops were constantly harassed by guerillas. The Molé Cabinet was not deceived by Clauzel's reports that the expedition had become "by an extraordinary turn of events" no more than an unsuccessful reconnaissance partrol, and dismissed him. The new Governor of Algeria, Damremont, was instructed to make peace with Abd-el-Kader and with Ahmed Bey, the leader of the Constantine area who had defeated Clauzel. It was hoped that France would thus keep a predominant position in Algeria by playing off two potential rivals against each other. The man chosen to negotiate with Abd-el-Kader was General Thomas-Robert Bugeaud, a blunt, straightforward soldier with no previous knowledge of Africa. Bugeaud allowed Abd-el-Kader to retain sovereign rights over parts of Western Algeria, and on his own initiative waived requests for tribute. By the Treaty of Tafna, in May 1837, France granted Abd-el-Kader the province of Oran (but not the town), the coastal port of Arzew and Mostaganem. Free on the western front, the French army turned on Ahmed Bey and finally occupied Constantine in October, after heavy fighting in which Damremont was killed. France was still eager to conclude a treaty with Ahmed Bey, but the latter lacked Abd-el-Kader's subtlety. Reluctantly, the French Government, saddled almost against its will with the province of Constantine, began the process of "direct administration" there, and a Frenchman was given the task of supervising the work of local caïds and khalifs.

But Abd-el-Kader was biding his time for a new trial of strength

against the French, raising fresh troops and fresh funds. He sorely
tried the patience of Molé, who was unwilling to take the
initiative for a new war, by disregarding the clauses of the Tafna
Treaty which were not to his advantage. His tribesmen began
sporadic attacks on the few French *"colons"* who had moved
into the fertile Mitidja plain around Algiers. A French military
expedition, from Constantine to Algiers, passed through the
mountain defile known then as the "Passage des Bibans" (today
it is a familiar landmark on the Algiers-Constantine road, known
as the "Portes de Fer") and Abd-el-Kader, his military preparations completed, used this as a pretext to restart the war. In the
spring of 1840 the French Government was determined to
destroy Abd-el-Kader, and as a first step successfully drove him
back to his Oran stronghold, occupying first Cherchell, then
Médéa and Miliana after costly fighting. In 1841 the Molé
Government cast round for a likely commander-in-chief, and
gave the task of ridding Algeria of Abd-el-Kader to Bugeaud.

Marshal Bugeaud and the beginnings of French Algeria

More than any other single Frenchman, General (later Marshal)
Bugeaud left his imprint on Algeria; many of Bugeaud's own
theories and policies were implicitly embodied, often unconsciously, by French army officers fighting in Algeria over a
hundred years later; until Bugeaud's appointment as Commander-
in-chief and Governor-General, colonisation had been haphazard and sporadic. It was thanks to Bugeaud that an increasing
number of Frenchmen moved to Algeria, confident that his
pledge to protect their homes and interests would be honoured.
He not only laid the basis for "l'Algérie Française" but also for
most of the problems implicit in the creation of a new densely-
populated colony, for unlike Morocco's Lyautey he lacked both
foresight and imagination.
   Bugeaud's previous fighting experience had mostly been
acquired in Napoleon's army during the disastrous Spanish war.

Forcibly retired for a spell in 1815, he had become a farmer in the Dordogne and, in 1831, been elected to the National Assembly. A conservative with no great breadth of vision but an instinctive understanding of the small farmer class of which he was a member, he possessed to the full the solid soldierly qualities of loyalty, doggedness and common-sense. He was popular with his own troops, despised by the intellectual writers and politicians of the day. He embarked on his new task with self-confidence, in spite of earlier misgivings about this "deadly Restauration present" (as he had once described Algeria) and never indulged in the literary histrionics of a Clauzel or a Changarnier. "Since we happen to be in Africa and want to stay there," he wrote, "we must see to it that the sacrifices this country has cost us have not been in vain." In a speech to the National Assembly before taking up his new appointment, Bugeaud explained why he had become a convert to Thiers' earlier policy of total conquest: partial occupation of Algeria had proved a "dangerous illusion" and the Tafna Treaty, for which Bugeaud himself bore part of the responsibility, had led to renewed fighting. Only the "complete domination" of Algeria would enable colonisation there to take place, and this alone would ensure that the conquest would be maintained. "We must lead a great invasion to Africa, in the style of the Franks and the Goths."

Bugeaud applied his previous Spanish experience to Algeria with remarkably successful, albeit savage, results. He formed his men into small mobile groups, ordered them to fight, not a series of regular battles, but a succession of ambushes. Outside Algiers there were no large towns in Algeria, no vital strategic centres. "The only interest which can affect (the Arabs) is the agricultural interest," wrote Bugeaud and to this effect French troops were ordered to destroy crops, to prevent the Arabs from sowing or cultivating their land.

The *razzia*, or scorched-earth policy, had already been used sporadically by the French army as a means of revenge over an elusive enemy. Bugeaud turned it into a doctrine of war. "We have burned everything, destroyed everything. How many women and children have died of cold and fatigue!" wrote Saint Arnaud, later a Marshal of France, then a young officer. "The carnage was frightful," another officer described. "Houses, tents, streets, courtyards littered with corpses . . . in the disorder, often in the shadòws, the soldiers could not wait to determine age or sex. They struck everywhere, without warning."

The conventions of war were ignored by both sides: in reprisal against the *razzia*, Abd-el-Krim's followers mutilated captured French soldiers and a French colonel, Pelissier, described how Algerian women themselves beheaded wounded French soldiers "then allowed themselves to be massacred, with a child at their breast, with the most awful resignation". Not for the last time, France lived in ignorance of the kind of conflict being fought in Algeria. Pelissier himself lighted fires at the mouth of a cave in which five hundred men, women and children had taken refuge, and all but ten were asphyxiated. *L'affaire des grottes* reached Paris, and became a scandal, denounced in the French Senate as "the calculated, cold-blooded murder of a defenceless enemy" and in *Le Courier Français* as "this cannibal act, this foul deed which is a blot on our military history and a stain on our flag". The Army in Algeria quickly learnt its lesson: barely two months later, Saint-Arnaud suffocated fifteen hundred Moslems in another cave, carefully left no survivors to tell the story, and in a confidential message reported to Bugeaud: "No one went into the cave; not a soul . . . but myself." Following Bugeaud's advice, the Government agreed that French newspapers should not have access to "too precise details, evidently easy to justify, but concerning which there is no advantage in informing a European public".

"It was not a pretty war, nor an amusing war," wrote Saint-Arnaud five years after Bugeaud assumed command. Neither was it a popular war. French public opinion was impatient both at its length and cost, and suspected that France's professional army was deliberately spinning it out, for "how else is one to become a general in peacetime?" Beaten in Algeria, Abd-el-Kader surrendered in October 1847. Taken to France, treated with honour and respect, he spent the rest of his life in comfortable exile in Damascus, on a sizeable French Government pension, where he became a close friend of Richard and Isabel Burton and, in 1860, saved some 12,000 Christians from being massacred by the Turks.

The "serious war" was over after seventeen years of intermittent but hard fighting. There were still assorted tribal leaders and "marabouts" to capture, and the Kabyles kept up resistance for several years. Crushed in 1857, they rose again in 1871, when they held the entire French Expeditionary force at bay for seven months, and the anti-French rebellion spread as far south as Touggourt and Ouargla. The Kabyle uprising, initially caused by a slighted Kabyle leader called Mokrani who regarded the end of military rule in Algeria and the appointment of a Jewish minister (Crémieux) as a sign that French authority in Algeria was weakening, soon became a fight for Kabyle autonomy. The repression was fearfully harsh: thousands of Kabyles were sentenced to death, usually by courts composed of *colons* who had themselves suffered at the hands of the rebels, a 36 million franc fine was imposed and 500,000 hectares of some of Kabylia's best land was confiscated.

The long, bloody conquest of Algeria had established a pattern of violence that would be evoked a century later with astonishing similarity. Despite the claims of contemporary nationalists, the legions of Abd-el-Kader were not in any modern sense a national movement. His people were more united by their religion than by any feeling of common destiny. But even in fighting for individual freedom, they betrayed signs of solidarity that were perhaps the seeds of later nationalism. "You are merely passing guests," Abd-el-Kader's men told the French. "You may stay three hundred years, like the Turks, but in the end you will leave." It would take generations of modernisation, a breakdown of the primitive tribes, before this xenophobic instinct could give way to a contemporary desire for a unified, self-governing state. Unintentionally and inadvertently, France was responsible for this transformation.

CHAPTER TWO

FROM THE CONQUEST TO "PRÉSENCE FRANÇAISE"

THE presence, on Algerian soil, of 1,070,000 non-Moslems is at the heart of the Algerian problem. Were it not for this large and vocal European minority, it is fairly certain that France would either have reluctantly capitulated before the surge of nationalism (as in Tunisia or in Morocco) or itself have prepared the way for self-government and later independence (as in France's former colonial territories in Black Africa). French liberals—and North African nationalists themselves—often contrast French stubbornness over Algeria with British common-sense over India. But India and Algeria are not really comparable: Britain, in 1947, had retained only a skeleton British-staffed administrative apparatus in India, and "Indianisation" of the administration, the armed forces and all other essential services had been going on apace for years. Indian generals of the rank of Brigadier headed mixed Indian and British brigades in Burma as early as 1943. In Algeria the French Army proudly announced the appointment of its first Moslem colonel commanding a regiment (French equivalent of a battalion) in 1959. Unlike Algeria, Indians were not only present but predominant in all walks of life. Nor was there, in India, a large "poor white" European minority, insecure and vociferous. Algeria can be compared more accurately with South Africa, where the Europeans are completely predominant, or with Kenya, where a white minority has acquired large estates through the legal spoliation of primitive Africans. Yet Algeria is neither South Africa nor Kenya. To be sure, the Europeans of Algeria are economically and socially predominant, but there are plenty of rich—and socially accepted—Moslems too; neither is Algeria a "White Highland": certainly the first French settlers obtained land by questionable means, and many later arrivals were granted land from government estates constituted by confiscated land. But many Europeans carved out domains for themselves out of swamps and waste land which no Moslem had ever cultivated or even used for grazing. Other arrivals—from Malta, Sicily, Greece and Spain—did not even belong to the hierarchy of landowners, however modest: in Algeria they followed their previous callings —as carpenters, tailors, masons or small shopkeepers, often without any initial state aid at all.

The "présence française" in Algeria is thus the outcome of more than a century of haphazard and unregulated colonisation, tempered less by French policy changes than by political and economic vicissitudes in France—and later in Europe—which forced an increasing number of Europeans to seek their fortunes in Algeria. The first settlers were, naturally enough, the officers, soldiers and camp followers of the French expeditionary force which landed at Sidi Ferruch in 1832. While the fate of Algeria was still in doubt, a number of speculators were already buying up property in and around Algiers from the terrified Moslems. Army leaders, General Clauzel among them, were wildly over-confident in their estimation of Algeria's potential wealth. Backed by military might, the first wave of speculators gradually forced the Moslems off their land in the rich Mitidja plain.

Laws governing Moslem land tenure were complicated and incomprehensible to nineteenth century Westerners. Property was inalienable (contrary to the special inheritance laws current in Kabylia) but no owner could be certain that his land would not be invaded by a swarm of remote kinsmen, all claiming a share of the crops or part of his pasture. In the Mitidja, farms were either owned by wealthy Moslem families from Algiers (and rented out to overseers who received a miserly one fifth of all produce) or held on special leases from the Turkish Government. The French conquerors found a variety of ways of edging the Moslems out: they behaved no worse than representatives of other dynamic nineteenth-century powers intent on colonial expansion, certainly far more humanely than the first white settlers in certain parts of Black Africa. But by applying western standards to the property they did acquire, they effectively drove out not only the former owners, but also the tribes which had enjoyed customary grazing rights.

Abd-el-Kader's seven year war reduced almost to nothing the efforts of the first French settlers in the Mitidja plain. Equally, it accelerated the Moslem drift away from French-held land to the Oran province farther west, then under Abd-el-Kader's control. With Abd-el-Kader's final defeat, the Moslem drift accelerated, this time no longer west but south, to the arid mountain areas below Blida, and Algeria acquired a new type of settler.

As early as 1832 some 400 Frenchmen, refugees from the banks of the Rhine, embarked at Le Havre, bound, as they thought, for the United States. After they had been at sea for several days, they discovered that a dishonest shipping agent was taking them to Algeria instead. Landed at Kouba and Delly Brahim, near Algiers, they lived for a while on army charity, petitioned unsuccessfully for their return to France, then made the best of it and settled on plots of land given them by the French army. In 1843, much against General Bugeaud's will, some Trappist monks founded a colony at Staoueli, a few miles west of Algiers, and soon turned it into a prosperous 1,000 hectare farm. A retired French army sergeant, Jacques Germain, bought some land south of Algiers and by sheer hard work turned it into some of Algeria's best farming country. General Bugeaud would have liked to have seen more French soldiers take up permanent residence in Algeria, but few were found to emulate Sergeant Germain. Bugeaud himself resigned from the Governorship of Algeria when the National Assembly refused to approve the costs of a Bugeaud-inspired plan to settle retired soldiers on Algerian soil on a massive scale.

For as long as the war lasted, settlers were almost as much of a liability to the French army as were Abd-el-Kader's men. General Bugeaud himself ordered all Europeans out of Boufarik (a mere fifteen miles south from Algiers) in 1846 on the grounds that his troops could not protect them effectively. Others were slaughtered by Abd-el-Kader's men or decimated by disease.

There is some truth to the French claim that the "history of the earliest French settlers in Algeria is written in the cemeteries". But by the 1860s most of the earliest rigours were gone. By 1853 French farmers had moved back to Boufarik and were petitioning the Algiers' authorities against the settlement of further "colons" in that area on the grounds that there was no more readily available land.

The end of the war, too, meant that thousands of acres belonging to Abd-el-Kader supporters were available for distribution, and Europeans readily came forward to stake their claims: in 1845 there were 46,080 Europeans in Algeria—mostly in and around Algiers, and in that year alone 1882 families applied for land concessions; in 1853 there were 140,000 Europeans (but only some 25,000 actual "colons"). Between 1847 and 1853 there occurred, too, in the French-colonised area around Algiers, a distinct social revolution among the remaining Moslems in the area: deprived of their customary grazing rights, tempted or swindled into parting with their small holdings, they gradually came to work for the Europeans as landless labourers. The same pattern repeated itself, at a few years' distance, in the areas around Oran and Bône.

Like immigrants the world over, the Europeans who settled in Algeria in the nineteenth century came from the least privileged strata of society. Some were sent to Algeria straight from state orphanages; in the early years of his rule, Napoleon III used Algeria as a convenient place to send political opponents, and Left-wing revolutionaries joined a motley collection of juvenile delinquents, prison offenders and refugees from France's eastern provinces. Successive wars and economic depressions brought more settlers throughout the nineteenth century and up to the present time: a large contingent of Frenchmen came to Algeria after the 1870 Franco-Prussian war; steadily, a trickle of France's poorest peasantry—from Corsica, Auvergne and the Cevennes—joined political refugees from the richer Alsace-Lorraine provinces. Later European crises brought other, non-French immigrants: Spaniards and Italians, fleeing poverty and later political oppression; Greeks, Cypriots and Maltese, eager to turn to commerce on French-held soil and acquire French nationality; settled Foreign Legionnaires and a sprinkling of political undesirables expelled from France because of their "royalist" views. At one point the French Government even considered the possibility of opening Algeria up to the Copts, the Maronites, the Irish, the Indians and the Chinese.

Between 1871 and 1880 French authorities set up 264 new "colonisation settlements" and Algeria's non-Moslem population rose steadily—from 245,000 in 1871 to 276,000 in 1880. By 1880 only 195,000 settlers had acquired French nationality. The rest were Spaniards, Italians or other nationals from the Mediterranean basin. By 1912 there were 781,000 Europeans, and a French Government report, compiled in 1917, came to the conclusion that only one European in five in Algeria was actually of French descent. But by that time France had granted all Europeans (and Algerians of Jewish origin) the privilege of acquiring French nationality automatically, and the number of European non-French nationals steadily declined, until today, out of the European population of just over a million, only some 200,000 have retained their previous nationality. But a glance at any telephone directory of any Algerian town will mirror the complex national origin of its European population. And not the least of France's troubles in Algeria has stemmed from the explosive national qualities inherent in these new citizens: from the Italian exuberance and the Spanish pride of these former immigrants whose panic-stricken reflexes to anything that smacks of change result from memories of an earlier exodus and a previous struggle to acquire status, a living, and a new nationality. There is more Spanish spoken in the poorer quarters of Oran than French. The *patois* of Bab-el-Oued, the European "east end" of Algiers (although it is actually west of the town, Algiers being the only town in the world whose slum drift has been in a westerly, not easterly direction) is incomprehensible to most Frenchmen, and contains a good deal of basic Arabic to it. The European living in Algeria is, most of the time, both envious and resentful of the French of metropolitan France, afraid, even in day-to-day business dealings, of being humiliated or swindled by his quick-thinking fellow countrymen from across the Mediterranean. Though school and university programmes are the same as in France, the Europeans in Algeria have little of what for want of another term has conveniently been called the Cartesian turn of mind: their judgements and reactions—in business, in love as well as in politics—are direct, emotive and—because reason plays little part in their decisions—subject to violent fluctuations. Bitter personal hatreds follow close on the most solid friendships; contradictory political opinions (and allegiances) are currently held by the same individual in the space of a few months. Albert Camus correctly diagnosed (and admired) some of his country-men's characteristics: a rejection of rational thought, a worship of things physical—the sun and sea, physical strength and beauty. Here too the Europeans of Algeria differ from their fellow-countrymen in metropolitan France, where the intellectual emphasis, in the last resort, counts far more than physical: one has only to walk down the Rue Michelet in Algiers to realise that, physically, the European student in Algiers is incomparably more healthy, more handsome and more physically alive than his Sorbonne equivalent. It is significant that, apart from Albert Camus, Algeria has produced few writers and thinkers of great talent (although a whole "new wave" of Moslem writers using French as their language has arisen over the last few years) but that France's greatest boxer, Marcel Cerdan, was born and bred in Algeria. (His death in an air crash was regarded in Algeria as a national calamity by Europeans and Moslems alike.)

It would have been difficult for a reflective, rational group of individuals to live cheek by jowl with the Algerian Moslems without acquiring sentiments of racial superiority. The whole history of French colonisation in Algeria encouraged the growth of such feelings from the start: the earliest settlers despised the Moslems for their archaic land tenure laws and primitive agri-cultural methods; wherever they failed in wresting arable land from the Moslems, they angrily watched such acreage wastefully cultivated. The Moslem way of life was unhygienic, barbarous and incomprehensible. The landless labourers whom the Europeans gradually acquired were shiftless, lazy and untrustworthy. The Europeans saw only these outward characteristics, and neither realised nor cared that Algeria, in the space of a few decades, had progressed from a medieval way of life to a modern one, and that some of the shiftlessness and fatalism displayed by the Moslems with whom they were in contact resulted from the stresses and strains of a social revolution. Probably the most revealing comment on the mentality of the Europeans in Algeria comes from a report by Jules Ferry, who helped to establish France as a great nineteenth-century colonial power. Writing in 1892, Ferry penned this judgement: "We have taken a close look at him, and have studied his private and public behaviour. We have found him very limited. Assuredly it is not his intellectual disposition which enables the colon to act, even in a limited capacity, as an arbiter where the fate of the natives is concerned. He has many virtues—all those of the hard worker and the patriot. But he lacks what may be described as the virtue of the victor, the balance of the spirit and of the heart, and the regard for the right of the weak which is in no ways incompatible with firm leadership. It is difficult to try and convince the European settler that there are rights other than his own in Arab country and that the native is not a race to be taxed and exploited to the utmost limits . . . the settlers proclaim that (the conquered Arabs) are totally incorrigible and utterly incapable of education, without ever having attempted, over the past thirty years, to do anything to drag them out of their moral and intellectual misery . . . The settlers are governed by no general policy in their attitude towards the natives. They fail to understand any other policy than that of containment. To be sure, there are no thoughts of destroying them; it is even claimed that there is no urge to drive them back. But there is no concern for their complaints, or for their numerical growth which seems to increase with their very poverty."[1]

[1] Jules Ferry: *Le Gouvernement de l'Algérie.*

CHAPTER THREE

THE FAILURE OF ASSIMILATION

THE Europeans who settled in increasing numbers in Algeria provided France with a problem which, in the course of some 140 years, has never been satisfactorily solved: their existence precluded the establishment of a nakedly colonial government apparatus, and as early as 1848 Algeria was divided into three departments, each headed by a Prefect as in metropolitan France. But the social, cultural and economic differences between Moslems and settlers were so great that "assimilation"—the declared goal of a whole succession of French political leaders from 1847 onwards—was regarded even by French liberals as a very remote goal indeed, and by the settlers themselves as a huge joke. After Abd-el-Kader's surrender, Marshal Bugeaud wrote: "The first duty of a conqueror is to provide good government" and—amongst the earliest administrators sent to Algeria, there was a good deal of missionary zeal, and a genuine concern to win over the Moslems to France by humane means. As early as 1841 Duvivier[1] wrote: "In spite of the savage war we are waging against them today, all the natives will be with us in thirty years time. Let us therefore adopt a policy not of containment but of confidence."

But such aims soon fell short of reality, for several reasons. The first was the (then common) belief that a colonial territory could be governed, for ever, by venal tribal leaders. Duvivier, for instance, wanted to "let the Arabs govern themselves, through their own leaders, duly bought by us". Such a system might work for decades, but it could scarcely be erected into a permanent system without fear of widespread discontent; and it is curious

---

[1] Franciade-Fleurus Duvivier, *Solution de la Question d'Afrique*.

that not only in Algeria, but in the Tunisian and Moroccan protectorates, and later in her African possessions, France continued to put her faith in a small class of pro-French *"hommes dévoués à la France"* when it was quite apparent, to the le st observant outsider, that these were bitterly hated by the people they were supposed to administer. The hotels of Vichy and Aix-les-Bains are still haunted by the luckiest of these survivals from another age. Terrorism and personal vengeance have taken their toll among those who failed to pull up stakes in time.

The second reason was that it was Algeria's misfortune that successive French régimes, from 1841 onwards, indulged in almost every conceivable experiment in government in their search for a satisfactory answer to the question: What should be the relations between metropolitan France and Algeria? First, and largely owing to French military influence, France put its trust in the "Arab Bureau". The Turkish hierarchy of khalifas, aghas and caïds was retained, but at every level a French Intelligence officer, acting as adviser, actually did all the governing, raising taxes and administering justice through a docile Moslem nominee. Since the French officer also had the task of looking after "internal security", he was in fact the undisputed master of his territory. In the same way, more than a century later, the last French Governor-General of Algeria, Jacques Soustelle, created the *"Sections Administratives Spécialisées"* (commonly known as the S.A.S.) whose duties closely paralleled those of the old Arab Bureau officers, and who inherited a good deal of the mystique of the Arab Bureau, down to the distinctive headpiece —the *"képi bleu"*, the symbol of France's *"mission civilisatrice"* in remote desert lands.

To a certain extent, the dilemma facing France was a double one; there was the clash between advocates of "containment" and advocates of "assimilation", and there was, too, running like a thread throughout Algeria's history since the French conquest, the conflict between the military, who claimed a pre-eminent role in governing the country, and the civilians; the attitude of

Napoleon III reflected the contradictory pulls of all these theories. After turning Algeria into a kind of jail for his political opponents, he tried administrative assimilation on a large scale, and the bottleneck which followed proved that Algeria could not be administered from Paris. Two years later he restored military rule in Algeria and appointed a Governor with full ministerial powers while Prefects of the Algerian departments were placed under the orders of the generals commanding the Bône, Oran and Algiers divisions. After a journey to Algeria in 1860 (the Empress was reported to have become "mad about the Arabs") he developed a romantic liking for the tribal chieftains he met, and began regarding himself as "emperor of the Arabs and of the French". Assimilation plans were scrapped, and Napoleon III's aim, as defined in letters to subordinates, was to "protect Algeria against the invasion of foreigners". It was a return to a policy of containment, if not of apartheid, but without the most flagrant injustices of the latter: the Moslems were assigned the basic tasks of growing wheat and breeding cattle, while the Europeans' functions in Algeria were defined as "commercial and industrial colonisation". Unlike South Africa, the "natives" were neither to be herded into special areas nor deprived of their lands: Napoleon III envisaged the establishment of more indirect controls to keep the Moslems going as active producers of basic commodities, and here his conception of France's role in Algeria was a remarkably enlightened one: he suggested that, to keep a satisfactory balance between the two communities, no further destitute "colons" should be admitted into Algeria, and the state should not act as banker in Algerian investment projects, but encourage private financial backing. It is certain that if this policy had been consistently followed, it would have kept the European minority in Algeria down to manageable size. Unfortunately rulings on the restricted entry of Europeans into Algeria soon fell into abeyance, and after 1870 the state continued to grant aid to new waves of immigrants. And however high-minded Napoleon III's aims were, they must be judged by their results, and these were catastrophic: always short of money, the

Emperor fell an easy prey to various foreign banks and investment trusts. In 1853 he gave the "Compagnie Genevoise" (a company formed exclusively of a number of Swiss banking interests) a 20,000 hectare concession in the Sétif area, provided the company recruited, and helped to settle, some 500 *colons* in ten new villages. Instead of abiding by these terms, the "Compagnie Genevoise" preferred to invest in cattle, without fulfilling its promise of building new villages or paying for the upkeep of newly established farmers. The company's attitude may have been a rational one: all agricultural experts agree that the "*hauts plateaux*" of the Constantinois area are more suitable for cattle than for agriculture. But the result was a net loss for France, and for Algeria: all profits were sent back to Switzerland, and no measures were taken by the French Government to protest against the violation of earlier agreements. Similarly, Napoleon III, with the passive or interested complicity of senior French officials, showed that practical gains meant more to him than high-minded statements of policy: some thirty financial groups obtained concessions for over 160,000 hectares of forest land. One company, the "Société Algérienne", received a 100,000 hectare concession in the Constantinois at a symbolic rental of one franc per hectare. The agreement specified that the company should invest 100 million francs in agricultural and industrial investment and at the same time contribute to Algeria's growing road and railway infrastructure costs. The company failed to meet its obligations, and no successful measures were ever taken to compel it to pay up. In 1868 a nation-wide famine (in which some 500,000 Moslems are believed to have died) led to anger and alarm in Paris and the appointment of a special investigation committee to determine what Algeria's economic and political needs were. The committee heard some 4,777 separate testimonies (mainly French) and came up with some sound ideas: the primacy of civil over military authority, the application of French law to Frenchmen and Moslems alike, and the establishment of legally recognised Moslem smallholders. But the reform plan—like so many others which were to follow—was never enforced. French political instability at home—and a tolerance of powerful lobbies of various kinds—reduced these attempts to nothing, just as a combination of lobbying and general conservatism was to reduce to nothing the Blum-Violette reforms of 1934. It is only in the light of such successive hopes and disappointments, spread over more than a century, that the Algerian rebellion can be understood. And though few Moslems recalled the terms of the original surrender treaty of 1830, according to which "the freedom of all classes of inhabitants, their property, their religion, their commerce will be unaffected", French colonisation procedures, throughout the nineteenth century, led to poverty and resentment: in various ways land spoliation continued long after the Algerian conquest and Algeria's tax system was far harsher for the Moslems than it was for the large companies.

The underlying reason for French unwillingness to force change on Algeria lay in Algeria's economic dependence on France and the benefits which almost everyone (except the Moslems) derived from such dependence: right up to 1944, the idea of Algeria's industrialisation was opposed because it would provide France with unfair competition: the European farmers of Algeria were afraid that industrialisation would lead to wage increases. All post-1944 industrial projects in Algeria until the rebellion began were presented to French public opinion as plans for the "*décentralisation*" of French industry. In agriculture, the *colons* succeeded in obtaining the benefits extended to farmers of metropolitan France (reserved markets and state subsidies) while paying substantially lower wages than their metropolitan colleagues. One-third of Algeria's agricultural produce consists of vineyards, and in 1953 Algeria produced 18 million hectolitres, of which 16 million were exported, mainly to France. As one parliamentarian had earlier pointed out, 64 per cent of all French wine-growers had estates of under 300 hectares, whereas in Algeria 757 large owners produced half of Algeria's total wine production, and the small landowners of the under 300-hectare category totalled a mere 27 per cent. But the power of the large wine growing individuals and companies was not only financial, but political: since it was natural for a European "notable" to become active politically, lobbying began, in the simplest possible fashion, with the duplication, in Paris, as deputies or senators, of the financially powerful French wine-growers in Algeria. Since these *notables* also controlled the regional agricultural loan boards, they were assured of the support and obedience of the smaller European landowners. This accumulation of privileges explains the intransigeance and the success with which the various European "lobbies" opposed reform in Algeria right up to the outbreak of the rebellion. When the usual lobbying methods failed to work, they resorted to threats: the riots of February 1956—when France's Premier, Guy Mollet, was pelted with tomatoes because he wanted to nominate a "liberal" general, Georges Catroux, as Minister for Algeria—were only one of a series of incidents and threats before which successive French Governments almost invariably bowed. As early as 1930 a large wine-grower and deputy, M. Fernand Brière, held a rally in Oran to protest against the possible restriction of wine imports into France, and reminded the government that American independence had resulted from England's will to tyrannise its colonisers in America. As late as 1947 Algeria's most prominent *colon* spokesman, Gabriel Abbo, told a French journalist: "You seem to fear only the possibility of an Arab insurrection. Bear in mind that there is another eventuality—that of the armed insurrection of the *colons*." And the Blum-Violette reforms were dropped when all European mayors threatened to strike and all Algerian-elected deputies and senators threatened to resign. If the outbreak of the Algerian rebellion was due to a century-old accumulation of resentments, the French Government's failure to impose its will on the Europeans of Algeria stemmed from a whole series of earlier defeats and compromises.

As General de Gaulle himself recognised, in a moving address to army officers at Blida on December 9, 1960, the Algerian tragedy stemmed from France's failure to grant concessions to the Moslems in time or prepare for the future. The violent opposition to successive Government proposals seems today incredible: it stemmed partly from the *colons'* consciousness of their own power and knowledge of weaknesses inherent in the constitutions of the Third and Fourth Republics, and partly from the feeling, common to powerful minorities, that concessions could only lead to further demands. By 1936 a mere 2,500 Moslems had applied for full French citizenship, and when Léon Blum and Maurice Violette proposed a modest change in existing laws to enable an increasing number of Moslems to enjoy political rights without giving up their *"statut personnel"* (i.e. without signing away their rights as Moslems to be tried by Moslem courts and be governed, in non-criminal jurisdiction, by Moslem law) parliament refused, just as, earlier, it had refused to grant full political rights to Moslems who had served in the French army and later, pressure groups led by *colon* spokesmen like Alain de Serigny were to refuse the "Collège Unique". Since this is not a chronological historical survey, but rather an attempt to find reasons for the origins and course of Algerian nationalism, it is sufficient to look at Algeria as it was, administratively, in 1954, on the eve of the rebellion: as French history textbooks were at great pains to stress, Algeria had been "part of France" since 1834, just as Britanny had been part of France since 1491, Alsace since 1649, Corsica since 1769 and Savoy since 1860. But in 1954 such a statement could hardly be taken seriously: true Algeria, like France, was divided into departments: but in the political, judicial, financial and administrative fields, its statute was entirely different. Algeria, in 1954, was—by the law of September 20, 1947, which itself modified only partially other, previous laws—governed by a Governor-General responsible to the Minister of the Interior. A local Algerian Assembly with legislative powers was charged with exclusively Algerian interests. This Assembly was composed of 120 elected delegates, of whom 60 were elected by one-tenth of Algeria's population, the remainder by the other nine-tenths. The elected delegates themselves were separated into two colleges. The first college was elected by all French citizens—i.e. all Europeans, plus the smattering of Moslems who had opted for French citizenship and the alienation of their rights as Moslems, plus a small number of "citoyens de statut local" (about 60,000) composed of officers and ex-officers, university, secondary or technical school graduates, officials, members of local Agriculture Committees and Chambers of Commerce, bachagas, caïds and other tribal officials, general and municipal councillors, members of the Order of the Legion of Honour or of other awards, members of selected trade unions and ex-servicemen. Each college sent fifteen Algerian deputies and senators to sit alongside elected representatives in the French Senate and National Assembly, and the Algerian Assembly's second college also nominated only half of the Algerian representatives to the (now defunct) Assembly of the French Union. The overwhelming majority of Moslems who voted to appoint members to Algeria's second college could nominate only half Algeria's general councillors, two out of five municipal councillors in communes administered on the French pattern by mayors. The "commune" system lent itself to further discrimination: Algeria was divided into "*communes de plein exercise*" (on the French pattern, with mayors and a municipal council, but the mayor was invariably French) and "*communes mixtes*": the "*commune mixte*" was a modified survival of the "*bureau arabe*": in "*commune mixte*" areas there was no mayor, and the local administrator was a French uniformed official, specially recruited and directly responsible to the Governor-General through the Prefect of his Department. He enjoyed full judicial, administrative and police powers, and was closely seconded by specially chosen bachagas, caïds and a "municipal council" whose Moslem members were nominated by the Department Prefect.

Such a system both helped to maintain European predominance in the Algerian Assembly and ensured that "direct administration" kept Moslems under tight control. Apologists for the "*commune mixte*" have advanced the usual arguments: that specially-selected, professional administrators were more competent to handle large numbers of primitive Moslems, still deeply influenced by tribal customs; that tribal leaders were the administrators' natural allies; and that no other system would have worked. But over the years—and particularly in the years leading up to the outbreak of the rebellion—the *"commune mixte"* system seems to have been a thoroughly evil, as well as a thoroughly inefficient system: the extent to which *"commune mixte"* administrators were informed of the happenings in their territory can be gauged from the fact that twenty-four hours before the rebellion broke out, in the Aurès mountains, the local administrator had pooh-poohed rumours of an impending clash, and insisted that there was nothing more serious going on in his territory than traditional tribal feuds and age-old banditry. Not that *"commune mixte"* administrators were necessarily inefficient, or corrupt men: but Algeria—and particularly the *"communes mixtes"*, which comprised the poorest parts of Algeria—were terribly under-administered. French officials had been forced, over the years, to delegate an increasing amount of power to tribal chiefs, who had quietly amassed fortunes from bribes. Algeria's administration was over-centralised, and while there were over 2,000 officials in Algiers itself, the French administrator of the *"commune mixte"* of Arris, in the Aurès mountains, exercised administrative control over 70,000 people in a mountainous area the size of southern England, with a secretary and a dozen French gendarmes. Many Moslems, in the remote Aurès and Kabylie mountains, had never seen a European before in their lives, and their sole contact with France was through a hated tax-hungry "bachaga" or "caïd". In Kabylia, the system was furthermore entirely alien to Kabyle mentality: the French administration had, in some parts of Kabylia, forced a tribal system on the Kabyles and designated "bachagas" and "caïds" despite extreme Kabyle reluctance to recognise any such alien authority, for Kabyles have always rejected the caïdal system in favour of rough-and-ready democracy in the form of popularly elected village councils.

In the *"communes de plein exercise"*, the influence of the powerful French pressure groups was sufficient to ensure the election of docile municipalities, and an investigation of local Algerian politics almost invariably leads to the reconstitution of a thread linking the powerful *colon* minority interests to individually elected local government bodies. General elections were something else: and thinking Frenchmen—including Algeria's last Governor-General, Jacques Soustelle—have stigmatised the conditions under which these elections were held before 1954. The elections for the Algerian Assembly in April, 1948, illustrate both the failures and the hypocrisy of France's senior civil servants in Algeria: by 1948 the nationalist-reformist movement was already strong in Algeria, but the elections returned 43 "independents" to 17 nationalists: the French administration in Algeria used every possible device to obtain this result. Two-thirds of the non-administration candidates were arrested on various charges during the electoral campaign, and their meetings, pamphlets and posters banned; in some communes, local police officials manned the polling booths; in some areas, where anti-administration feeling was strongest, no voting took place at all but "*commune mixte*" officials reported returns favourable to government candidates; in other areas, where the Moslems had refused to vote owing to the arrest or disappearance of nationalist candidates, the army moved in and forced them to vote; in some cities, where results gave an overwhelming proportion of votes in favour of nationalist candidates, results were not communicated to Algiers in time. The day after the vote, the Governor-General of Algeria, Marcel-Edmond Naegelen, a highly-respected French socialist, issued a statement thanking the Algerian population "for having accomplished its electoral duties calmly". Similar irregularities occurred right up to the outbreak of the rebellion, and explain—if they do not entirely excuse—the present extreme suspicion of today's Algerian nationalists towards any solution to the Algerian problem based on a referendum without some kind of outside control—a suspicion which later electoral consultations after the advent of General de Gaulle did nothing to alleviate. Jacques Soustelle himself, in a Government Report in May 1955, summed up his thinking on the end products of such elections: "The pseudo-deputies, commonly referred to as 'pre-fabricated', put in office thanks to the electoral fraud, most often illiterate and frequently dishonest, representing nothing and nobody, have no

influence in their voting areas and do not even repay the Administration for having created them. Few mistakes have been more
tragic than that which consisted in distorting our own laws to
bring into prominence discredited personalities without any
intellectual or moral value."

CHAPTER FOUR

ALGERIAN NATIONALISM: THE BEGINNINGS

"It is to be foreseen—and indeed I regard it as a historic truth—
that in the more or less distant future North Africa—modernised,
civilised, living its own autonomous life—will detach itself from
metropolitan France. When this occurs—and it must be our supreme
political goal—the parting must occur without pain and the nations
must be able to continue to view France without fear. The African
peoples must not turn against her. For this reason, we must, from
today, as a starting point, make ourselves loved."

(Marshal Lyautey, in a speech at Rabat,
April 14, 1925)

IN most Middle Eastern and Afro-Asian countries once subject to
colonial rule, there is usually a point, an event, a date before
which one can pause and say: nationalism began here. Not so
with Algeria, partly because of its unique status, partly because,
lacking the homogeneity of a Tunisia or a Morocco, it followed
various trends and was influenced by a number of Moslem personalities in contradiction with each other. Indeed, it would be
unfair to call the first signs of Algerian political discontent
nationalism at all. As both the *colons* and the present-day nationalists agree, Algerian political leaders explored all possibilities of
reaching agreement on the basis of "integration" with France,
and every European in Algeria seems to have learnt by heart
Ferhat Abbas's famous phrase about seeking an Algerian nation
and not finding it. As early as 1912 a Moslem paper published in
Djidjelli, *Rachidi*, asked for full French citizenship rights in return
for French-imposed conscription laws in Algeria. In 1922 Abd-
el-Kader's grandson, the Emir Khaled, himself a former captain
in the French army, protested against discrimination against
Moslems in the army's promotion system, demanded selection in
civilian and military fields based on merit alone. (For so doing,

he was temporarily exiled.) Ferhat Abbas's own goal, for a long time, was to be a Frenchman with full rights without abandoning anything of his Moslem heritage.

Such was one trend in the course of Algerian nationalism, moving only gradually towards the concept of independence after successive failures and disappointments, faked elections and growing disillusion with France. The other trend is more direct, more extreme: as early as 1925 Hadj Abd-el-Kader (more commonly known as Messali Hadj), then a member of the French Communist Party's central committee, founded *L'étoile Nord-Africaine* and demanded "total independence, the withdrawal of all occupation troops and the creation of a national army". Yet another trend was provided by a prominent Algerian religious leader, Sheikh Abdelhamid Ben Badis, who founded, in 1931, an Algeria-wide *Ulemas* (religious teachers) Association, whose members proclaimed that ". . . Islam is my religion, Arabic my tongue, Algeria is my country . . . and independence is a natural right for all people on earth".

Perhaps, in the thirties, it was the Ulemas Association of Ben Badis rather than the Messalists or the moderate followers of Ferhat Abbas which exerted most influence in Algeria: official religious teaching, in Algeria was—and remains—State-controlled. The imams were paid for out of the Algerian budget. Naturally, they were chosen for their "reliability" and were under the close supervision of Prefects, European mayors and *"commune mixte"* administrators. But side by side with the official state-appointed religious teachers, there sprang up hundreds of "free" schools. Ben Badis, through his paper, *Al Shihab* (Dawn), campaigned for the end of state supervision in religious matters, widespread teaching of Arabic, and a free Arab press. He also raised funds from the Moslem community to set up an increased number of "free" schools, and founded, in Constantine, the "Ben Badis Institute" to train Moslem teachers, some of whom were selected to finish their studies in Middle Eastern universities. If, today, the Algerian "National Liberation Front" seems aggressively Moslem compared to Tunisia's Neo-Destour movement and Morocco's opposed political parties, it is largely due to the success of the *medersas* (religious schools) of Ben Badis and his doctrinaire teachers.

But the growth of Algerian nationalism does have something in common with Tunisian and Moroccan nationalism: for all the insistence of Ben Badis on the importance of Arabic and Islam, it drew its strength and vitality not from the Middle East but from Europe. In Paris the Messalists, the "moderates" and the disciples of Ben Badis mingled freely with young Tunisian and Moroccan nationalists. In the late twenties and early thirties, names of speakers at "anti-colonialist" rallies and Moslem student meetings in Paris and Brussels read like later Tunisian and Moroccan cabinet lists: Ahmed Balafredj (later Moroccan Foreign Minister), Allal el Fassi (the extreme Moroccan nationalist mystic and poet), Habib Bourguiba himself. It would be wrong to draw hard and fast lines between different categories of nationalists: they influenced each other. But since today's Algerian nationalism is incarnated by the "National Liberation Front", whose titular head was, until August 1961, Ferhat Abbas, and to a lesser extent by the rival "Mouvement Nationaliste Algérien" (M.N.A.) led by Messali Hadj, one should take a close look at both men, bearing in mind all the while that the rebellion which broke out on November 1, 1954, did so without their leadership, consent or even their knowledge.

Ferhat Abbas was born on October 24, 1899, at Taher, in the department of Constantine, grandson of a landowner whose property had been expropriated after the French conquest, son of an influential pro-French *"bachaga"* who held the rank of Commander in the Order of the Legion of Honour. The Abbas family was proud of its close ties with France, and made a fetish of speaking French at home (today Ferhat Abbas speaks halting, simple Arabic, reverts to French whenever he can). Ferhat Abbas' father wanted his children (three boys and one girl) to be raised as Europeans, an ambitious aim in Taher which contained little that resembled European culture. Ferhat went to a local school when he was ten, and spent most of his time as a child wandering around Taher's barren hillsides with Moslem shepherds.

At Djidjelli *lycée*, where he obtained his *baccalauréat*, Ferhat Abbas began to get some notion of what it meant to be a Moslem, however respectable, in a country colonised by Europeans. Northern Constantine, then as now, is an impoverished, economically marginal area where relations between Moslems and Europeans are often strained. The then Mayor of Djidjelli was a diehard Frenchman, a believer in European supremacy, whose toughness made Moslems shudder. Abbas spent two years in the army as a conscript (he rose to the rank of sergeant in the medical corps), and his growing impatience with discrimination, he claims, crystallised one day in 1922, when he read an editorial in a French paper called *L'Afrique Latine* which rejected all Moslem pretensions to belonging to Algeria.

After military service Abbas went to Algiers to enrol in Algiers University Chemistry School. Here, for the first time, he mingled with young "*evolués*" of his generation. He was made aware of material French achievements in Algeria, of the modernity of European life. But as a Moslem he and his fellow-students felt they were second-class citizens unless they gave up their personal Koranic status: most of these young Algerians were not religious, and cared very little whether they would be judged in Koranic courts, or adhered to religious inheritance laws. But the "personal status" was a symbol: to discard it was a sort of surrender.

In an attempt to bridge the gulf between his French and Moslem leanings, Abbas agitated actively for equality, plunged into politics and became president of the Algerian Moslem Students Association—a post which taught him the basic rules of political organisation (Abbas still considers this post one of the most important he ever had, and insists that it be mentioned prominently in every biographical note). He was an avid, perhaps none too discriminating reader; Anatole France, Victor Hugo, Michelet's *History of France*, Jean Jaurès, the Declarations of the Rights of Man. Like many a contemporary Moslem tasting French political thought, Abbas tended to think of himself in the nineteenth century tradition of socialist humanism. At the same time, he studied the origins of Islam—not in their Arabic texts but in French translations—and tried to blend the beliefs of the West with the experience of the Middle East. Significantly, when he first began to write, at the age of twenty-one, he took as pseudonym *Kemal Abancerage*—a transparent evocation of the Turkish nationalist and the Chateaubriand hero who sacrificed happiness for glory. In the beginning, his whole political life swung like a pendulum between realism and romanticism.

Though he managed to find time to become a qualified chemist, Abbas was first and foremost a professional student politician. He wrote articles for political newspapers, travelled frequently to France and met Tunisian and Moroccan nationalist contemporaries. Simultaneously, he strove with success to assimilate himself personally into the European life of Algeria. He was a good mixer, an excellent debater, a fine after-dinner speaker; he divorced his Moslem wife (whom he had married by family arrangement early in life), moved to Sétif, a drab town half-way between Algiers and Constantine, and became a leading member of Sétif society. His chemist's shop there (now boarded up) is still pointed out as a Sétif landmark. He met Marcelle Perez, the wife of a local doctor, and married her after her divorce. (Madame Abbas, a handsome woman of Alsatian descent and bearing, is herself a symbol of Ferhat Abbas' divided loyalties between France and Islam: from an old *colon* family, she has remained intensely loyal to Abbas, despite family opposition and the hardships of exile.) But beneath the surface, younger Algerian nationalists note with a wry smile, Madame Abbas has some of the instinctive reactions of a *"piednoir"*. *"Il est parfois difficile,"* one nationalist said recently, *"de savoir ce qu'elle fait dans notre galère."*

Ferhat Abbas' political career began in 1934 with his election to office as Municipal Councillor of Sétif, as a member of the *"fédération des élus musulmans"* which advocated Franco-Moslem assimilation. Previously he had published a short booklet, *Le Jeune Algérien*, defining his position. "What nationalism really means," he wrote, "is the fight for our economic and political emancipation

... we have once and for all swept away all dreams and illusions in order to link our future firmly with French achievements in this country." And further on comes his oft-quoted phrase: "If I had discovered the Algerian nation, I would be a nationalist and I would not blush for it as a crime. Men who die for a patriotic ideal are honoured and respected. My life is not worth more than theirs. But I would not die for an Algerian fatherland because such a fatherland does not exist. I cannot find it. I questioned history. I questioned the living and the dead. I searched through the cemeteries: nobody could speak to me of it. You cannot build on air."

The only hindrance to equality, Abbas argued, was the colonial system which had created a juridical caste difference between European and Moslem. A Spaniard, an Italian or a Maltese could become a Frenchman in Algeria with the minimum of formality. A Moslem could not unless he ceased to be a Moslem—i.e. substituted French law for Koranic law. His aspiration, at the time, was to see Algeria transformed "from a colony to a province". "There is nothing in the Holy Book," Abbas wrote, "to prevent a Moslem Algerian from being *nationally* a Frenchman, his arms strong, his intelligence keen, his heart loyal, conscious of national solidarity. There is nothing, but colonisation."

In the same year *Le Jeune Algérien* appeared, the liberal Governor-General of Algeria, Maurice Violette, made a memorable speech in the National Assembly: "These Moslems, when they protest, you become indignant; when they approve, you become suspicious; when they keep quiet, you become afraid. Gentlemen, these men have no political country of their own. They do not even claim their religious country. They crave to be admitted to your country. Should you refuse, you may well fear that they will soon create one."

In 1936 Léon Blum's Popular Front government came to power, and with it came a proposal from Maurice Violette, the new Minister of State, for a Bill to admit Algeria's Moslems "to the political rights of French citizens, without any modification of their status or their civil rights". It was hardly a radical project, since it aimed at "political emancipation" of a mere 21,000 Moslems the first year and would integrate others slowly and progressively. Followers of Messali Hadj attacked it violently, called it an "instrument of colonialism . . . designed to divide the Algerian people by separating the élite from the masses". Algeria's Europeans were just as hostile. A congress of 300 mayors from all over Algeria overwhelmingly (298 to 2) voted against the plan, threatening to suspend all municipal government if it were put through. Abbas and a handful of "integrationists" threw themselves into a campaign to back Blum and Violette, even went so far as fighting Messalist hecklers in meeting halls. But all their efforts failed. The French Senate, sensitive as ever to pressure from Algerian Europeans, voted down the Bill. Not long afterwards the Popular Front fell and a new government took severe measures, by decree, to prevent "all disorders or manifestations against French sovereignty, all active or passive resistance to the laws, decrees, regulations or order of the public authority". The failure of the Blum–Violette reforms was a serious blow to Abbas. In 1938 he created a party, the *Union Populaire Algérienne* (U.P.A.), attracting moderates like himself who advocated political emancipation within the French framework. But it seemed clear that assimilation was a lost cause: in April 1938 came Ferhat Abbas's first clash with authority: following a U.P.A. meeting, he was charged with obstructing the police and given a small fine. But Abbas had not lost faith in France: when war broke out, he enlisted (at the age of forty) in the medical corps, issued a romantic farewell to his political friends: "If I am killed, someone else will continue my task. *Vive la France! Vive l'Algérie!*"

Returning to Sétif after France's 1940 collapse, Abbas drafted a mild reform plan for Algeria which he sent, in letter form, to Marshal Pétain, obtaining a polite letter of acknowledgement but nothing further. Algeria in the second world war was a bastion of Vichy: its Europeans were for Pétain and against de Gaulle in their overwhelming majority. One of the protagonists of the successful Gaullist and U.S. plot to overthrow the Vichy régime on the eve of the American landings in Sidi Ferruch has himself estimated that the Gaullist "coup" in Algiers was carried out by not more than 200 men. The Vichy régime, in France and Algeria, was in the main reactionary, authoritarian and avowedly anti-Semitic: in Algeria the Crémieux law was abrogated, and Jews, like "*statut personnel*" Moslems, became subject to a "*numerus clausus*" in schools and universities; the Vichy régime left "moderates" like Ferhat Abbas alone, concentrating its police measures on the more extreme Messalists, who were jailed by the hundred. As in her colonial areas elsewhere, France suffered a significant loss of prestige with the 1940 capitulation, aggravated by severe hardship amounting in some areas to famine caused by the reduced communication between Algeria and metropolitan France. The 1942 landings in North Africa had the same impact in Algeria as in Morocco and Tunisia: the U.S. troops not only brought with them the material benefits of a modern industrial nation, which they distributed generously, and a display of armed might compared with which French army units looked puny and out-of-date, but also spread their own native brand of orthodox American anti-colonialism.

Ever sensitive to atmosphere, Ferhat Abbas realised that something had changed in Algeria itself. First Admiral Darlan, then General Giraud had called on the Moslems to contribute to a "generous" war effort. Abbas replied in a message to French authorities signed by himself and some of his former U.P.A. supporters: "The Algerians agree to take part in a war for the people's liberation, provided this be carried out without racial or religious discrimination; provided that—despite past sacrifices and past promises—they should not be deprived of their freedom and of essential liberties; and provided a congress of elected representatives and of representatives of all Moslem organisations be convened to draft a political, economic and social statute." By 1943, almost by default, Abbas had become Algeria's most important nationalist: Messali Hadj was in jail, and the religious leaders had lost their former importance. Abbas was received by Robert Murphy, Roosevelt's personal representative. Contrary to French reports current ever since, Murphy did not encourage Abbas' demands for political change in Algeria, but explicitly stated that he was interested in getting as much Moslem support for the war as possible. The mere fact of being received by Murphy gave Abbas added self-confidence and a new policy: "The Algerian people," he proclaimed, "is conscious of its personality and no longer conceives the end of the problem of its liberation in a form other than the Algerian Fatherland . . . Henceforth an Algerian Moslem will ask nothing else but to be an Algerian Moslem." On February 10, 1943, Ferhat Abbas and fifty-five Moslem lawyers, doctors, teachers and professional politicians signed the "*Manifeste du Peuple Algérien*".

The Manifesto was a further step away from assimilation: still a moderate, Abbas proposed self-determination, asking for an Algerian Constitution guaranteeing liberty and equality of all inhabitants without distinction of race or religion, recognition of Arabic as an official language on a par with French, agricultural reform, freedom of the press and of the right of association, free and compulsory education, freedom of religion and the application of the principle of the separation of Church and State. Shortly afterwards, an additional supplement called for "an Algerian state". By June 1943, General de Gaulle's "Committee of National Liberation" had established itself in Algiers and Abbas had some hopes that the Manifesto would serve as the basis for discussions with France's new Government-to-be. But the new Governor-General, Georges Catroux (whose attempted nomination by Mollet in 1956 as Governor-General was to spark off European rioting and discredit France's Government when Mollet relented and nominated Robert Lacoste instead), took exception to the supplement. When Abbas refused to attend a meeting called to discuss a counter-proposal drafted by Catroux, Abbas was arrested, sent to enforced residence in a village in Southern Oranie. In the climate of 1943 it was difficult for Catroux to behave otherwise. The concept of an "Algerian state" was anathema not only to Europeans in Algeria, but to the immense majority of Frenchmen in metropolitan France, brought up to believe that Algeria was part of France.

Perhaps Abbas himself realised his mistake: while under house arrest, he affirmed his "patriotism and fidelity to France", maintained his desire for political, economic and social reforms "within the fold of the French community". Freed in December, Abbas made contact with Messali Hadj, himself under house arrest at Reibell, some fifty miles south-west of Algiers. In March 1944 Abbas announced the creation, in Sétif, of the "*Amis du Manifeste de la liberté*" (A.M.L.) which included not only Messali and a number of orthodox Moslem religious leaders, but minor nationalists of various hues. Its aim, it proclaimed, was "to render familiar the idea of an Algerian nation and to render desirable the constitution in Algeria of an autonomous republic federated to a renovated, anti-colonial and anti-imperialist French republic". Within four months Abbas had a weekly French-language newspaper, *Egalité*, and claimed 500,000 supporters. An A.M.L. congress a year later showed that plans for a moderate united nationalist front were premature: encouraged by the congress in Heliopolis which had given birth to the Arab League a few days before, the extremist religious nationalists and Messali's followers outvoted and outshouted Abbas and his partisans, pushing through motions proclaiming Messali as "the uncontested leader of the Algerian people", dismissing all proposals for federation with France. The congress was nearly a fatal blow for Abbas, but its consequences were swallowed up in an event which, in one form or another, has marked every single Algerian Moslem alive at the time: the Sétif riots in May 1945 and their unbelievably severe repression by French forces and hastily-organised armed European vigilantes.

On May 8, 1945, a group of Sétif Moslems was authorised to parade on V-E Day, provided the marchers eschewed politics, carried no banners and shouted no slogans. They were to leave the main Sétif mosque at 9.15 a.m., walk to the War Memorial to lay a wreath and disperse in orderly fashion. Many of the Moslems either disobeyed orders or had not been informed of them. Several thousands appeared that morning, carrying French, British, Russian and American flags, signs reading "Down with colonialism", "Free Messali", "We want to be your equals", and

"Long live a free Algeria". Cheering and shouting, they made their way down the Avenue Clemenceau, and ran into the police. There were scuffles as gendarmes tried to take the banners away from the demonstrators. In the midst of the fighting, shots rang out, fired by a panic-stricken policeman. Part of the mob scattered and dispersed. Others continued to fight the police with stones. Small bands took off through the town armed with clubs, axes and knives, savagely attacking Europeans; that day twenty-nine Europeans were killed and forty-nine wounded. By noon the movement had spread north, to the rugged Babor mountains of Kabylia. The "uprising" of Sétif was enough to ignite this area too. Encouraged by the wildest kind of rumour—that all Algeria was in revolt, that an Arab government had been proclaimed in Algiers—Moslems roamed the countryside killing, pillaging and burning. The explosion was brutal and utterly unprepared for, in some places inexplicable: in some villages Moslems attacked Europeans they had lived on good terms with since boyhood. For three days the 200,000 Europeans of Kabylia, the Constantinois and the Sétif areas lived in fear, isolated amid 3,500,000 angry and unpredictable Moslems.

The repression, when it came, was a holocaust—"ferocious, pitiless, in truth inhuman by its lack of discrimination".[1] In Sétif martial law was proclaimed and any Moslem not wearing an armband was summarily shot. Throughout the countryside units of Senegalese, Spahis and Foreign Legionnaires killed and pillaged as the Moslems had done. The cruisers *Dugay-Trouin*, *Tigre* and *Tempête* shelled coastal villages, and fighter planes and bombers strafed *"mechtas"* (native settlements). In some towns Europeans organised their own shotgun justice, and in one village, besieged by Moslems a few days previously, 219 Moslems were shot out of hand.

How and why the Sétif explosion occurred has never been satisfactorily explained. An investigating committee was dissolved forty-eight hours after it had been established. Followers of Messali Hadj were certainly spoiling for a fight. There was

[1] Charles-André Julien—*L'Afrique du Nord en Marche*.

another factor, neglected at the time, regarded since as perhaps most important of all: owing to the war, essential imports from France to Algeria had dropped to a trickle and Algeria's exports (wine, tomatoes) were likewise curtailed. Algeria's European community managed to survive the war without exceptional hardship. For the Moslems, with a far lower standard of living, the story was quite different. In some areas of Constantine and Kabylia, they were at starvation level. The Sétif riots may have been sparked off by a handful of Messalist agitators: but their root cause may well have been an unorganised, savage "Jacquerie" caused by intolerable living conditions which had nothing to do with local politics.

Total European casualties numbered about one hundred, with a high proportion of officials. The true figure of Moslem dead in the subsequent "police action" to restore order has been contested ever since. The official French figure is 1,005. Privately, French army officers with direct experience of the repression suggest 6,000 to 8,000. Some reporters (including Cy Sulzberger of the *New York Times*) put the figure at 18,000. Ex-premier Georges Bidault once mentioned the figure of 20,000 and Algerian nationalists themselves claim that between 40,000 and 50,000 Moslems were killed. Whatever the figure, it was disproportionately brutal, and it is more than likely that the thousands killed did not necessarily coincide with the 50,000 Moslems believed—by French authorities—to have joined in the uprising.

On that eighth day of May, Ferhat Abbas was in Algiers, to pay his respects to Governor-General Yves Chataigneau for the allied victory in Europe. He was nevertheless arrested and jailed, his new A.M.L. banned. Of the 4,560 Algerians arrested alongside Abbas, 99 were sentenced to death, 64 to life imprisonment. The after-effects of the Sétif uprising cannot be underestimated. Every one of the "new wave" of Algerian nationalists prominent in the "National Liberation Front" today traces his revolutionary determination back to May 1945. The moderate, French-educated Algerians who had hoped for progressive evolution towards self-government had their hopes dashed by French violence. Among the current leaders of the F.L.N. (many of whom did not know each other in 1945) there is general agreement: each of them felt after May 1945 that some form of armed uprising would sooner or later become necessary. Individually, or with a small circle of fellow-conspirators, they began to think or talk about the idea of an underground apparatus.

No conspirator, Ferhat Abbas was released in March 1946, proclaimed a new federal platform conceived in his political prisoner's cell, announced the formation of a new party around it. He advocated "neither assimilation nor new masters nor separatism", but an Algerian state, with its own government and flag, linked to France in a common defence community. He called his party the "*Union democratique du Manifeste Algérien*" (U.D.M.A.), and when he put up candidates in the June 1946 elections to the French Constituent Assembly his triumph was resounding: his movement—unopposed by other nationalists, still either in jail or outlawed—got 71 per cent of the vote.

Recognising—after Sétif—the urgent need for reform in Algeria the French Government itself had made considerable efforts towards a liberal framework for Algeria. Already, in March 1944, an ordinance permitted Moslems to become French citizens without renouncing Moslem marriage rites or inheritance laws; in September 1947 a new statute was promulgated (after heated parliamentary debate) creating the two-college Algerian Assembly. But Algeria remained under the overall responsibility of the Interior Minister, was governed by a Governor-General, and the double college system in fact meant that the Europeans controlled the whole Assembly. The elections to the Algerian Assembly in April 1948 stage-managed by Marcel-Edmond Naegelen, brought it into disrepute as it was being established. Paris socialist deputies who observed the election called it "a slap in the face for democracy". Then and later, Algeria's administrators failed to appreciate that repeated fraud at the polls would eventually backfire against them. The European in Algeria laughed at the thought of an "*élection à l'Algérienne*". The Moslem merely bided his time. Whatever faith he might have had in the democratic process was slowly destroyed. At the same time, below the surface of the country, a young, dynamic, dedicated group of political agitators were convincing themselves that the bullet spoke louder than the ballot. Soustelle himself, in his report on Algeria in 1955, condemning successive electoral frauds, warned that the political discontent of the small Moslem élite was joining the social and economic discontent of the masses, and "a meeting of the two constitutes an enormous explosive force".

Ferhat Abbas and Hadj Abd-el-Kader (known as Messali Hadj) were, from the start, different and likely to clash. Whereas Abbas came from the prosperous pro-French bourgeoisie, Messali was from working-class stock. Whereas Abbas was, sentimentally at least, a nineteenth-century liberal, Messali was by temperament both a mystic and an extremist. A soldier in the first world war, Messali stayed on in France and married a Frenchwoman, eking out a living as a factory-worker with occasional spells as an itinerant salesman at fairs. An early member of the French Communist Party, he attended the Communist school for promising members at Bobigny, and—though he broke with the Communists early in his political career—he never quite forgot his early training. In 1930 he attended the International Congress in Moscow, then returned to Paris where he founded a nationalist newspaper, *El Ouma* (the Nation), which was banned by French authorities. From 1929 onwards, Messali lived under the constant threat of arrest. He was first jailed (for two years) in 1933, for trying to reconstitute the banned *L'étoile Nord-Africaine*, then again in 1935 for inciting conscripts to desert. In 1935, between prison spells, he founded the *Union Nationale des Musulmans Nord-Africaine*, which in turn was banned in 1937. The Blum Government of 1936 allowed Messali to return to Algeria (from Switzerland, where he had fled to avoid further imprisonment) and Messali embarked on a triumphal tour of Algeria. Gradually Messali was moving away from the communists, but fell for a moment under the influence of the communist-turned-fascist Jacques Doriot. His "Parti du Peuple Algérien" (P.P.A.), formed in 1937, immediately obtained a large following among the poorer Moslems, and Messali was once more arrested and sentenced to two years imprisonment for "disorderly acts against the sovereignty of the state". The Vichy régime was to concentrate its activities on the P.P.A.: Messali, whose two-year prison spell was up at the beginning of the war, was arrested again and placed under enforced residence; the Vichy Governor-General of Algiers brought fresh charges against him, and in 1941 he was sentenced to sixteen years hard labour. Messali was imprisoned at Lambèse in Algeria, along with several Tunisian nationalists (including the present Tunisian vice-premier, Bahi Ladgham). Released by General Giraud in 1943, he was once more sent to forced residence at Reibell where he began having secret contacts with Abbas. His victory over Abbas at the 1945 congress of the "*Amis du Manifeste de la Liberté*" showed that at this date he was still the dominant figure in Algerian nationalism, and the only personality to command fanatical support among the Algerian masses. But just as the Sétif uprising saved Abbas from political oblivion, so it put an end to Messali's short-lived triumph: along with thousands of other Algerians, Messali was arrested (though his connections with the Sétif uprising could not be proved) and deported to Brazzaville where he remained until 1947. The Sétif uprising turned Messali, overnight, into a staunch anti-communist: the reprisals struck his own former P.P.A. sympathisers worst of all, and in Sétif, European communists were among the organisers of the repressive militia. As anti-communist French left-wingers have since pointed out, the French Government which "covered" the reprisals included Maurice Thorèz, then vice-premier, and Charles Tillon, then Air Minister. The Sétif uprising left the field free in Algeria for other, younger nationalists who continued to pay lip-service to Messali while in fact imposing their own policy. Since 1945 Messali has been an important figure-head, and still commands the loyalty of a large fraction of Algerians in France as well as in certain parts of Algeria. But he, like Abbas, was to play no direct part in the events leading up to the rebellion of 1954.

CHAPTER FIVE

THE NATIONALIST UNDERGROUND:
1950–54

FROM the Sétif uprising to the outbreak of the Algerian rebellion in 1954 was a time of eclipse for Ferhat Abbas and Messali Hadj: but for a small group of Algerian Moslems, mostly in their twenties, it was a time of preparation and underground organisation. With the war, a new generation of Algerian Moslems had emerged. Unlike Abbas, who had grown up in the "ambiance" of bourgeois liberalism, and unlike Messali Hadj, whose youth had been spent in the Red Belt around Paris, these young Algerians were practical, disciplined, and believers in the efficacy of collective organisation. Some of them had served in the French army during the Second World War, and had acquired some measure of cosmopolitanism and a knowledge of Marxist revolutionary techniques. Impatient with the intellectuals' habit of interminable political conversation, of hollow manifestoes and constantly suppressed political movements, they respected strength and force. They functioned under the pressure of desperation. They became adepts at revolutionary warfare while remaining strangely, almost childishly, ignorant of many aspects of day-to-day life which most Europeans take for granted. "I never had a chance to know adolescence," the F.L.N.'s present Foreign Affairs minister, Belkacem Krim, said once. "I belong to the Algerian generation that passed from the total innocence of childhood into the maturity of the man." Men like Krim had fought bravely in the French army in the second world war, and had sincerely believed that at war's end, Algeria would be given a "new deal".

Instead, in May 1945, they witnessed some of the bloodiest repression in Algeria's history, their disappointment heightened by relative French indifference: Europe was busy celebrating the

end of the war, and no French newspaper deemed it necessary to
send a special correspondent to the Constantine area until long
after the repression had ended. Following Sétif, they witnessed a
series of gross electoral frauds, and the failure of either Abbas or
Messali's movements to check the Algerian Administration's
behaviour. Discouragement warmed into anger, and anger inspired a plan of action. In 1947 a group of some half-dozen young
nationalists, all of them in their twenties, using their membership
of Messali Hadj's legal M.T.L.D. party as a cover, conceived the
idea of a para-military organisation that might one day go into
action. The founders met secretly throughout 1947, and put
together what they called their *"Organisation Secrète"*. There was
no single recognised leader of the group, but its strongest personality was Ahmed Ben Bella, then twenty-eight, a merchant's
son from the Moroccan border town of Marnia. Ben Bella had
fought well with the French army in Italy, was demobilised with
the rank of sergeant-major. Other organisers were Aït Ahmed
Hocine, a Kabyle jurist, who had been involved in nationalist
movements since his schooldays; Mohamed Boudiaf, a French army
veteran; Lakdar ben Tobbal, a miller's son from Eastern Algeria;
Abdelhafid Boussouf, aged twenty-one. The *"Organisation
Secrète"* members raised a small clandestine army of some 500 men,
and put them through vigorous training without arousing French
suspicions. Gradually, they were joined by a nucleus of politicians
who, like them, theoretically belonged to Messali Hadj's
M.T.L.D., recognised Messali's popularity among the Algerian
masses but were increasingly impatient of his autocratic party
direction. The first "underground" politicians were: Mohamed
Lamine-Debaghine, a doctor, Abdelhamid Mehri, a student of
classical Arabic at Tunis university—the only man in the movement to be fluent in literary Arabic, M'Hammed Yazid, the son
of a retired French army officer and secretary-general of the
Moslem students association in France. Their acknowledged leader
was Mohamed Khider, a former Algiers trolleybus conductor
who had been among Messali's earliest followers, elected to
France's National Assembly in 1946. As a French deputy, he

enjoyed parliamentary immunity. Still in the planning stage throughout 1948 and 1949, the "O.S." rarely went into action. Once, in 1949, more as an exercise than for any other reason, an underground unit in Mostaganem dynamited a monument to the nineteenth century Algerian hero Abd-el-Kader just before it was due to be unveiled at an official French ceremony; a few months later, in Oran, Ben Bella himself led a masked raid on the Central Post Office, and got away with 3,070,000 francs—the O.S.'s first solid treasury.

Meanwhile, in Kabylia, a former French army corporal, Belkacem Krim, was organising a Kabyle "maquis" of his own, and he was brought into the O.S. too. At first Krim was not too attracted by the structure of the O.S., which he considered slightly "amateurish".

The O.S. did not remain secret for long: in the spring of 1950, French police uncovered an O.S. plot in Bône, and within two weeks Ben Bella and an accomplice were jailed, while hidden arsenals were discovered all over Algeria. Some of its leaders escaped to France, or took to the Algerian "maquis". Mohamed Khider, the only deputy among them, escaped to Cairo before his parliamentary immunity could be lifted. So did Krim, Ben Tobbal, Aït Ahmed and Krim's deputy, Omar Ouamrane. The *colons* of Algeria were only slightly worried by news of the plot. As their mouthpiece, *L'Echo d'Alger* said, on April 21, 1950: "The combined forces of justice and public order will continue unfailingly until the destruction of every single germ of revolt on our Algerian soil." But the French Government was sufficiently worried by the discovery of the O.S. ring to appoint as new Governor-General of Algeria, in 1951, a former Paris Prefect of Police, Roger Léonard.

The collapse of the O.S. created chaos among Algerian nationalists everywhere. In an atmosphere of failure, the members of the M.T.L.D. began feuding among themselves, one bloc proclaiming its loyalty to Messali Hadj, the other declaring itself for moderate reformism under Ferhat Abbas. Many of the anti-Messalist members of the M.T.L.D. were, however, performing a feint. They wanted to throw observers off their track, and imagined that the spectacle of dissension among M.T.L.D. ranks would give the impression of a general weakening in the nationalist ranks.

In March 1952, before he had been brought to trial, Ben Bella escaped from Blida jail and joined other members of the O.S. in Cairo. Within Algeria, liaison was gradually built up with what remained of the former O.S. network. "We realised," said one leading O.S. member recently, "that a revolutionary army doesn't have to be organised a long time in advance. You start with a handful of professionals and your followers can become soldiers when the time is ripe. You are too vulnerable if you maintain a large body of men."

While the M.T.L.D. continued its haggles in congresses and meetings, nine young men—the *club des neuf*—were preparing to get a solid organisation started. Six of them—Ben Boulaïd, Didouche, Ben M'hidi, Boudiaf, Bitat and Krim—were either already in Algeria or returned there from the safety of Cairo. Khider, Aït Ahmed and Ben Bella remained in Cairo, entrusted with the task of obtaining Egyptian arms and financial support.[1] The *club des neuf* became, in March 1954, the *Comité Révolutionnaire pour l'Unité et l'Action* (C.R.U.A.), itself the immediate forerunner of the National Liberation Front. C.R.U.A. members met constantly throughout 1954, in Berne and in Algiers. By July, the C.R.U.A. members co-opted by the original *club des neuf* had been warned that a revolt was imminent. By mid-September the C.R.U.A. members had divided Algeria into six *wilayas* (zones), and decided on commanders for each one. Meanwhile, the M.T.L.D. had openly and irrevocably split: some of its members remained with Messali, others were drawn to the new secret revolutionary movement. On October 10 the six "interior" chiefs of the C.R.U.A. met for the last time. They decided to start the revolt at 1 a.m. on November 1. It was All Saints' Day, a holiday, and they thought it a good moment to catch French forces

---

[1] By 1961, Belkacem Krim was the only active survivor of this "club"—of the remaining eight, four were under arrest and four had been killed in action.

napping. "It is difficult," one veteran C.R.U.A. member said recently, "to recall exactly what we felt when we learnt that the revolt was about to begin. Certainly, if we had known the extent of the bloodshed, the sacrifices and the length of the conflict we would have been even more awed. But I think if we had known all these things we would still have gone ahead." The moment was certainly timed—albeit unconsciously—to anger and embarrass not only the Government of Pierre Mendès-France but French public opinion as a whole: a few months previously, the cream of France's army had surrendered at Dien Bien Phu at the close of an eight-year war which had bled France's professional army white; in Tunisia some half-hearted Tunisian "fellaghas" had tied up several thousand French troops and in the eyes of the Arab world they had been responsible for extracting from Mendès-France the offer of Tunisian internal autonomy (though this offer would have come spontaneously from the Mendès-France Government even had there been no violence); in Morocco the French-imposed "puppet" Sultan Ben Arafa had survived one attempt on his life and trembled within his palace walls, while angry Istiq-lal demonstrators shrilly demanded independence and Riff tribesmen prepared for a guerilla war. The Algerian C.R.U.A. leaders felt certain that violence in Algeria would provoke France into making a liberal offer where former peaceful political means had failed. They underestimated both the umbilical cord linking Algeria to France in the minds of the great majority of public opinion in metropolitan France, and the diehard courage, tenacity and obstinacy of the European inhabitants of Algeria. They underestimated the military forces against them and the means France was prepared to place at the French army's disposal. Above all, they underestimated the sacrifices which nearly every single one of Algeria's nine million Moslems would have to endure, the wealth of destruction, the damage done both to the French and Algerian body-politic as the war dragged on. They underestimated, too, Algeria's importance as a pawn in the Cold War, and naïvely failed to realise that France's allies, however disapproving, would neither interfere nor proffer advice until French public opinion had reconciled itself to the eventuality of Algerian independence. "We were young, we were hopeful, perhaps we were a shade ruthless," a veteran C.R.U.A. member said recently in Tunis. "But in the context of 1954 was there really any other alternative?"

CHAPTER SIX

THE OUTBREAK OF THE REBELLION

GENERAL DE GAULLE's famous Brazzaville speech, in 1944, and the very text of the post-war French Constitution of 1946 had implied that France recognised the drive towards independence which, at war's end, was becoming the major preoccupation of all overseas territories not under communist rule. Algeria had provided a sizeable contribution of volunteers in the last two years of the war (though nearly all Europeans had remained Pétainists from the time France fell in 1940 until the very moment General de Gaulle established his National Liberation Committee in Algiers): Marshal Juin's successes, at the head of a French division in Italy, were largely due to the gallantry of Algerian and Moroccan *tirailleurs*. The Sultan of Morocco, Sidi Mohammed, had remained loyal to de Gaulle (and as a reward was made a Companion of the exclusive "Order of Liberation"). Tunisia had witnessed some of the fiercest fighting of the North African campaign, and the Tunisian Neo-Destour leader, Habib Bourguiba—whatever diehard French propagandists may have implied since—resisted all Italian blandishments to throw Tunisia on the side of the Axis powers in return for freedom. From prison, in 1942, Bourguiba managed to smuggle out a message to his friends in Tunisia in which he affirmed his faith in an Allied victory and cautioned them against Italian overtures. France's African territories had been the first to rally to de Gaulle, and made possible the epic progress of General Leclerc's column from Fort Lamy to the Mediterranean.

Nine years after the war, and for a variety of reasons, France had dissipated her capital of goodwill: on the eve of the outbreak of the Algerian rebellion, a costly unnecessary war was still raging in Indo-China; Tunisia had obtained the promise of internal autonomy only after considerable violence and Tunisian disappointment at the spectacle of internal French dissensions, while in Morocco nationalist agitation was at its height.

The reasons for successive post-war French failures overseas have been the subject of careful analysis. The best remains Herbert Luethy's *L'Heure de son clocher*. While it would be presumptuous to try to summarise this important book it should be pointed out that the reasons which explain French failures in Morocco, Tunisia and Indo-China also contributed to French failure in Algeria, right up to General de Gaulle's return to power. From 1945 onwards, it was obvious that successive French Governments, hamstrung by a divided, boisterous and irresponsible National Assembly, were no longer able to initiate and execute a given policy: the very outbreak of the Indo-China war is fraught with ambiguities due to local initiatives taken by French commanders in the field and by de Gaulle's representative there, Admiral Thierry d'Argenlieu. The Sultan of Morocco's exile, in 1953, was decided by a small group of officials and officers in Morocco itself, and accepted with misgivings after the fact by the French Government. In Tunisia the "liberal" policy of Robert Schuman, France's foreign minister during most of this period, was constantly called into question by his own subordinates in Tunisia and in the Foreign Ministry, backed by a loose coalition of self-interested *colons* and local officials. Occasionally the consequences of such government impotence were grotesque: as when M. Schuman, while Foreign Minister, learnt of the arrest and exile of a recently appointed moderate nationalist Tunisian government by listening to an early morning news broadcast.

There is a tendency among foreigners to neglect France's very real achievements from 1945 to 1954: her economic recovery, the courage and industry with which Frenchmen faced the task of rebuilding a badly mauled France, the French drive towards unity in Europe. Unfortunately, France's most competent technicians and politicians during this period tended, like Clemenceau before them, to neglect all problems outside France's physical frontiers. Government by all-powerful civil servants had drawbacks as well as advantages: at best the French system gave a technocrat immense powers which, utilised for the good, resulted in France's rapid recovery from the Second World War. The same powers, misused by high officials unchecked by any effective hierarchy, or who took advantage of governmental instability to cut across recalcitrant or weak ministers, resulted in a series of French disasters in Indo-China, Tunisia and Morocco. Towards the end of the Fourth Republic the contamination of unchecked indiscipline had spread to the very base of the French administrative pyramid: one of France's last Residents in Morocco, Gilbert Granval, recalled how disapproving switchboard operators in Rabat Residency deliberately delayed his calls to Paris because they, like the majority of Europeans living in Morocco, disapproved of his policy; later, de Gaulle's Delegate in Algeria, Paul Delouvrier, was to fight similar obstruction from minor officials in the Algerian Delegation, in the army and police.

Lack of discipline, at all levels of France's adminstration which dealt with overseas policy, was paralleled by French governmental reluctance to face or acknowledge the existence of unpleasant facts. The revelation of such facts became the privilege of the left-wing opposition press. Since such facts were unpalatable, it became customary to brand those reponsible for their publication as traitors. Perhaps one of the most disquieting symptoms of the Fourth Republic's "malaise" was the immense gulf which existed between the public and private utterances of prominent French politicians. "Double-think" was not the prerogative of French politicians alone: thus, at the very moment France's commander-in-chief in Indo-China, General Henri Navarre, was submitting reports showing that the only possible alternatives, after the fall of Dien Bien Phu, were either internationalisation of the war or negotiations with Ho Chi Minh, he was issuing public communiqués claiming that French forces were well prepared to withstand a direct offensive on Hanoi; Premier Edgar Faure, in 1955, went so far as to leave his own Resident in Morocco, Gilbert Granval, in ignorance of his decision to restore Sultan Sidi Mohammed to the throne, and in 1956 Premier Guy Mollet, having pledged himself to a liberal Algerian policy in pre-election speeches was forced, for a number of reasons, to carry out a completely different policy, and even underwrote the folly of the "kidnapping" of the Algerian rebel leader Ben Bella in October 1956.

Contrary to what most of France's career officers still believe, the Indo-China war had little immediate effect on the events leading up to the Algerian rebellion: the protagonists of "direct action" in Algeria, between 1950 and 1954, were only remotely aware of the gradual French collapse in Indo-China and of the rear-guard battle waged by successive French governments to preserve the trappings of power in Viet Nam—which led France to grant to the puppet emperor Bao Dai what it had refused to grant, three years previously, to Ho Chi Minh. Plans for "direct action" were already well advanced when Mendès-France put a stop to terrorism in Tunisia by his dramatic journey to Tunis on July 31, 1954, and outlined his plan for Tunisian internal autonomy. In any event, there was a fine line drawn between what was politically acceptable in France under certain circumstances and what was not: there have been no more vocal or ruthless opponents to the policy of negotiation with the Algerian rebels than ex-ministers Georges Bidault, Jacques Soustelle, André Morice and Robert Lacoste: yet they all, in the National Assembly debate on Tunisia in 1954, voted in favour of Mendès-France's Tunisian policy. France's foremost partisan of "*la présence française en Afrique du Nord*", Marshal Juin himself, accompanied Mendès-France on his dramatic Tunis journey in 1954; and the Government which granted Morocco its independence included the "*Centre des Indépendents*" leader Roger Duchet. What is extraordinary is not that all the above-mentioned personalities were later to be effective opponents of any liberal Algerian settlement, but that they condemned as treason a policy they had themselves supported and, in certain cases, implemented. With questionable hindsight they attributed all later Algerian disturbance to the "disastrous" North African policy of Mendès-France and were at pains to disassociate themselves from it. Yet it seems today a commonplace truth that, even if the "direct action" minority had

not existed, some kind of change in Algeria was virtually certain
after Tunisian and Moroccan independence: the protectorates had
not come into existence to guarantee the security of France's
Algerian possession. Bound by racial, linguistic and religious ties
to their neighbours, the Algerian Moslems could not fail to compare their status with that of Tunisians and Moroccans. To ignore
the consequences of Tunisian and Moroccan independence was to
ignore the world-wide nationalist current which occurred almost
everywhere in French, British, Dutch and Belgian overseas possessions since 1945.

Yet, when the rebellion took place, the immediate reaction of
the lucid Mendès-France Government was to answer force with
force: troops were despatched to Algeria despite on-the-spot
assurances, from senior officials, that all was well; Mendès-France's
Interior Minister, François Mitterand, warned that France's only
negotiation would be war. The reason was, partly, that the
rebellion was sparked off by a tiny minority and did not spread
to Algeria as a whole for over a year; partly that the Mendès-
France Government realised that it could not give way in Algeria
to a small terrorist group without alienating French public
opinion as a whole. For France, on November 1, 1954, was bliss-
fully unaware of the conditions prevailing in Algeria which were
to turn the rebellion headed by a tiny minority group into a full-
scale war. Public opinion was far more aware of the tragic Indo-
China issues, and disgruntled French career officers were beginning
to return to France filled with disgust at French half-measures
there which made a real "policy of force" impossible; in Algeria
attention had been focused a few months previously when
hundreds of people were killed in the Orleansville area earthquake:
but this disaster—which led to considerable fund-raising from
metropolitan France to help both Moslem and European victims
—had only emphasised the good relations existing between the two
communities: papers were full of stories showing how Europeans
and Moslems, beyond any racial or language barrier, had helped
each other. Indeed, for local officials and army officers stationed
in North Africa, the surprising thing was that with Tunisia and

Morocco seething at its borders, Algeria should have remained so calm. The Europeans resident in Algeria saw in this calm, not the ominous lull before the storm, but proof that in Algeria at least "*la manière forte*" was a practical and adequate safeguard against subversion.

The spot chosen for the outbreak of the rebellion was the Aurès mountain area of eastern Algeria—probably the poorest part of a desperately poor country: the rebels' main arsenal, the Benchaïba farm near the small town of Arris, was filled with shotguns, flintlocks and weapons picked up in the wake of tth German, Italian and Allied armies of the Second World War. On the night of October 31 some 150 men gathered in the Benchaïba farm, picked up their weapons and spread out over the barren countryside: some headed for the small village of T'kout to attack the French gendarmerie. Others set off for the small lead mine of Ichmoul armed with explosives.[1] The main group was dispatched to Batna, the largest (22,000) town in the area, to snipe at two French army barracks there.

A few days previously the French Commissioner for the "*commune mixte*" of Arris, in the Aurès mountains, had been summoned to Algiers to report on rumours of a forthcoming terrorist "coup" against the army and the administration. The Resident-General in Algiers, Roger Léonard, only half believed these rumours: there was little real knowledge of the existence of a still active secret terrorist group: since the discovery of the "*Organisation Secrète*" in 1950 it was thought that most of those Algerians implicated and not jailed had fled to Cairo where they had only a minor nuisance value. "No, I don't see what you mean," the Commissioner from Arris told high officials in Algiers. "All is quiet at the moment."

At 1 a.m. on November 1 the quiet was shattered—and not only in the Aurès mountains. In Batna a rebel group moved into the centre of the town and killed two French army sentries. At

[1] They were ignominiously driven off by a Moslem night watchman armed with an old shotgun.

Kenchela, east of Batna, two more soldiers were killed. On Monday morning a bus was ambushed between M'Chouneche and Arris and three of its occupants—a French schoolteacher, his wife and a "caïd" holding the honorary rank of captain in the French army—were murdered. In all, rebels struck in seventy different places all over Algeria. How the rebellion broke out, who had planned the attacks was, at the time, a mystery. "Their spontaneity," said *Le Monde*, "gives rise to the belief that one is in the presence of a concerted action." Characteristically, Cairo Radio took advantage of the news, though even Egyptian Intelligence officers had little real knowledge of what was being planned. "At one o'clock this morning," a bulletin announced, "Algeria began to live a worthy and honourable life." First reports suggested that the rebels were none other than Tunisian "fellaghas", operating from the comparative safety of the Tunisian frontier. But Jacques Chevallier, the liberal Mayor of Algiers (and Secretary of State for War in the Mendès-France Government), who toured the area with ex-premier René Mayer, deputy for Constantine, reported on his return that the Aurès was "practically in a state of insurrection". Helicopters were being used to fly supplies to Arris, cut off by the rebels and inaccessible by road; Foum Toub, near the Timgad ruins in southeastern Algeria, was besieged by a rebel group for three days. Roadblocks hindered army relief columns—and in any case French units in Algeria, totalling a mere 50,000 men, were neither numerically sufficient nor adequately trained to deal with the situation. French army columns were rushed to the Aurès area, and the Mendès-France Government began air-lifting gendarmerie and paratroop units to Algeria. Simultaneously, in an understandable but futile attempt to check the rebellion, police closed in on suspects—mostly Messalists of the M.T.L.D. who had had no part in planning the rebellion, and arrested 160 of them in France and Algeria.

That France was faced with something more than "fellagha" raiding parties or action by Messali Hadj's men was established by a tract distributed all over Algeria on November 1, a copy of which eventually fell in French hands. "Algerian People" it read:

"reflect on your humiliating, colonised condition. Under colonialism, justice, democracy and equality are nothing but a snare and a delusion. To these misfortunes must be added the bankruptcy of the parties claiming to defend you. Side by side with our brothers to the East and to the West who are dying that their Fatherland may live, we call on you to reconquer your freedom at the price of your blood. Organise yourselves to give aid, comfort and protection to the Forces of Liberation. To take no interest in the struggle is a crime; to oppose it is treason. . . . Long live the Army of Liberation! Long live Independent Algeria!"

Another sign that in Algeria an organised force was in motion came with the discovery of a "National Army of Liberation" "standing order" explaining that enlistment was open to all men between the ages of eighteen and forty and that those drafted for service were required to remain at their homes until called for.

The leaders of the November 1 rebellion, having succeeded in their main goal—which was to spread panic and disorder throughout Algeria—quickly capitalised on their activity by announcing, through tracts and secret proclamations, the creation of the "National Liberation Front" and its military arm, the "National Liberation Army". The F.L.N.'s goal was defined as: "National independence, through

(1) the restoration of the Algerian state, sovereign, democratic and social, within the framework of the principles of Islam

(2) the preservation of all fundamental freedoms, without distinction of race or religion."

The first tract embodying this goal also contained a reference to France, though—at the time—few thinking Frenchmen took it seriously. "To limit bloodshed," the same tract read, "we propose an honourable platform for discussions with the French authorities:

(1) the opening of negotiations with authentic spokesmen of the Algerian people, on the basis of the recognition of Algerian sovereignty 'une et indivisible'

(2) the introduction of an atmosphere of confidence brought about by the freeing of all those detained, by annulment of all arbitrary measures, and by ending all legal action against the combatant forces.

(3) the recognition of Algerian nationhood by an official declaration abrogating all edicts, decrees and laws by virtue of which Algeria is 'French soil'.

"In return for which:

French cultural and economic interests will be respected, as well as persons and families

all French citizens desiring to remain in Algeria will be allowed to opt for their original nationality, in which case they will be considered as foreigners, or for Algerian nationality, in which case they will be considered as Algerians, equal both as to rights and duties

the ties between Algeria and France will be the object of agreement between the two powers on the basis of equality and mutual respect."

The position of the F.L.N. was to remain remarkably faithful to this earliest statement of policy for the following seven years. Coming as early as November 1954 this tract, too, was proof that rebel organisation had gone beyond immediate military plans to the elaboration of long-term political goals.

Among those surprised, puzzled and dismayed by the new violent trend in Algeria was Ferhat Abbas himself, still leader of the U.D.M.A. and an influential, almost clubby, member of the second college of the Algerian Assembly. In a party statement, made four days after the rebellion's outbreak, Abbas recalled that his party had

"constantly sought to attract the attention of the authorities to the need to put an end to the colonial régime and to satisfy the legitimate aspirations of the population . . . Our appeals to reason and to wisdom have unfortunately found no echo in governmental spheres. The U.D.M.A. reasserts its doctrinal position, which is to seek, in an atmosphere of understanding, a solution acceptable to all. In view of the present situation, the political bureau calls upon the European and Moslem populations to keep their heads, to analyse the facts with lucidity so as not to yield to panic and passion."

Three weeks later Abbas attempted to make a speech in the Algerian Assembly but was denied the right to do so by the speaker, the late Raymond Laquière. In the speech (subsequently released to the press)—Abbas stated there would have been no "fellaghas" in Arris if the local population had been allowed to administer its own affairs. "Take care," Abbas had intended to say. "Is it not to be feared that these are premonitory signs of the great upheaval that could be upon us in a few years' time—the general uprising of the proletariat?" Still by tradition and sentiment a man of compromise, Abbas added: "The extension of the unitary Republic is contrary to the nature of things . . . the only course remaining to us lies in a union of peoples, a great human community gathered around France . . . Let us sanction the existence of this Algerian state, which we will direct together. With democratic France remaining in our midst, peace and security will be assured, as well as the conditions of prosperity . . ."

But continued ambushes, murders and successful attempts to blow up railway lines continued, and—as in Cyprus—terrorism bred its own poison: the increasing, indiscriminate brutality of the military forces, ill-equipped to put down subversion in an unfamiliar land. Despite reinforcements, French troops had only slight successes against the rebels—though elaborate, division-scale operations were mounted, with little result other than that of alienating the local population through indiscriminate shellings and shootings of suspects. Not for the first time, French officers pondered on the ethics of this very special kind of warfare officially dubbed "police action". Theoretically, the death of every rebel was still subject to a meticulous police enquiry, and—still in theory—the French soldier who shot him was liable to questioning. In practice of course things were different, but the very abyss between theory and practice was not conducive to high military morale. Nor was it conducive to good relations between European members of the Algerian Assembly—who rejoiced, almost to a man, at news of *ratissages* and successful military operations against the rebels—and their Moslem colleagues.

The month after the rebellion began a group of forty-six "second college" Moslem delegates to the Algerian Assembly adopted a resolution protesting against "illegal searches, arbitrary arrests and inhuman brutalities to which prisoners . . . are subjected" and demanding that "a policy of complete equality of rights and duties be quickly put into effect in Algeria within the framework of French democracy and the removal of any extra-legal system". Cautious in the extreme, the resolution nevertheless foreshadowed the dissolution of the Algerian Assembly which was to lapse without providing new members in fresh elections—impossible to organise in a rebel-torn country—thus removing one of the last sounding boards of Algerian opinion. Strangely, this measure was to be proposed by a new Governor-General appointed by Mendès-France himself, whose name was to become a symbol of hope for the Europeans of Algeria two years later but was anathema when he landed in Algiers on January 26, 1955—Jacques Soustelle.

CHAPTER SEVEN

JACQUES SOUSTELLE AND THE ALGERIAN REBELLION

FEW Frenchmen have had more impact on French politics in the last decade than Jacques Soustelle, the distinguished ethnologist, lecturer at the Musée de L'Homme and expert on Aztec and Mayan civilisations. Born of Protestant working-class stock in Montpellier, singled out by his brilliance while still a University student, Soustelle was a prominent pre-war anti-Fascist intellectual of the left but not of the slavish extreme left which followed the French Communist Party at the time of the Soviet Treaty with Nazi Germany. Caught on a cultural mission to Mexico at the time of France's collapse in 1940, he was among the first of the small devoted band to rally to de Gaulle: General de Gaulle used him, to great effect, first as an eloquent, persuasive lobbyist for the cause of Free France, then as head of the Free French secret service, where he displayed considerable talent for organisation and a surprising bent for the job. After a brief spell as Information Minister, Soustelle resumed his teaching career, and kept in politics by standing for Lyons as "social republican" (Gaullist) deputy in every legislature since 1946. At the time of his appointment as Algerian Governor-General, Soustelle was regarded as a far-to-the-left liberal member of the Gaullist parliamentary group.

Soustelle's difficulties began even before his appointment became effective: ten days after his nomination, the Mendès-France Government fell, having lost its parliamentary majority in the face of a coalition of former supporters—led by the ex-premier and deputy for Constantine, René Mayer—who feared and distrusted Mendès-France's North African policies without offering any valid alternative to them; for the next two weeks

France was without a government, but eventually the new premier, Edgar Faure, asked Soustelle to remain in office.

On arrival in Algiers, Soustelle was boycotted by the Europeans, except for Jacques Chevallier, the liberal mayor of Algiers and member of Mendès-France's former cabinet: the Europeans, conscious of their power, believed then—and were to be reinforced in the belief later—that they could make or break any Paris-appointed Governor-General. The record supported this view: from Violette through Naegelen to Léonard, history had shown that a Governor-General's chances of implementing a policy against the views of the Europeans of Algeria stood little chance of success and that he himself stood little chance of political survival. Conscious, then as later, that they alone determined the truth, the Europeans placed the men sent to govern Algeria into two categories: those who, after a spell in office, began to understand the "realities" of the Algerian situation, and the irrecuperable, stubborn ones who did not and who were invariably eased out of office by a combination of lobbying in Paris and passive resistance in Algiers. To the average European in Algiers, Soustelle appeared to belong to the second category.

Soustelle immediately saw that the Algerian rebellion was far more widespread than was realised in France at the time. After an extensive tour of Algeria, he reported in a later book[1] that

the rebellion was then tending to become an endemic evil, that of permanent and diffuse guerilla warfare with ambushes, isolated attacks and individual assaults . . . Isolated at first, these attacks on Moslems soon became more and more frequent and atrocious, accompanied, the better to strike the imagination, by gruesome effects: revolting mutilations, threatening messages pinned to the clothes of victims.

When I made my first trip to the Aurès, the first of many, terror had taken hold. No one spoke. The Administration and the Army had seen information dry up as soon as any informer, any native suspected of friendly relations with the authorities ran the fear of assassination or mutilation. Fear closed mouths

[1] Jacques Soustelle, *Aimée et Souffrante Algérie*.

and hardened faces. . . . The population as a whole, without throwing in their lot with the rebels—there has never been a general uprising—remained frightened and noncommittal.

Along with the extent of the rebellion, Soustelle was struck by Algeria's poverty, its top-heavy administration (which concentrated several thousand civil servants in Algiers while areas as big as half of France were left in charge of one French administrator with a handful of policemen), and the indifferent results of the French army's large-scale operations.

Soustelle's first policy speech—to present the Algerian budget for 1956 at the Algerian Assembly—was greeted with mixed feelings by the Europeans of Algeria. Soustelle's attitude was on that occasion no different from that of the previous Mendès-France Government, which had also pledged itself to put down the rebellion. Pacification, he said, would be his first aim. But he did introduce a new notion:

"No uncertainty," he went on, "must be allowed to remain as to our inflexible determination to preserve Algeria from the terrible destiny that some are seeking to prepare for it. France is at home here, or rather, Algeria and all her inhabitants form an integral part of France, one and indivisible. All must know, here and elsewhere, that France will not leave Algeria any more than she will leave Provence and Brittany. Whatever happens, the destiny of Algeria is French. This means that a choice has been made. The choice is called 'integration'; it is to make Algeria each day more completely a province, different from the others, certainly, but fully French."

Integration, like "assimilation" before it, was greeted by Europeans and Moslems alike with distrust. The Europeans were not prepared to surrender their existing privileges. The Moslems looked for concrete examples of integration and found none; "integration" was a fine word—with none of the questionable undertones of "assimilation"—and a good one to brandish in the face of mounting outside criticism. It was to become, two years later, a rallying cry for the Europeans who had, all their lives, rejected and fought everything that integration stood for. It was based on the conception, irrational and obviously untrue, but current in all French history books for decades, that *"l'Algérie, c'est la France"*. It was a generous attempt to give substance to a juridical fiction, and at the same time an obvious defence mechanism to avoid the recognition of any form of nationalism. (The Portuguese have been using the same device in their African possessions for years to deny the existence of any Portuguese "colonies".) Perhaps the very ambiguity of the term caused Soustelle to select it. If taken at all seriously, it was a long-term goal, implying a psychological revolution in the minds of both Moslems and Europeans, as well as a gigantic financial effort on the part of France herself. At the time, neither the ambiguities nor the implications were seriously considered, and Soustelle himself was faced, on the morrow of his speech, with the down-to-earth problem of putting a stop to terrorism in a steadily deteriorating political and military climate.

From the moment Soustelle landed in Algiers, the F.L.N. had intensified its activity, and as the months went by the rebellion spread alarmingly from the Aurès mountains, first to the Southern Constantine department, then to Kabylia. Far from being free to implement his integration promises, Soustelle was faced with the problem of tackling a growing, violent independence movement backed by terrorism, with inadequate and untrained troops. However generous Soustelle's motives were, in practice his decisions did not tend to make Algeria more like France in any way: on the contrary they emphasised already existing differences. On April 1, largely at Soustelle's urging, the French National Assembly passed the first Algerian "state of emergency" Bill, delegating special powers to the prefects in Algeria, including the right to restrict the movement of persons and vehicles, to establish "special security zones" by decree and send undesirables and suspects into enforced residence. The Bill also provided for night searches and arrests, the control of the press, radio, cinema and theatre. The French Ministry of Justice also ruled that military courts should try persons for crimes committed before October 30, 1954. Parliament passed the first state of emergency Bill with some reluctance, and a government promise that under no circumstances would detention camps be systematically established (this promise went by the board a few months later). The Bill was effective for six months: since then it has, in an increasingly thorough way, been revised and prolonged.[1] Some of the provisions of the Bill affected Algeria's inhabitants only indirectly: thus, for two years, a government official refused to allow the film *The Bridge of the River Kwai* to be shown in Algeria (on the grounds that it showed Europeans in humiliating circumstances) and the film *Ill Met By Moonlight* (which describes the kidnapping of a German general by some British and Greek partisans in wartime Crete) has never been allowed to be shown at all; the Bill affected Europeans in other, more important, ways: the import of medical supplies, wireless sets, batteries and the like was strictly controlled, the sale of "war surplus" items heavily restricted. Far more important than these petty controls were the *"mesures d'exception"* which struck indiscriminately at Moslems, guilty and innocent, independence-minded or not. While these measures began taking effect, the Afro-Asian independent countries, meeting in Bandoeung (from April 18 to 24), gave the nationalist movements in Tunisia, Algeria and Morocco great encouragement: the North African Neo-Destour, F.L.N. and Istiq-lal representatives did not have full delegate status, but were active behind the scenes and intellectually as impressive as any of the delegations from fully independent countries. An Egyptian motion, unanimously adopted, proclaimed the rights of Tunisia, Algeria and Morocco to full independence and called on France to seek peaceful settlement with her North African possessions "without delay".

Side by side with the newly enforced security measures, Soustelle attempted to reform the Algerian administration. He realised, with most members of the Faure Government in Paris,

---

[1] Until February 1961, when the decree was abrogated, but other measures taken which in fact prolonged most of the "emergency" powers.

that if the worst consequences of the rebellion were to be avoided, Moslems would have to be brought into public life and into positions of increased administrative responsibility. Soustelle's plan, which was to become that of his successors too, involved partial decentralisation of the adminstration, the creation of new departments, increased electoral responsibilities for the Moslems (including parity of representation for the Moslems in the towns). Before his spell as Governor was over, Soustelle had succeeded in getting some of these measures accepted (including the creation of a Bône department). But even the most timid reforms caused a storm of protest from the European mayors' association and the three main European settler associations, the *"Rassemblement des Français d'Afrique du Nord"*, the *"Union Française Nord Africaine"* and the *"Vigilance Africaine"*. None of these groups was a political party: their sole doctrine consisted in opposing all measures which could conceivably lead to a decline in European privileges in Algeria. Their membership varied according to months and even weeks: when French interests in Algeria seemed particularly threatened, there was a rush of new members. The European *"clientèle"* of these groups was very similar to that of the later *"Front National Français"* and the *"Front de l'Algérie Française"*. It is probable that the very same person who joined the "Rassemblement" or the "Union" in 1955 and '56 joined the *"Front National Français"* in 1959 and the *"Front de l'Algérie Française"* in 1960. Leaders of these lobbies successfully milked the Europeans of Algeria of considerable sums; indeed, one of the later contributing causes to French settler anger and disillusion in 1961 was the realisation that such groups, with large funds at their disposal, had been relatively ineffective, and occasionally downright corrupt.

One of Soustelle's reforms was to have considerable repercussions: this was his decision to create a new corps of administrators, drawn from the French army but engaged in a whole series of civilian duties. The under-administration of Algeria was, to a large extent, reponsible for the rebellion's earlier successes: in some areas, particularly in the Aurès, Nementcha and Djurdjura mountains, no European official had been seen within living memory. As one captured rebel put it around this time, "We thought that France had given up interest in Algeria . . . our only contact with France was through corrupt tax-gathering 'caïds'."

Soustelle's partly successful answer to this situation was the establishment of the *"Sections Administratives Specialisées"*, followed, later, by the *"Sections Administratives Urbaines"* (S.A.U.) for urban areas. The S.A.S. officers (usually lieutenants or captains) dealt with every conceivable aspect of adminstration, from teaching, improving agricultural methods and health to administering justice. The organisation of the S.A.S. was entrusted to General Parlange, and the army continued throughout the years to appoint and supervise the running of the S.A.S. though each S.A.S. officer was under orders, not from the local military commander, but from the Prefect of his department. Whoever has seen an S.A.S. officer at work in a remote Kabyle village will recall the selfless devotion of such men, often living in considerable danger and isolation, displaying all the ingenuity and skill which is characteristic of French officers with limited funds at their disposal but an unlimited supply of courage and "systeme D.".
Unfortunately, the S.A.S. system contained its own inevitable drawbacks: first of all, it was created and administered by a general who had himself been trained as a native affairs officer in Morocco, and had inherited fairly rigid ideas as a result of service in this fine, but somewhat out-dated corps; secondly, S.A.S. officers stepped into their job after hasty training, with no time to learn Arabic, with the result that in some parts of Algeria (though not in Kabylia where, thanks to old-established French schools and the Kabyle habit of seeking work in France, nearly all the men spoke French) they were entirely dependent on interpreters; lastly, and perhaps most important of all, the S.A.S. officers could not afford to specialise in exclusively constructive work, such as helping villagers to rebuild their houses, improve their agriculture and see to it that "mandats" (money orders) from France arrived regularly and were actually received by families entitled to them: the very shortage of officers and men in Algeria compelled the S.A.S. officers to act not only as good Samaritans but as policemen and soldiers

too. Part of the benefits of their activities were lost as the S.A.S. officers, with locally raised Moslem militiamen, also acted as military detachments in support of army units engaged in putting down the rebellion. In many cases the result was similar to that described by Winston Churchill in his autobiography and telling of his experiences as a subaltern on India's North-West Frontier: as in India, where army commanders and civilian assistant commissioners often clashed, the S.A.S. officers—inevitably preoccupied first and foremost with the welfare of the local population—frequently were at odds with local army commanders intent only on hunting out and destroying the rebels, even if this meant that in the process Moslem villages and civilians were to suffer. Unlike India, the army commander almost invariably had the last word, and indeed it would have been impossible for a lieutenant or a captain to go against the orders of a unit commander of the rank of colonel or above. In other ways, too, Moslem confidence in the local S.A.S. officers was tempered by suspicion and fear: inevitably, as the rebellion continued, the S.A.S. officer tended to become increasingly concerned with security duties; holding absolute power in a small area, he could be a tremendous influence for either good or evil. An S.A.S. officer could, for instance, increase or diminish the number of rations brought in to non-self-supporting villages, decide who would work on public projects, could close down shops and administer justice himself. Naturally, there was a tendency to use this power to stamp out the rebellion and punish those suspected of helping it, even if such justice sometimes went wrong. As a tribute to the S.A.S. officers as whole, it should be stated that abuses were rare, and that where S.A.S officers were active, there were few of the atrocities and excesses which marred the French army's reputation.

There was one aspect of the S.A.S. which did not escape the Moslems: and that was its resemblance to the Tunisian and Moroccan corps of "native affairs officers". Perhaps unwisely, instructions given to S.A.S. officers included orders (and the necessary funds) to build a "bordj", or fort—partly for their own security, partly to impress on the Moslem population that the implantation of French officer-adminstrators was a physical and inescapable fact. Many of the S.A.S. officers deplored the fact that they had to live in a "bordj" and would have preferred to live among the Moslem villagers in spite of the discomfort involved. A "bordj" may have been a symbol of French strength; it was also a symbol of "direct administration". In medieval Europe, a village could at least seek refuge in the castle of the protecting lord. But the "bordj" was meant primarily as a dwelling place for the S.A.S. officer himself, his family and Moslem militiamen. Like the *képi bleu*, the distinctive headgear which the S.A.S. officer inherited from the corps of native affairs officers, it was a symbol of a glorious past.

Such administrative changes were in full swing when there occurred, on August 20, 1955, a series of uprisings which were to fill Europeans with horror and cause, in a minor way, a re-enactment of the events which surrounded the Sétif uprising of 1945: on the second anniversary of the exile of Morocco's Sultan Sidi Mohammed, a series of Moslem uprisings occurred all over Algeria and Morocco: at Oued Zem, in Morocco, some 2,000 maddened Berber tribesmen massacred nearly ninety European civilians. In the Philippeville area itself massacres occurred on a similar scale. In Philippeville uniformed "fellagha" appeared in the streets of the town, marching six abreast through the Moslem quarter with their green and white flag; at El Halia near Philippeville Moslems rose against the Europeans with hideous savagery, encouraged by every conceivable kind of rumour—that the Egyptian navy was about to land Egyptian troops on the coast, that the United States was entering the rebellion on the side of the F.L.N. As in Sétif, the massacres were followed by equally hideous shotgun justice: in Philippeville itself, Europeans, in vigilante committees, summarily executed Moslems and buried them surreptitiously while armed civilians held over-inquisitive correspondents at bay; in the countryside, fear-crazed Moslems, fleeing both F.L.N. bands and enraged Europeans, fled from their villages and started roaming over the mountains. For the first time it was found necessary to appoint a French colonel as overall civilian and military commander of the Philippeville and Collo areas. Soustelle appealed to the Moslems to return to their villages, and assured them that justice would "spare the innocent". But the August 20 massacres left an indelible impression on Europeans and Moslems alike: not the least marked was Soustelle himself, who visited hospitals and homes in the most seriously affected areas. Confronted with physical violence at close quarters, Soustelle was appalled by the savagery with which those reponsible for the uprising had butchered and mutilated their victims. Though he has been at pains to deny it since, it seems that his uncompromising hostility to Algerian nationalism has its roots in his memories of the Philippeville and El Halia victims.

The following month brought fresh troubles for France: for the first time, the question of Algerian rebellion was raised in the United Nations: an Afro-Asian request stating that colonial rule had prevented the Algerian people from exercising its right to self-determination and stressing the "imperious necessity for negotiations between the French Government and the true representatives of the Algerian people" was at first rejected by the Assembly's General Committee, then admitted by the Assembly itself (by 28 votes to 27, and 5 abstentions). Then, as later, the French Government took the view that the United Nations had no right to discuss an internal matter "involving part of the territory of the French Republic". Acting on instructions from the French Government, France's leader to the U.N. Delegation, Antoine Pinay, withdrew in protest. A few weeks after the vote, French forces in Algeria were faced with a further extension of the rebellion—this time to the Oran department, hitherto a haven of peace and security. Meanwhile, a group of Moslem deputies, senators, councillors of the French Union and delegates to the Algerian Assembly had affirmed their faith in "the Algerian national idea". A manifesto, known as the "*manifeste des 61*" was forwarded to the French Government. Some of the signatories could be taxed with opportunism. Others, like Ahmed Francis (who later joined the F.L.N. along with Ferhat Abbas, and became a "minister" in the Algerian "provisional government") had long hoped to bring about political change by legal means. Publication of the manifesto both encouraged the rebels to continue and had a considerable effect on French public opinion in France.

Despite Soustelle's efforts, the F.L.N. rebellion had emerged, at the end of 1956, immeasurably stronger than at the beginning of the year. It had witnessed its first diplomatic success in the United Nations, and countless minor military skirmishes against a heavily-equipped, but less mobile French army. Police and army activity against the rebels contributed to its very success: the lack of discrimination with which arrests were made and villages destroyed, the increasingly brutal interrogation measures practised by troops and police, the blind conservatism of most European settlers, all helped to turn the mass of the Moslem population into prudent *"attentistes"*, intent on keeping out of trouble if possible but increasingly willing to support the rebellion. By the end of 1956, F.L.N. organisation had grown from its rudimentary form to a relatively complex network of tax-gatherers, political commissars and judges, backed by local commandos enjoying the tacit support of the Moslem population. Logistically speaking, the F.L.N. had improved its position partly from financial gifts from the Arab League countries and partly from arms purchases from its own funds, and it was able to move supplies into Algeria from across the Tunisian border without overwhelming difficulties. Ominously, the year ended with the first bomb explosions in Algiers itself.

CHAPTER EIGHT

FRENCH ELECTIONS AND AFTER

THE French Government's decision to put forward general elections by six months was taken in the hope that a new National Assembly would be more manageable. The decision caused fresh fears and increased unrest in Algeria: the Algerian Assembly, by an overwhelming majority, voted in favour of postponing elections, on the grounds that "the exceptional circumstances . . . make it impossible to conduct sincere and free electoral operations" and refused to vote election appropriations: from January 2 onwards, Algerian seats in the National Assembly just lapsed, and the Algerian Assembly itself was soon to become an empty, ghost-ridden building, used infrequently from 1956 onwards as a convenient spot to record election returns.

French political observers predicted a swing to the left, and the Europeans of Algeria feared above all things the emergence of a socialist government which would begin negotiations with the rebels. Fear acted as a binding factor in the case of fifty-two different (and occasionally rival) ex-servicemen's associations which had also become powerful, vocal lobbies of European opinion. They banded together in a single "*Comité d'entente des anciens combatants, victimes de la guerre et cadres de reserve*", which was to become one of the most powerful of all European pressure groups in Algeria.

The elections in France resulted in further confusion: the socialists, radicals and Catholic "popular republicans" all lost a little ground; the (Gaullist) "social republicans" lost 51 out of 71 seats, and 51 new, brash, unsophisticated "Poujadist" deputies appeared on the scene for the first time. Though it was obvious that some kind of socialist coalition would be required, the difficulties of

government leadership with such a National Assembly were
increased rather than diminished.

On January 13 the new "Comité d'Entente", acting like other
European lobby groups before it, demanded that the new
government

"solemnly proclaim its irrevocable determination to maintain
French sovereignty in Algeria

"re-establish law and order . . . by all means at its disposal

"order the execution of all sentences imposed by the courts,
particularly the death sentences

"make energetic representations to foreign nations in order that
all encouragement and material aid to the rebels be stopped."

The last demand could cause some embarrassment to the new
government: over the past few months French N.A.T.O. units
had quietly been taken out of Germany to serve in Algeria, and
the streets of Algiers were full of private cars owned by officers
bearing the blue-and-white German occupation number plate;
Sikorsky helicopters, badly needed in Algeria, had been turned
over by the United States Air Force to the French Air Force in
Stuttgart. One of France's best divisions, the *"septième division
méchanique rapide"*, had been sent to Algeria complete with its new
equipment (which proved totally inadequate for guerilla warfare
and had to be scrapped). The French Government had, in the past,
stated that French units leaving for Algeria had left their American
equipment behind. As many first-hand witnesses have since
testified, the claim was not true, and was to cause considerable
resentment among both the French army and the F.L.N. It became
not uncommon for a French junior officer, wearing equipment
inscribed with the tell-tale "U.S." markings, to ask visiting
journalists angrily: "Why do our American allies not help us in
this war against communism?" Just as it became increasingly
common for the F.L.N., from its Tunis headquarters, to draw
attention to "United States aid . . . received by the French army
in its war of extermination against the Algerian people". The
Suez operation complicated matters still further: one of its results

—and not the least from the F.L.N. point of view—was that Nasser was able to lay his hands on the huge, obsolescent British Army stores along the Suez canal, and as time went on the F.L.N. received large consignments of British arms (mostly Lee-Enfields) and British equipment. French army intelligence officers, with a fine contempt for the obvious, even went so far as to allege that Britain was somehow knowingly supplying the rebels with arms, and many times I was confronted, on a visit to a French unit on operations, with a rack of captured Lee-Enfields and an angry *"regardez, monsieur le journaliste"*. It was invariably impossible to convince anyone that the arms had fallen into the F.L.N.'s hands as a result of the Suez landings.

Faithfully reflecting the fears of the European community in Algiers, Soustelle went to Paris shortly after the elections to point out to French political leaders that premature federation (which was then in the air) would make integration impossible for ever, and lead directly to secession. Soustelle urged that the new National Assembly make a "solemn proclamation", a kind of pledge to achieve full European and Moslem equality within a given time limit, followed by an "aman", or pardon to all rebels not accused of crimes of violence. For Soustelle, integration had become more pressing than ever, though at no time did he suggest how a genuine integration policy could be pursued in the midst of a full-scale rebellion and against the wishes of most Moslems and the entire European community. Soustelle's insistence on "real integration", including the introduction of similar credit and wage scales as well as similar power and transport costs, to say nothing of a common electoral roll, caused the spokesman of the *"Union Française Nord Africaine"* to accuse him of preparing "a criminal conspiracy to prepare for our obliteration". Partly to reassure the Europeans in Algeria, partly to explain his policy to France, Soustelle made a broadcast speech in which he outlined his integration policy more fully than ever before.

"Since Algeria must become an integral part of France," (he said on January 12), "it is imperative that this exigency become

more real each day for the good of all. This means that the
specific personality of this province of the French Republic be
solemnly recognised and guaranteed with all respect for its
traditions, for its religion and for its culture. This means, too,
that among the French of Algeria, whatever their racial origin,
whatever their religion, as also between them and their fellow-
citizens of metropolitan France equality must reign—the
equality of rights and duties, of advantages and sacrifices, from
Dunkirk to Tamanrasset.

"I am profoundly convinced that this is the only way to
salvation. . . ."

As expected, the new government was headed by the socialist
leader, Guy Mollet, who was sceptical of Soustelle's integration
policy. During the election campaign there had been considerable
socialist pressure for direct negotiations with the rebels, and the
socialists had joined with the Mendès-France fraction of the
radicals in a common "republican front". Mendès-France was
anathema to the Europeans of Algeria. Was he not blamed not
only for the Indo-China catastrophe but also for the loss of
Tunisia and Morocco? Confronted with a likely change in
Governors (Soustelle's term was to expire on January 31) the
Europeans of Algeria suddenly realised that Soustelle was a more
acceptable alternative than any socialist-appointed successor.

In January, too, occurred a significant statement by Ferhat
Abbas, by this time living in Paris. Interviewed by the Tunisian
paper *Action*, Abbas said:

"I am in no ways qualified to negotiate with France. The men
who lead the action are alone entitled to do so. My party (the
U.D.M.A.) and I have thrown our entire support to the cause
defended by the National Liberation Front. My role, today, is
to stand aside for the chiefs of the armed resistance. The methods
that I have upheld for the last fifteen years—cooperation, discussion, persuasion—have shown themselves to be ineffective;
this I recognise. . . .

"I shall take no political action unless I am instructed to do so by the National Liberation Front. And for this contingency to arise, the military problem will first have to be solved by negotiation."

The Europeans' fears were confirmed when the announcement came of Soustelle's successor, General Georges Catroux. An immensely respected soldier, Catroux had been one of the first army officers to join de Gaulle; he was not only a Gaullist (and the Chancellor of the Order of the Légion d'Honneur, one of the highest posts France can confer) but an avowed liberal. He had resigned from the national council of the Gaullist "*Rassemblement du Peuple Français*" in 1952 because of his disappointment at the R.P.F.'s attitude towards Tunisian and Moroccan problems. A disciple of Lyautey, he had publicly sided with the eminent French writer François Mauriac, a relentless critic of French North African policy. General Guillaume, while France's Resident-General in Morocco, had in fact barred Catroux from visiting Morocco. Last but not least General Catroux had been the French Government's emissary to Antsirabé, in Madagascar, to negotiate the exiled Moroccan Sultan's return. At the time of his appointment, he was seventy-nine years old.

From the moment of the announcement of Soustelle's successor, the European associations and lobby groups began preparing for his reception. Their anger and their fears were reinforced by the interpretation, in most of the French press, of the meaning of this appointment. "General Catroux's departure for Algeria," said *le Monde*, "can only reflect the determination of the new French Government to seek there as well a peaceful solution, necessary not only for Algeria, but also for the equilibrium of North Africa as a whole."

But Guy Mollet's investiture speech provided neither the dramatic reversal of policy expected by the Europeans of Algeria or a real repudiation of integration. His Algerian platform was a tissue of generalities, and only his promise to "recognise and respect the Algerian personality" attracted attention: the rest was a mixture as before of vague good intentions. He described his objectives as the re-establishment of peace, the organisation of the co-existence of the two Algerian communities, the establishment of "indissoluble links" between Algeria and metropolitan France, the promise of administrative and social reform, while "adapting . . . the army to its task". General Catroux himself went to some lengths to dispel the settlers' fears in an interview granted to *le Monde*. Rejecting integration "which the Moslems today no longer accept", Catroux said government policy would "take into account the specific character of the country, with its two communities . . . there can be no question of conceding to Algeria a solely Moslem personality," Catroux added. "First this would fail to recognise the importance of the metropolitan contribution to the country's development. In addition, there is no historical basis for the recognition of a national Algerian state . . ." Catroux added that he was prepared, in Algiers, to meet "*interlocuteurs valables*" but not rebel spokesmen, and that "there could be no question of allowing the bonds that link Algeria to France to be impaired. If the government is resolved to secure for the Moslem community its rights, it does not under any circumstances intend to turn the country into a national state, inevitably marked for independence. Nor can there be any question of reducing the French to minority status . . ."

Catroux's statements had little effect on the Europeans: looking for loopholes, they came across a passage in the *le Monde* interview in which he stated he would try to assess the real strength of the rebellion. In January 1956 it was particularly strong, though the larger towns had as yet been spared. Besides, nothing that Catroux said could convince the Europeans that he would not begin negotiations with the leaders of the rebellion. Catroux's appointment made them cherish the presence of Jacques Soustelle, and on the day of Soustelle's departure (on February 2), tens of thousands of Europeans (and a handful of Moslems) crowded the "gare maritime" and the docks where he was to embark on the French steamer *El Djezaïr*, carried him in triumph and shouted "do not leave us". The demonstration was directed as much against General Catroux as it was for Soustelle, and the air was full of cries of "A bas Catroux" and "A bas Mendès". Nobody paid any attention to the fact that hostile slogans were being shouted at Algeria's Governor-elect, Soustelle least of all. The crowd had blocked Soustelle's official "cortège" of Spahis and limousines, and threatened to keep Soustelle in Algiers by force. Demanding silence, Soustelle shouted: "If you want me to continue to defend French Algeria" ... (cries of "yes, yes") ... "then let me leave." By his own admittance, Soustelle's farewell reception—like his inspection of the victims of the El Halia massacre—was to have serious consequences: for the first time Soustelle found himself the hero of a wildly cheering compact mass of people. There is no doubt that this episode went to his head. After his departure, he became the leader, in Paris, of the European community in Algiers whose shortcomings and blind conservatism he had been the first to denounce.

The farewell ceremonies for Soustelle were a kind of dress rehearsal for the welcoming ceremonies planned for Catroux, and on February 6 the Premier, Guy Mollet, made his historic arrival in Algiers (Mollet had previously announced that he, personally, would install Catroux as Algerian "Minister-resident"). What happened on February 6 was to confirm the European community of Algeria in the belief that it could dictate policy to Paris by street demonstrations and violence—a belief which lasted until the failure of "barricades week" in January 1960 and the nationalist Moslem counter-demonstrations of December 1960. Ignoring the warnings of the ex-servicemen's "Comité d'Entente" Mollet laid a wreath at the war memorial in Algiers' town centre: tens of thousands of Europeans, mostly youths, packed the square and the adjoining main streets. While Algiers' police stood by, they pelted the unfortunate Premier with cabbages and tomatoes. Members of Mollet's immediate entourage, and the squads of gendarmerie and "Companies Républicaines de Securité" did their best to hold off the mob. The police—nearly all of them local men, whose own hierarchy was strongly politically tainted—failed to do their duty, and there were some grounds for the belief that the demonstrations had actually been planned with the tacit consent of senior Algiers police officials. Seriously shaken, Mollet returned to the "Palais d'Eté", the ornate Moorish-style residence of Governors of Algeria, and here too a crowd broke through a good-natured police cordon and began tearing up the garden of the "Palais d'Eté", putting the flag in front of its main entrance at half mast. No Government would have allowed such a mob to behave in this way with impunity in Paris, but then, as later, France's government leaders obscurely felt that the European demonstrators in Algiers were entitled to some special immunity. The effect on the Moslems was of course deplorable: to them it was evident that there were two scales of justice—one for the Europeans, who were allowed the utmost leeway and enjoyed the tacit approval of the police force; and one for the Moslems, against whom both police and army had no hesitation in opening fire.

The importance of February 6, 1956, cannot be underestimated: the European demonstrators felt that there was nothing that street violence could not achieve; it encouraged them to perfect this technique, which they were to use to such effect two years later, on May 13, 1958; it showed them that they were not alone in their struggle against Paris authority, and that sizeable elements in the police itself were on their side. If the police could be won over, why not the army too? The results of such behaviour were immediate: where more stubborn, ruthless men would have stuck to their guns, Mollet preferred to bow to the crowd. It was not only a matter of physical courage, for Mollet was not a coward; rather was it a measure of the existing Algerian vacuum: the Moslems were in no position to express their thoughts, and Mollet's own expressed Algerian policy was couched in the vaguest possible terms; the authority of any Premier in the Fourth Republic was shaky in the extreme. Perhaps Mollet instinctively realised that, for a successful show of force against the European demonstrators, he would need the kind of power and stability which no Fourth Republic government leader could possess; the February 6 demonstrations had shown an unsuspected tenacity and toughness among the Europeans of Algiers, and Mollet, himself a lifelong socialist, had been struck by the fact that the mob's anger cut across class divisions: the rioters included workers and small shopkeepers, mechanics and petty officials who, on the other side of the Mediterranean, would doubtless have voted socialist. For all these reasons, he preferred to surrender before battle was really joined: that evening, he announced the resignation of General Catroux who had remained in Paris. Wild with delight, the *"Comité d'Entente"* issued what amounted to a series of ultimatums to Mollet, and that stormy petrel of extreme right-wing politics, Maître Jean-Baptiste Biaggi, appeared on the scene, welding various European association representatives into a short-lived "Committee of Public Safety". It seems incredible that a newly-appointed Premier, enjoying the confidence of a large majority (420 votes to 71 in the National Assembly) should have failed to react to this situation. No arrests were made among the European activists. Biaggi was not asked to leave Algiers for over a week. No senior Algiers police officer was dismissed or even transferred. It was known that some of the demonstrators had come into Algiers from outlying districts by car, and that their vehicles contained arms to stage a real armed revolt should Mollet persist in Catroux nomination. No enquiries were made into local European leadership which ordered the arms to be on hand or into the obvious links between European associations in Algiers and Jean-Baptiste Biaggi's bully-boys of the extreme right in Paris. On February 9 Mollet announced the appointment of fellow-socialist Robert Lacoste, a bluff, hearty labour leader well to the right of the party itself, to Catroux's job. It was a logical choice to make: there was nothing about Lacoste which could possibly irritate the European population of Algiers. That same day, in what seemed to some as an orgy of self-abasement, Mollet made a broadcast specially destined for the Europeans of Algeria:

"You have been depicted as colonialists," he said. "I do not share this view. There is, no doubt, a small selfish minority ready to defend its own interests and political positions to the desperate end. . . . There is also the immense mass of the European population: farmers, workers, tradespeople, teachers, doctors, who have been established in Algeria for several generations and have their homes, their families and their dead in Algeria. Since my arrival, I have heard the voice of all of them and have been greatly moved by it. In their eyes, Algeria is the best country in the world: it is their small homeland, it is what they are most attached to. They see France only as it is reflected in Algeria. . . .

"These men . . . believed that France was going to abandon them. I understand their despair. . . . That is why I say to you in all sincerity that, even though for me the experience was painful, the unfortunate demonstration on Monday had a wholesome aspect. It provided many with an opportunity to express their attachment to France and their fear of being abandoned. If that is what the immense majority of the men and women at the War Memorial wanted to make known, I assure them that they have been heard. France will remain present in Algeria. The bonds linking metropolitan France to Algeria are indissoluble. . . ."

The reaction of the Moslems to this speech can be imagined. True, in the same speech, Mollet repeated his pledge to "make the Franco-Moslem community a living reality . . . You aspire to a régime of freedom. This freedom, only republican France can guarantee it." To the Moslems it appeared that the only freedom the Mollet Government was able to confer was that of allowing the European minority to do whatever it wished.

CHAPTER NINE

THE COLLAPSE OF THE
FOURTH REPUBLIC (1)

THE change of Government in France, brought about by the general elections of January 2, 1956, began disastrously for Algeria with the collapse of Premier Guy Mollet's authority in Algiers when confronted with a spirited European mob and the passivity of the police force. The note was irrevocably set by Mollet's surrender, and was to lead, eventually, to the May 13 demonstration two years later which overthrew the Fourth Republic altogether. Between February 6, 1956, and May 13, 1958, the authority of the French Government, both in France and Algeria, was progressively and increasingly sapped.

Evidence of France's dwindling power to control events in Algeria was not lost on the Moslems: occasionally this defiance of authority took on a particularly overt form, as when, just after the February 6 riots, thousands of Europeans, led by their European mayors, gathered in Algiers in protest against the Mollet Government to lay a wreath at the tomb of the Unknown Soldier at a time when gatherings of more than three people were nominally forbidden; Poujadists and students successfully compelled shopkeepers to close their shops, and the administration did nothing to punish the instigators of the strike. Local French newspapers, and some French observers, noted that during European demonstrations on February 6 and after, no Moslems were actually molested by the crowds and deduced that this meant that the Europeans enjoyed tacit Moslem support. Senior officials in the French Government can hardly have believed this outrageous theory: nevertheless, such was the atmosphere in Algiers at the time that I personally had it repeated to me on any number of occasions by officials who should have known better. If this belief was held by any responsible officials in Algeria, it was proof of the appalling capacity for wishful thinking shown, then and later, by administrators and senior army officers who chose to elude the real complexities confronting them in favour of a simpler, happier, traditional "Image d'Epinal" in which right and wrong, good and bad, were comfortably and irrevocably distinguished as in a children's fairy tale where everybody lives happily ever after. On any number of occasions, civilians and officers alike could have gauged the true nature of the situation in Algeria by questioning men of proven experience whose testimony was not likely to be false. In Algiers itself, Archbishop Duval was seconded by some priests—in particular the Abbé Scotto, the "curé" of Bab el Oued —whose long-established friendships with Moslems and whose lifelong experience in Algeria enabled them to speak with some authority of the serious situation existing in 1956, of the danger of an extension of terrorism, of the Moslems' disgust and despair at obvious double standards of justice, and of the threat implicit in French weakness towards the European mob, which encouraged them to take the law more and more in their own hands. For reasons which may have had something to do with Robert Lacoste's avowed anti-clericalism, such men were regarded as suspects, and their advice and warnings deliberately ignored until too late.

Nor, at a higher level, did Mollet himself realise what he was doing when he allowed the French army in Algeria to "use political propaganda weapons" as well as the conventional means of putting down the rebellion: by allowing the army a measure of political control, Mollet himself opened the door to the extremists in the French army who helped overthrow the institutions of the Fourth Republic and had to be thoroughly cowed by General de Gaulle before the latter could feel strong enough to attempt to solve the Algerian war without being, himself, destroyed by the army elements which had helped him to power.

Partly, Mollet's own predicament was due to the rebellion's increasing strength during and after the February riots: during 1956 and the first few months of 1957, the rebels got nearer than at any other time to the actual physical control of certain parts of Algeria: men of the F.L.N. were physically present in any number of mountain villages in Algeria, openly drilling and even playing football, with plenty of time to take cover or disappear as soon as the "guétteur" signalled the presence of a patrol or a spotter plane; this was the time of large-scale desertions in Algerian Moslem units in the French army, of successful ambushes on the roads, of widespread destruction of farms, wine crops and telegraph poles. It should be noted, however, that in February 1956 urban terrorism in its full horror was still to come. Apart from two bombs in Moslem cinemas in December 1955 (which may have been the work of counter-terrorists) Algiers itself had as yet suffered few casualties.

Could the French Government have believed, in the light of growing rebel strength, and following the display of French weakness during the February riots, that its leaders would accept cease-fire terms with nothing more substantial than the promise of elections to come within a three-month period? Such was the proposal outlined by Premier Mollet in a broadcast made on February 26.

"France," he said, "recognises and respects the Algerian personality. Algeria is and will remain indissolubly linked to France. The final status of Algeria will under no circumstances be determined unilaterally. It will result from free discussion with the elected representatives of the Algerian population. . . .

"In accordance with its promise, the Government will immediately initiate the announced measures for economic and social progress and administrative reform. To this end, a Bill conferring upon it the necessary special powers will be submitted to the National Assembly tomorrow. . . .

"I now turn to the Moslems, to all the Moslems of Algeria: in the name of the Government, I renew and clarify before them a solemn commitment: the guns will be silenced, and elections organised within the three months that follow the cessation of the fighting and of acts of violence . . . today you

have a way to make your aspirations known and freely to choose
your representatives . . . are there any among you, who by
their refusal to put an end to the fighting are prepared to assume
before the world and before history the tragic responsibility of
making the situation irreversible, for preventing your peaceful
emancipation, and for destroying Franco-Moslem brotherhood?
France, loyal and generous, offers you justice and equality. . . .
I cannot believe that this appeal, which I make with utmost
my conviction, will go unheeded. . . ."

That the rebels would agree to end the fighting must have
seemed improbable to France's best informed officials in Algeria:
it must be remembered that, then as later, there was profound
distrust, among virtually all Moslems, for abstract promises which
had gone by the board so often. To offer the Moslems the chance
of going to the polls once more to choose their elected representatives was, in Moslem eyes, to go once more through the whole
cycle of "élections à l'Algérienne" which had been broken by
the outbreak of violence. Even had the offer been couched in
more attractive terms, its rejection was still certain, for in private
conversation officials and officers made it quite clear that they
thought in terms of "pre-fabricated" elections, with all rebel
sympathisers barred. In this context, the phrase "organised
elections" in Mollet's speech had sinister undertones not realised
in Paris. In April, as if to emphasize the failure of Mollet's offer,
the Algerian Assembly was dissolved by decree and its prerogatives temporarily vested in the Minister for Algeria.

As one of Algeria's foremost experts, the ethnologist Germaine Tillon, has noted,[1] that the rebellion did not become a
mass movement until April 1956. The F.L.N. gained increased
support at this time for several reasons: one of them indubitably
was Tunisian and Moroccan independence (achieved in March
1956); another was the disgust and despair already noted following
the successful "diktat" of the Europeans to Mollet in February;
probably the most immediate reason, however, was the news of
the first two capital executions of two Algerian rebels, sentenced

[1] *Les Ennemis Complémentaires*, Editions de Minuit, 1960.

to death for bearing arms against France. The two men, Ferradj and Zabanah, were executed in March: the day after their execution, in a wave of armed attacks by Moslems, 47 European civilians were killed or wounded. Urban terrorism had started in Algiers in full earnest, and this was only the beginning; one of the Moslems shot down as he attacked Europeans in the streets of Algiers was called Achour. He lived in a crumbling tenement building in the Algiers Kasbah, at number three, rue de Thèbes. In July, a powerful bomb exploded at this address, a few minutes before curfew, destroying the entire building, killing 53 Moslems, including women and children, and making 280 people homeless. Officially, the Algiers Government-General announced that the bomb had been placed in the building as a result of rival gang warfare between the F.L.N. and its rival nationalist movement, the M.N.A. In private, officials admitted that they believed the bomb was the work of European counter-terrorists, led by an Algiers doctor called Kovacs, who had organised an efficient counter-terrorist organisation with the help of various Algiers police officials. (These suspicions were to harden when Kovacs was found to be the instigator of the later attempt on the life of General Raoul Salan, then Commander-in-chief of French forces in Algeria.) Understandably, since a number of police officials were themselves involved in counter-terrorism, enquiries into the bomb outrage on the rue de Thèbes building got nowhere. It did, however, provide the F.L.N. with arguments for carrying on the rebellion by indiscriminate urban terrorism, and such was the hideous climate in Algiers, in the latter part of 1956 and in 1957, that those Moslems who had sincerely disapproved of the F.L.N.'s earlier violence in 1955 sided almost unanimously with the rebel leaders: in the Kasbah, in the overcrowded Barberousse prison, news of each successful piece of urban terrorism was greeted with exultation, and the chief terrorist leader in the Kasbah and his lieutenant, Yacef Saadi and Ali Ammar, known as "Ali la Pointe", became national heroes. On September 30 the first F.L.N. bomb exploded in Algiers—in two fashionable cafés, the '*Caféteria*" and the "*Milk Bar*", frequented mainly by European students and

Algiers' "Jeunesse dorée". One European was killed and 52 wounded. Bombs were to follow thick and fast: On January 27 of the following year, 4 people were killed and 50 wounded in a similar explosion; in February, a time-bomb in Algiers sports stadium exploded after a football match, killing 9 and wounding 45; in June time-bombs concealed in the base of lamp-posts near a bus stop in the centre of Algiers exploded at noon on a Saturday, killing 10 and wounding 86. Six days later, a time-bomb exploded in the "Casino de la Corniche", a dance hall, during a crowded Sunday afternoon dance, killing 10 and wounding 90.

Germaine Tillon has given an extraordinary account, first in *L'Express*, later in a collection of essays,[1] of her two meetings in Algiers with Yacef Saadi and Ali la Pointe at the height of the terrorist scare. Germaine Tillon was in Algeria as a member of a committee looking into conditions in detention camps for Moslem nationalists. Her previous book, "L'Algérie en 1957", had stressed the gradual "pauperisation" of Algeria's Moslems and their economic dependence on France. During June 1957 she was told, through a Moslem woman friend, that "a number of people" would like to meet her to discuss this book. She accepted, and found herself in the presence of Saadi, Ali "la Pointe" and a few other terrorist leaders. One of the questions Yacef Saadi asked, with—it seemed to Germaine Tillon—considerable humility, was one most Frenchmen were asking themselves: "How will it all end?" "I was very pessimistic" [wrote Germaine Tillon] "and answered brutally: There is no reason for it to end —ever. The F.L.N. will never beat the French army and even if the French army manages to stamp out the rebellion for a time, it could not do so for ever. If in the distant future, France gets tired of the drain in men and money and decided to halt its activities, it seemed to me that it would be impossible for Algerian workers to retain the privileges they enjoyed at present on the French labour market; in which case the whole country was sentenced to a speedy and necessarily bloody regression. I also explained that while, on paper, there were eight million Algerians

[1] *Les Ennemis Complémentaires.*

to one million Europeans, representing a balance of forces of eight to one, such calculations were in fact meaningless, that the potential strength of a country was not necessarily a question of numbers but far more of its technical strength and its investment potential. This being the case, there was a kind of equivalent balance of forces between the two groups which made the situation even more insoluble. If there had been fewer Europeans the Tunisian solution would have been possible, if there had been fewer Moslems, integration could have been achieved without overwhelming difficulties. At this point Yacef blurted out: 'Then I shall never be a free man!' The tone was not aggressive or angry, but one of positive despair . . ."

Germaine Tillon went on to explain that the committee she belonged to had come to Algeria to enquire into atrocities and to prevent them from happening, and mentioned F.L.N. atrocities and mutilations. "I could not help but point out to him (Yacef) that he was able to see for himself how unfair it was to attribute collective responsibility to a community for crimes committed by a few of its members, and what was unfair *vis-à-vis* himself was also unfair *vis-à-vis* ourselves.

"After two and a half hours' conversation along these lines, Yacef said something, with a smile, like: 'You see we are neither criminals nor murderers.' Very sadly, but very firmly, I answered: 'Yes you are; you are murderers.' He was so astounded that he remained for a moment quite speechless . . . then his eyes filled with tears and he said: 'Yes, Madame Tillon, we are murderers.' He told me some details about the bombing of the Casino, and said that when he had heard of it he had cried for three days and three nights . . . I remember then having said: 'In the eyes of a certain section of opinion, terrorism justifies torture. In the eyes of another section of opinion, torture and capital punishments are the justification of terrorism. It is a vicious circle and quite inextricable.' At one stage of the conversation, Yacef Saadi made a violent gesture and said: 'Ah, those bombs! I would like to see them all at the bottom of the sea.' I replied with something like: 'I would help you dump them there.' Very overwrought, he replied: 'It's the only way we have of expressing ourselves.' It seems to me he said this phrase over and over again, while I repeated, over and over, that 'innocent blood calls for vengeance' ... almost abruptly he said: 'I promise you that from now on the civil population will be spared.' " Highly moved, Germaine Tillon pressed him to define this promise, and asked him whether it would stand even if further executions took place: "In that case," Yacef Saadi replied, "I cannot guarantee a thing."

Germaine Tillon returned to Paris and reported her conversation to a highly placed official on Mollet's personal staff, explaining that the pressure of Moslem opinion was such that terrorist leaders were forced to stage fresh bombings every time an Algerian nationalist was executed, and suggesting a general suspension in the carrying out of death sentences. Whether her suggestion came to anything or not is, by now, of academic importance: but the fact remains that, between her talks with Yacef Saadi and the carrying out of the death sentence on three Algerians ten days later, there was not a single terrorist bomb outrage in Algiers. In a later meeting, Yacef Saadi told Germaine Tillon that he had given instructions that there should be no reprisals for future executions, and he seems, more or less, to have kept his word, until his own arrest a few months later. Tillon's meeting with Yacef Saadi showed that even at the height of terrorism, F.L.N. leaders involved in the most ruthless forms of warfare showed that they too had their "crise de conscience". Even the top F.L.N. terrorist leader in Algiers during 1956, Ramdane Abbane, who could have stepped straight out of a Malraux novel and whose whole life was dedicated to violence, seems to have felt pangs of conscience before ordering indiscriminate urban terrorism. It is not my intention to whitewash F.L.N. terrorism, or to excuse the summary executions and mutilations suffered by Moslems at the hands of the F.L.N. But an account of the rise of terrorism in Algiers, and of the reasons why it took its hideously violent form, would be incomplete without a mention both of European counter-terrorism which started the bombings and of Yacef Saadi's pathetic pledge and bitter tears.

Germaine Tillon's encounter with Yacef Saadi and Ali la Pointe can only be fully understood if the background to their conversations is summarily drawn in: Algiers, from the summer of 1956 onwards, was a fearsome city to live in, all the more fearsome in that the principal activity of its European inhabitants was that of accumulating wealth as fast as possible. The rebellion was bringing undreamed-of prosperity to many; real estate values were spiralling; government spending on public works and new housing, the presence of large numbers of soldiers, officials and oil men in Algiers, all resulted in easy profits and high profit margins. Algiers was a boom town, with no real desire for the rebellion to stop. But it was a front-line town, too, since the rebellion was now striking at the heart of Algiers, and the slightest backfiring of a car caused people to start nervously; it was a town full of rumour, but its inhabitants lacked real curiosity about certain aspects of the activities being carried on there: daily, truckloads of Moslems were seen entering buildings in El Biar suburb temporarily occupied by paratroops units. What happened to these Moslems seemed of little concern to Europeans, even when the ranks of their own employees were thinned by arrests. Replacements were found without much difficulty from among the large numbers of Moslem unemployed. The Europeans' own lack of curiosity about the activities of the paratroop regiments was paralleled by the lack of concern of the Algerian Minister himself. On January 7, 1957, Lacoste turned over the responsibility of all police and security measures to General Jacques Massu and his Tenth Parachute Division. It was difficult for him, after that date, to intervene without being rebuffed. As a number of senior "para" officers were apt to remind civilians, they had not wanted the job in the first place. They had been entrusted with the task of stamping out terrorism in Algiers "by any means". The least that civilian officials could do, they implied, was to keep their noses out of army affairs and let the "paras" clear up the mess. Lacoste himself, in characteristically gruff fashion, was not above expressing the same point of view when confronted with enquiring reporters. "Let us get on with the job," he told me on the one occasion I met him. *"Je ne vous demande qu'une seule chose, à vous autres journalistes étrangers: c'est de bien vouloir ne pas venir nous enmerder."* Such bluff self-confidence could be of use in Paris, to bolster up the morale of an embarrassed Government. It was out of place in Algiers, where there was all too much evidence at hand to show that the "paras" very special form of police investigation cut a wide swathe through innocent and guilty alike, breeding even more hatred. From day-to-day observation of the activities of Robert Lacoste and his staff, it was difficult to avoid the impression that, for the "Ministre-Résident", movement was a substitute for action and bluster a form of permanent self-defence. An experienced politician, M. Lacoste approached Moslems and Europeans alike more like an S.F.I.O. bigwig oozing bluff self-confidence among a group of socialist party members than as a minister faced with crushing responsibilities in a desperate situation. His clubby geniality made him popular with most Europeans, from the modest "piednoirs" of the "poor white" urban areas to the powerful newspaper owners and lobbyists who found to their surprise that a socialist minister could express bluntly patriotic sentiments as well, if not better, than they themselves. Like former men in his position. Lacoste met only those Moslems whom his subordinates wished him to meet. Like his predecessors, Lacoste was virtually a prisoner of his own tentacular staff: as time went on, it became increasingly obvious that various departments nominally responsible to him were in fact acquiring an autonomous life of their own. During his tenure of office, both the efficiency and discipline of the "Gouvernement-Général" staff deteriorated still further.

CHAPTER TEN

THE GROWING PAINS OF THE REBELLION

THE time has come for a closer look at the growing structure of the F.L.N., both in Algeria itself and in exile. The successes of the rebellion (which caused the French Government to send its conscript army to Algeria and increased its forces there to 400,000 men by the end of 1956), together with the existence of a mass movement in Algeria in favour of the F.L.N. from April 1956 onwards, did not mean that its growth proceeded without inner clashes. In a factual account of rebel dissensions from 1954 until 1958 based largely on police reports and F.L.N. correspondence seized by the French army, Serge Bromberger[1] has made a valuable contribution to this aspect of the rebellion.

The course of revolutionary movements seldom runs smooth: a "resistance movement", inadequately supplied, whose means of communication with the outside world were uncertain, whose leaders were constantly on the move, could not but give way to the stresses and strains related by Bromberger. Correspondence between the F.L.N. leaders of the interior and the "*délégation extérieure*" inevitably tended to dwell on those aspects of the rebellion—arms shortages, leadership clashes, ethnic rivalries—which were causing most concern. In the same way, volumes could be written on the differences of opinion and personal rivalries which existed in France from 1940 to 1945 between the various resistance groups inside France and General de Gaulle's Free French Headquarters in London. But to write the definitive history of the French Resistance solely in those terms would be misleading. Even so, the parallel is not entirely fair: during the Second World War, the French Resistance Movement was immeasurably better equipped to withstand such strains than was

---

[1] *Les Rebelles Algériens*, Plon.

the F.L.N. Liaison officers and reinforcements in men and material were parachuted into France with increasing frequency from 1943 onwards; an efficient radio system kept all parties in constant touch; and German defeats, first in North Africa, then on the Russian Front, were a constant spur to action.

In Algeria, none of these conditions existed. Tunisian and Moroccan independence greatly facilitated the activities of Algerian nationalists, but did not provide the same kind of logistical support as was provided by Britain during the war. There were no proper radio links, and messages from Algiers to Tunis had to be carried by men on foot, often taking up to three months for delivery when their bearer was not killed or captured. (The setting-up, in 1958, of the "Morice Line" along the Tunisian–Algerian border was an additional barrier to communication.) The rebels were not part of a world-wide conflict: they were isolated men in a world not, at that time, particularly preoccupied with Algeria. Nor did they, at this period, benefit from the active sympathy of the communist bloc. For the first five years of the rebellion they could rely only on themselves, on grudgingly provided aid from Arab League members and on pious declarations of sympathy from the Afro-Asian bloc at the United Nations Organisation.

There were other aspects inherent in Algeria itself which could not but lead to interior clashes: Algeria's historical lack of unity, the absence of any established political forces there, the predominance of tribal clannishness, the lack of any historical precedents and the intellectual and cultural limitations of the main protagonists themselves were all factors which were to encourage internal divisions. It must be remembered, too, that most of the leaders of the F.L.N. were themselves the disgruntled former supporters of Messali Hadj's nationalist party, that Messali Hadj had publicly condemned the rebellion in 1955, and that for some time after the rebellion began F.L.N. leaders remained suspicious of those adherents of Ferhat Abbas's U.D.M.A. who wished to join them. Much has been made of the internal rivalries of the F.L.N. and there has been a natural tendency to compare Algerian nationalism with Tunisian and Moroccan nationalism and find it wanting. But in Tunisia the Neo-Destour party was, long before it resorted to violence in 1952, tightly organised and united around Habib Bourguiba, while in Morocco all sections of Moroccan opinion, Arab and Berber, united around the exiled father-figure of Sultan Mohammed V. The astonishing thing about the F.L.N. throughout its growing pains, was not that rivalries and dissensions occurred but that it was able to survive without any major split. In the long run, the long underground experience of the F.L.N. may have proved an advantage: whereas in Morocco independence brought disunity and bitter rivalry among former friends, the Algerian rebel leaders were forced to weather their difficulties while still in a hard-pressed, clandestine, revolutionary stage.

Quite apart from the operational hazards and difficulties, problems of organisation and internal unity came in the wake of the November 1954 outbreak. Shortly after the initial uprising, the "chaouia" tribesmen of the Aurès mountains (Wilaya number 1) rose against their leaders and refused to accept orders imposed from outside their own tribes. Since there was not one "chaouia" tribe, but hundreds of sub-tribes, mostly divided against each other by centuries of village feuding, the operational value of the "chaouia" tribesmen dropped sharply, especially after the commander of the number 1 Wilaya had been murdered by his own men. Another difficulty arose from the F.L.N.'s chronic arms shortage: as far as possible, F.L.N. commandos attempted to become self-sufficient by collecting the arms and equipment of those French troops they killed in battle. With a growing number of volunteers this source proved insufficient, and Wilaya (division) commanders began the habit of trekking to Tunisia and Morocco to obtain arms where they could. On the world arms market, the F.L.N. became a major customer. It bought small arms and ammunition from Belgium, Italy, West and East Germany as well as from Czechoslovakia; in addition, consignments of arms began pouring in from Egypt and Syria, and later from Iraq. These arms were either smuggled across the

Egyptian border into Libya, and thence to Tunisia, or shipped in directly to a Tunisian or Moroccan port.

But once the arms were in Tunisia or Morocco the problem remained that of bringing them into Algeria and of distributing them fairly. It was obvious that the Wilaya commanders nearest the Tunisian or Moroccan borders were better placed to receive fresh arms consignments than Wilaya commanders in the centre of Algeria, and the reluctance of the "frontier" Wilaya commanders to allow consignments through and their tendency to increase their own reserves at the expense of the Wilayas of the centre led to bitter recriminations. (Thus, for a year and a half after the rebellion began, the Wilaya number 3 (Kabylia) was still mainly armed with shotguns while F.L.N. units in the Oranais and Constantinois areas were far better equipped.)

There were other problems: the question of overall leadership frequently arose during the first year and a half of the rebellion, and in various ways was to be implicit in all difficulties facing the F.L.N. right up to 1961. The outbreak of the rebellion had been planned and executed by the "*Club des Neuf*", who had pledged themselves by solemn pact not to take any decision affecting the course of the Algerian rebellion without consulting all members of the "Club". But as time went by, such a resolution could not be implemented without the greatest difficulty: some of the original members of the "*Club des Neuf*" were killed in action, and one of them (Rabah Bitat) was arrested early on in the rebellion. By August 1956 only two of the original members of the "Club" were still operationally active in Algeria: Belkacem Krim (of the Wilaya number 3) and Larbi Ben M'Hidi (of the Wilaya number 5). The other survivors of the "Club", whose unquestioned leader was Ahmed Ben Bella, were part of the F.L.N.'s "*délégation extérieure*" in Cairo, dealing with the F.L.N.'s finances, arms supplies and diplomacy, and communications difficulties precluded physical consultations. Moreover, since the rebellion began, new leaders had appeared on the scene, lacking the glorious aura of the rebellion's founder-members, but making up in enthusiasm and competence what they lacked in

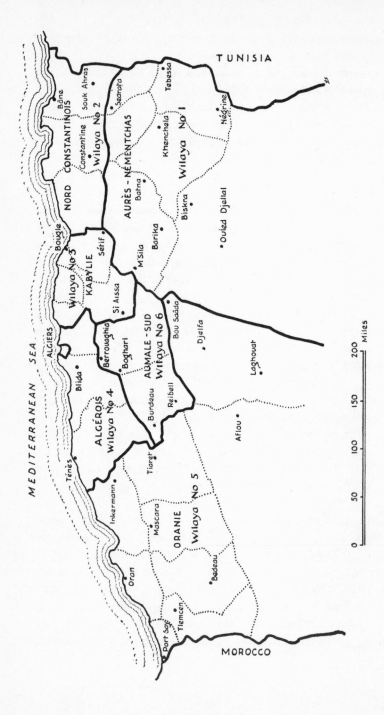

MEDITERRANEAN SEA

TUNISIA

MOROCCO

NORD CONSTANTINOIS

Wilaya No 2

AURÈS - NÉMENTCHAS

Wilaya No 1

KABYLIE Wilaya No 3

ALGÉROIS Wilaya No 4

AUMALE - SUD Wilaya No 6

ORANIE Wilaya No 5

Bône
Souk Ahras
Constantine
Sétif
Bougie
ALGIERS
Blida
Ténès
Inkermann
Oran
Port Say
Tlemcen
Mascara
Badeau
Tiaret
Burdeau
Rebell
Berrouaghia
Boghari
Si Aissa
M'Sila
Barika
Biskra
Batna
Khenchala
Négrine
Tébessa
Saarata
Ouled Djellal
Bou Saada
Djelfa
Laghouat
Afiou

0   50   100   150   200
Miles

"*ancienneté*". Foremost among the "new wave", of F.L.N. leaders who came to prominence in 1956 was Ramdane Abbane, a young Kabyle who had once been clerk in a "*commune mixte*" and had flung himself into the struggle with almost religious zeal. In 1956, when Belkacem Krim was commander of the Number 1 (Kabylia) Wilaya, Abbane became his political adviser and chief of staff. Abbane was one of the few "intellectuals" of this early phase of the rebellion—he had passed his "baccalaureate", a literate, persuasive organiser with a natural political flair. He possessed to the full that necessary if unpleasant attribute of born leaders—the ability to manipulate subordinates without any sentimental regard for personal relationships—and as a political and military tactician he was remarkable, though his sombre, sad personality reflected his rigid belief that just as France had conquered Algeria through violence, nothing but violence could ever force her to relinquish it. Largely through Abbane's realisation that the F.L.N. must be as broadly based as possible, a number of prominent Algerian nationalist sympathisers found their way to Tunis and Cairo, and he was instrumental in persuading Ferhat Abbas and Ahmed Francis to leave France in April 1956.

By the summer of 1956 both the "*délégation extérieure*" and the Wilaya commanders of the interior agreed that they should meet to discuss urgent problems. The Wilaya commanders were reluctant to leave Algeria. Finally, despite the overwhelming problems involved, the "Soummam Conference" was held in August 1956 but members of the "*délégation extérieure*" were unable to attend, the meeting-place having been changed at the last minute for security reasons. Only three of the six Wilayas (though the three most active ones—Nord Constantinois, Kabylia and Algerois) turned up in force, complete with delegations. The Wilaya number 5 was represented by its leader, Larbi Ben M'Hidi; the Wilaya number 6—which at this time was largely a paper creation—had no representatives to the conference and number 1 Wilaya members were not present though a delegation (of doubtful representation) had been consulted before the talks began.[1] In all some 250 men met for several days under the noses of the French army in a deserted hut in the Soummam valley.

The Soummam Conference marked the apogee of Abbane's influence within the F.L.N.: its resolutions bore the imprint of his style as well as of his thinking. The results of the Soummam Conference were to have a lasting effect on the F.L.N.'s future orientation, even though some of the resolutions adopted by those attending it were by-passed by later F.L.N. leadership. At the Soummam Conference, the delegations established an overall "Execution and Coordination Committee" (C.C.E.), whose members were three of the Wilaya commanders attending—Larbi Ben M'Hidi (Wilaya number 5), Zighout (Wilaya number 2) and Krim (Wilaya number 3) as well as Ramdane Abbane and the imprisoned trade union leader Aïssat Idir.[2] They also established a *"Conseil National de la Révolution Algérienne"*, composed of delegates from all over Algeria, who were to act as a kind of sovereign parliament, representing the Algerian people as a whole; the meeting also ratified Abbane's proposals that the *"délégation extérieure"* should be responsible to the "forces of the interior" (i.e. to the newly constituted C.C.E., which was to meet semi-permanently in Algiers) and not vice versa; that collective leadership should be implicitly accepted at all levels; and that military decisions should be subordinate to political aims.

Such were the communication difficulties between the interior and the *"délégation extérieure"* that Ahmed Ben Bella did not learn the full decisions of the Soummam Conference for several months—on the eve, in fact, of his arrest by the French. From his French jail, Ben Bella spent some considerable time upbraiding Larbi Ben M'Hidi and Ramdane Abbane for their betrayal of the solemn *"Club des Neuf"* pact. In a sense, it can be supposed that Ben Bella's arrest prevented, by averting, a full-scale split between the F.L.N. partisans of Ramdane Abbane and the *"délégation*

---

[1] The "number 4 Wilaya" (the Algerios area) was represented by Omar Ouamrane, though there is some doubt as to whether he was its ranking leader at the time.

[2] Who later died in an Algiers military hospital of burns probably inflicted by paratroop "interrogators".

Other members were Youssef ben Khedda, who was later appointed 'Premier' in 1961 and Saad Dahlab who succeeded Krim as Foreign Minister at the same time.

extérieure". Eventually this internal rivalry between two men, one of them Arab, the other Kabyle, abated: the F.L.N.'s "C.C.E." was forced in turn to seek refuge in Tunis and the question of interior primacy did not arise again for some considerable time while the principle of "collective leadership" advocated by Ramdane Abbane was adopted. The fate of Abbane himself was tragic, and remains shrouded in mystery; after the flight of the remains of the C.C.E. to Tunis, Abbane became increasingly opposed to the F.L.N.'s collective policy; according to some, he was eased out of the C.C.E. and left virtually inactive in Tunis for some time, though he still continued to work on economic blueprint for an independent Algeria. According to others, he asked to be sent back to Algiers to reorganise a terrorist network; went back despite the opposition of most of his colleagues, found that security precautions in Algiers and the memories of Massu's police repression so strong that no one would co-operate, and returned to the Tunisian border. Then his track is all but lost. The time was February to April 1958, and heavy fighting was then going on at the frontier between well-organised F.L.N. troops and the paratroopers guarding the Tunisian frontier (one of the regiments involved, the *Premier Régiment Etranger Parachutiste*, the crack paratrooper Foreign Legion Regiment, later disbanded for its role in the "Generals" Insurrection of April 1961, lost a third of its strength, including its commanding officer, in dead and wounded on the Tunisian–Algerian border during this period). Abbane is believed to have taken part in the fighting and to have been seriously wounded. He returned to Tunisia, where he died. The discretion surrounding his death has led some observers to believe that Abbane was "liquidated" by the F.L.N.: its leaders have naturally denied this, but readily admit that at the time of his death he was in disgrace. It is said that many of the F.L.N.'s later "Provisional Government" never forgave Abbane his prominent part in organising the Soummam Conference; in turn Abbane was deeply suspicious of the survivors of the "*Club des Neuf*", and openly accused Ben Bella of wanting to assume dictatorial powers; in the long run, Abbane owed his eclipse, and perhaps his death, to the principle of collective leadership which he had himself proclaimed as a major principle of policy at the Soummam Conference; by the end of 1957, there is strong evidence that his uncompromisingly violent stand and his insistence on the efficacy of indiscriminate urban terrorism met with sharp opposition from most of the other F.L.N. leaders in Tunis and led to his downfall.

The Soummam Conference, achieved despite Ben Bella's opposition, had immediate results: in the first place, the rebel organisation was quite naturally exhilarated at having staged a major policy conference on Algerian soil, and the news that such a meeting had taken place spread throughout Algeria.

Secondly, some of the Conference decisions were immediately implemented: the C.C.E. moved to Algiers, and the "Zone Autonome d'Alger"—headed by Youssouf Ben Khedda—became, for the next few months, the most active area in the whole rebellion. Encouraged by their own successes, the C.C.E. members, mostly at the prodding of Ramdane Abbane, decided to go ahead with indiscriminate urban terrorism despite the reservations of some of its members. The "battle of Algiers" began in earnest and was to last for a whole year, until the arrest, in October 1957, of the last surviving member of the F.L.N.'s terrorist network.

The avowed aim of the C.C.E. and of the leaders of the "Zone autonome d'Alger" was to bring the city of Algiers to its knees by indiscriminate terrorism, and they very nearly succeeded. The Algiers Kasbah was a superb natural hiding place; despite French claims that at no time were more than 4,500 Algerians directly concerned with terrorism (out of a total Moslem 450,000), it seems certain that the terrorists benefited from the complicity of a huge majority of the Moslem population, as well as from the aid of a small number of Europeans. Among those arrested and convicted for having taken a major part in terrorist activity during this period were employees of the Algiers gas and electricity services; postmen and post office clerks; students, doctors, tradesmen, customs officials, even Moslem police officers and a prominent "bachaga", the Bachaga Boutaleb, whose nationalist sympathies overcame his basically pro-French sentiments. Practically no Moslem representative of Algiers society was lacking, from the most humble welders and dockers to the wealthy members of the tiny Algiers Moslem "bourgeoisie" and including that well-known element of Kasbah society, the pimps and petty racketeers. The efficient and well-organised Algiers terrorist network could not have operated without the tacit support of the Moslem population as a whole.

That this whole episode is one of the grimmest in the entire history of Algeria no one, least of all the F.L.N. itself, will deny. As the civilian casualties (including Moslems) increased, public opinion turned against F.L.N. leadership both in France and in the world at large; French public opinion in particular was shocked by accounts of deaths and mutilations suffered by civilians, and hardened against the idea of negotiations with those who had ordered them; cold-bloodedly, an F.L.N. spokesman at the U.N. once replied, as I questioned the efficacy of such methods: "You must realise that every time a bomb explodes in Algiers we are taken more seriously here." Looking back on this period, it is easy to see how great the temptation was for the F.L.N. to use its considerable means to wage a war of this kind. But, seen in perspective, the "battle of Algiers" certainly did the F.L.N. cause more harm than good: it alienated French public opinion for years. It was instrumental in bringing General Massu's paratroopers into Algiers as a permanent police force and in causing M. Lacoste, the "Ministre-Résidant", to hand over most of his prerogatives to the army, and by so doing it delayed, for years, all serious chances of negotiations. Those who were responsible for starting the "bataille d'Alger" did not realise that rather than cause a French surrender it would increase French determination to hang on to Algeria at all costs and that all questionable French army methods in dealing with F.L.N. suspects would henceforth be justified by the inevitable excesses of urban terrorism.

Only by forgetting the victims of the "battle of Algiers" can this episode be treated as it must have appeared to its protagonists:

as a desperate adventure, a constant battle of wits against immeasurably superior forces and hopeless odds. Scores of times terrorist leaders were cornered by police and General Massu's paratroopers; scores of times they escaped, disguised as women, hidden in cisterns or passing from one crumbling Kasbah house to another through an elaborate network of secret passages. In the fearful cat-and-mouse game played by the paratroopers and the terrorists, no holds were barred: the terrorists deliberately chose attractive young girls to place explosives in crowded cafés, while the paratroopers resorted to every conceivable form of torture to obtain information. There were moments, in the "battle of Algiers", of unbelievable horror and violence, as when two terrorist leaders, Mourad and Ramel, were cornered in a house in the Kasbah and surrounded by paratroopers: they fought it out to the end, lowering hastily primed explosives down into the street below in baskets to blast the paratroopers, finally blowing themselves up with their final stock of bombs when they realised the situation was hopeless; similarly, when Ali la Pointe was surrounded, paratroopers, taking no chances, blew up the house in which he was cornered: the detonation set off Ali's own stock of bombs and blew up the whole street, killing 25 people, including 8 children as well as Ali's two runners, aged eighteen and thirteen.

On January 7, 1957, with F.L.N. terrorism at its height, M. Lacoste had handed over all police and security responsibilities to General Jacques Massu. On January 27 Massu's tenth Paratroop Division moved into Algiers just as the F.L.N. was about to stage an eight-day "insurrectional strike". One "para" regiment at least was to remain in Algiers until February 1960. The use of paratroopers as policemen could be defended in the light of the worsening terrorist situation. But Lacoste's decision to hand over responsibility lock, stock and barrel could not. By doing so, Lacoste himself avoided dealing with the moral problem of justifying torture as a means of obtaining information. As army officers were quick to point out, the problem was not Lacoste's but theirs, and detailed instructions from the French Government on what was, and what was not, permissible did not come in time.

The result was that the "battle of Algiers" became, for the paratroopers who fought it, and for France itself, a pyrrhic victory: it is estimated that out of the Kasbah's total population of 80,000, between 30 and 40 per cent of its active male population was, at one stage or another of the "battle", arrested for questioning and questioning came to involve the use of torture as a basic instrument, as a time-saving device to obtain quick results. It is certain that without torture the F.L.N.'s terrorist network would never have been overcome; it is equally certain that the degrading effect on those who used it and its hideous consequences on the thousands of innocent Algerians subjected to it outweighed in importance the "battle of Algiers" itself. For some months French public opinion was unwilling to believe reports concerning the behaviour of French paratroopers in Algiers; Henri Alleg's *La Question*, describing his experiences at the hands of a paratrooper unit, was the first of a whole spate of accounts of the same kind. The disappearance of a young communist mathematics lecturer, Maurice Audin, suspected of sheltering wanted Algerians, drew attention to another regrettable aspect of the "battle of Algiers": that thousands of Algerians either died under torture or were summarily executed without a semblance of trial. As time went on, the Algiers *"Délégation Generale"* gradually accumulated a "dossier" on the extent of such disappearances. Though it has never been released, I have reason to know that it estimates at several thousands the number of Algerians "shot while trying to escape". French public opinion is, at the present time, far more conscious of the excesses which became widespread during this period, and were to continue, in sporadic form, for the rest of the Algerian war: what was surprising was the degree of ignorance and indifference on the part of the Europeans of Algiers, living as they did in close proximity to the schools and other commandeered buildings in which torture was constantly being carried out.

A year after the Soummam Conference, the results of the F.L.N.'s decision to indulge in indiscriminate urban terrorism could be clearly seen: of the Algiers-based C.C.E., Larbi Ben M'Hidi had been captured and killed (summarily executed after torture), and its survivors forced to flee Algiers. The head of the "Algiers Autonomous Zone", Youssouf Ben Khedda, had fled to Tunis. The F.L.N.'s entire terrorist network was out of action, its politico-administrative sections badly mauled, its fund-raising network destroyed, and the entire Moslem population of Algiers cowed beyond belief. The paratrooper practice of making extensive use of hooded informers (who pointed out F.L.N. sympathisers as they streamed out to work from the heavily guarded Kasbah precincts), and of raising a French-protected militia from turncoat F.L.N. members to terrorise the Moslem population of the Kasbah and hunt out all remaining suspects, was to have a lasting effect on the Moslem population of Algiers. French paratroop commanders pointed to the relative peace and quiet which returned to Algiers after October 1957 as evidence that their methods had successfully stamped out all vestiges of F.L.N. influence. That the Moslems of Algiers were frightened into docile passivity for some time after October 1957 was a fact, as it was a fact that many Moslems blamed irresponsible F.L.N. leadership for having brought them to this pass. But that the "battle of Algiers" was ever forgotten is improbable: when the Moslem crowds in the Kasbah and elsewhere in Algiers rose on December 10, 1960, to the cry "Vive l'Indépendence" and "Vive Ferhat Abbas" they did so in part to show that they remembered the humiliations and sufferings imposed upon them during the "battle of Algiers", to exorcise the ghosts of paratroopers, traitors and informers and to show that despite the defeat suffered at the hands of General Massu's paratroopers the Kasbah was still a nationalist stronghold.

Back in Tunis in the summer of 1957 the surviving F.L.N. leaders took stock of the situation: the physical and psychological damage caused by the "battle of Algiers" was readily conceded. In Algiers itself the F.L.N. had lost its cadres, and its best troops had suffered, in the words of a prominent F.L.N. member, an Algerian "Dien Bien Phu"; one of the F.L.N.'s ablest and most dedicated leaders, Larbi Ben M'Hidi, had been captured and killed; elsewhere in Algeria, the arrival of strong French reinforcements had put a brake on earlier F.L.N. successes. F.L.N. units had, in many areas, become unwieldy and more vulnerable as their numbers swelled with untrained volunteers; better, heavier weapons had led to a decrease in mobility. And though the F.L.N. managed to rush supplies through in huge quantities right up to April 1958, the French decision to build an electrified "Morice Line" along the Tunisian–Algerian border threatened to cut off Tunisia as a source of supply. A meeting of the "*Conseil National de la Révolution Algérienne*" was arranged to take place in Cairo, and the C.C.E. became a nine-man affair, the direct precursor of the later Algerian "provisional government". Its members were: Belkacem Krim, Ferhat Abbas, who had joined the F.L.N. only two months previously, Ramdane Abbane, Lakdar Ben Tobbal (who had commanded the number 3 Wilaya after the death of its former commander, Zighout), Abdulhafid Boussouf, who had succeeded Larbi Ben M'Hidi at the head of number 5 Wilaya, Lamine-Debaghine, an ex-Messalist who had been persuaded to join the F.L.N. by Abbane, Abdulhamid Mehri, who had until this time been the F.L.N.'s representative in Damascus, Omar Ouamrane, an ex-Wilaya commander and arms specialist, and Mahmoud Cherif, a former French army officer who had fought with distinction in Indo-China. With Ben Bella and three other members[1] of the "*délégation extérieure*" in a French jail, Belkacem Krim was the only "founder-member" left still in activity—a sign of the tremendous toll taken during the first two years of its existence.

Disturbed by the failure of the "battle of Algiers" and the worsening situation elsewhere, the new C.C.E. somewhat naturally began to cast around for assistance from almost any quarter. After the abortive Suez expedition, Egypt could be counted on for increased support. So could other Middle Eastern states, despite the F.L.N.'s distaste for the "feudal" régime of Saudi Arabia. For the first time since the rebellion began its leaders began to realise how long and arduous a path they still had to travel before independence could be achieved.

[1] Mohammed Khider, Aït Ahmed, Mohammed Boudiaf.

CHAPTER ELEVEN

THE COLLAPSE OF THE FOURTH REPUBLIC (2)

FRENCH authority gave way to the Algiers mob on February 6, 1956, and set the pattern both for future mob pressure and for future French Government humiliations. Before its final collapse, in May 1958, the French Government weathered two further serious incidents which prepared the way for final collapse.

On October 22 (only a few weeks after secret contacts between the F.L.N. and some French socialist party representatives, discreetly mandated by M. Mollet to find out the extent of F.L.N. intransigence) one of the F.L.N.'s ranking leaders, Ahmed Ben Bella, was kidnapped while on his way from Rabat to Tunis to attend a North African conference there along with Tunisia's Premier, Habib Bourguiba, and King Mohammed V of Morocco. The circumstances of the kidnapping marked a turning-point in France's relations with Tunisia and Morocco, as well as a turning-point in the rebellion itself. By October 1956 both Moroccan and Tunisian leaders were gravely concerned by the Algerian rebellion and its consequences on Tunisia and Morocco. Both countries had obtained independence in favourable circumstances: the presence of an affluent, dynamic European minority in both countries was economically beneficial; most Europeans, after a period of bitterness and resentment, had accepted the fact of independence with remarkable equanimity. Both Tunisia and Morocco were eager to retain their cultural and economic links with France, and individual relations between Europeans, Tunisians and Moroccans were at first excellent. The Algerian rebellion, however, threatened to destroy this *entente:* in both Tunisia and Morocco there was strong popular support for the Algerian rebels. No Tunisian or Moroccan Government, however strong, could fail to take this into account—not even Bourguiba, for whom the overwhelming majority of Tunisians had respect bordering on veneration. Algerians in Tunisia and Morocco discreetly played on the feelings of the two newly-independent countries, comparing the activity of the Neo-Destour, and of the Moroccan Istiq-lal in the period preceding independence with their own present struggle. The French Government itself realised how unrealistic it would be to demand of Tunisia and Morocco the complete boycott of the F.L.N. Slowly, as the rebellion increased in scope and in power, Morocco (and to a far greater extent) Tunisia came to be used as a rear-echelon F.L.N. base. Neither Tunisia nor Morocco could possibly have refused such hospitality, though both countries were seriously perturbed by the consequences implicit in the presence, on Tunisian and Moroccan soil, of large numbers of Algerian "volunteers".

Such consequences could, and did, take several forms: France, partly bowing to the pressure of French public and parliamentary opinion, was led to reduce its material aid to Tunisia and Morocco; the Europeans in Morocco and Tunisia lost some of their sense of security and started leaving in large numbers; the presence on Tunisian and Moroccan soil of Algerian volunteers led to a worsening in diplomatic relations and the threat of a direct French attack on F.L.N. "enclaves" there; caught in this dilemma, both the Tunisian and Moroccan Governments began using the presence of Frenchmen in their countries as pawns, putting pressure on France to avoid the worst economic reprisals which would affect Frenchmen too.

Moroccan and Tunisian difficulties were well known to the French Foreign Affairs Ministry. Nor can it have been unaware of the genuine concern of the Tunisians and Moroccans at the continued presence on their soil of an increasing number of Algerians. But few attempts were made to examine the situation dispassionately, and full rein was given to those vocal elements of French public opinion which happily attributed every single rebel success to dastardly Tunisian and Moroccan leadership. Just as Mendès-France became, in a surprisingly short space of time, the national scapegoat for Indo-China, so Bourguiba (and to a lesser extent King Mohammed V) were made responsible for the continuing Algerian rebellion.

The situation became dramatic in October 1956—thousands of Algerian refugees began fleeing across to Tunisia as battles raged in the Aurès mountains and along the Algerian–Tunisian border; the Algerians who crossed over into Tunisia were destitute, and became an additional burden for the Tunisian economy; the setting-up of the "Morice Line" led, by 1958, to the permanent closing of the border and to the existence of something very much akin to a war zone; in the hills along the Tunisian border, F.L.N. training camps and rest centres were set up, which periodically raided Algeria from the safety of their Tunisian bases. The number of uniformed F.L.N. rebels along the Tunisian border seems to have varied between 8,000 and 20,000. Though they were kept out of sight, and hardly ever ventured into Tunisian towns in uniform, they were a permanent threat to security: in all, Tunisian armed forces and National Guardsmen numbered less than 18,000 men, (a mere 16,000 after some 2,000 Tunisian troops had been sent to the Congo in September 1960). Such numbers were inadequate to guard the frontier and ensure the safety of European residents in Tunisia; reluctantly, Bourguiba ordered the evacuation of Europeans living in the "frontier zones" in 1958.

The problems facing France and her former Tunisian and Moroccan protectorates were fully apparent by October 1956. At this time, both Bourguiba and King Mohammed V believed a solution could come through the establishment of a Franco-North African Community in which both Tunisia and Morocco would join, along with an autonomous Algeria to be promised full independence by stages. A Tunis conference with F.L.N. leaders was planned for October 1956, and both Tunisia and Morocco agreed to propose their joint good offices to France if there seemed any likelihood of the F.L.N. accepting such proposals as a basis for discussions with France.

On the face of it, such a chance of ending the Algerian war appeared almost too good to be true. But this was to ignore the lack of authority—and the contradictory North African policy—

inherent in the Mollet Government. Certain elements within the government were favourable to negotiations. Others were opposed to any solution other than military victory to be followed by timid reforms: the true extent of the rebellion seems to have been ignored, and much was made of over-optimistic army reports (on November 20 Robert Lacoste was to make his famous *"dernier quart d'heure"* statement). The French army in Algeria was rapidly developing a policy of its own, and contempt for the institutions of the Fourth Republic was as ingrained among most regular army officers as it was among the Europeans of Algeria.

Preliminary meetings between Ahmed Ben Bella and King Mohammed took place in Rabat in October. Then King Mohammed flew to Tunis, unaccompanied by Ben Bella and his three colleagues of the F.L.N.'s *"délégation extérieure"*. (As a Moroccan spokesman pointed out at the time, King Mohammed wanted, as far as possible, to avoid giving offence to France by appearing to give Ben Bella and the *"délégation extérieure"* official recognition.) Ben Bella, Aït Ahmed, Mohammed Boudiaf and Mohammed Khider boarded a chartered "Air Atlas" plane on October 22. They were accompanied by Mohammed Lacheraf, a former Sorbonne Professor and F.L.N. sympathiser with no official rank in the F.L.N. hierarchy, by several French reporters and the North African representative of the *New York Times*, Thomas Brady. The plane was piloted by a French crew. While in the air, the pilot received orders from French Intelligence authorities in Algiers, relayed by the aeronautics staff at Algiers airport, to land in Algiers instead of Tunis. He obeyed, and circled over the Mediterranean until it was time to land. As the plane came to a halt, it was surrounded by armoured cars and steel-helmeted French troops. When the news was made public that evening, there was wild revelry in Algiers.

In Tunis the announcement of Ben Bella's kidnapping was greeted with consternation. In Paris Mollet briefly wondered whether he should resign: as with previous Tunisian and Moroccan initiatives before independence, the news of Ben Bella's capture had come to his ears too late for him to stop the operation. Lacoste himself also claimed that he had been taken unawares, but decided to underwrite his subordinates' initiative; in so doing he achieved what he prized most of all—a degree of popularity among the European population of Algeria. Only Alain Savary, Mollet's Secretary of State for Tunisian and Moroccan Affairs, and Pierre de Leusse, France's newly appointed Ambassador to Tunis, fully realised the implications of the capture, and resigned in disgust.

French Government leaders were well aware of the Tunisian and Moroccan proposals, and King Mohammed had even, in guarded terms, discussed them with France's Ambassador in Rabat. The implication of Ben Bella's arrest were clear to all those in Tunis waiting for the conference to begin: either certain elements in the French army in Algeria had got wind of impending negotiations, and had forced down Ben Bella's plane to destroy any hope of a negotiated Algerian settlement, or else they had acted with the complicity of at least some of the members of the French Government. In either case, by "covering up" for its subordinates, and by refusing to return Ben Bella to Morocco, the government had shown that it had neither the authority nor the will to take any steps which could possibly lead to an Algerian settlement. Ben Bella and his three assistants were the guests of King Mohammed at the time of their arrest, and the latter regarded their arrest as a personal affront and as a French betrayal. After Ben Bella's arrest, both Bourguiba and King Mohammed resigned themselves to the inevitability of a long war, while the F.L.N. interpreted France's "act of piracy in the air" as a sign that no Fourth Republic Government could be trusted, even if its intentions appeared conciliatory. It was symptomatic of French wishful thinking at the time that Ben Bella's arrest was regarded as a blow from which the F.L.N. would never recover: despite his capture, and the mass of (doubtless valuable) correspondence seized on the plane, the arrest intensified, rather than diminished, the F.L.N.'s aggressiveness. It also hardened the F.L.N.'s position: to a renewed (March 1957)

French offer of a cease-fire to be followed by "free" elections, an F.L.N. spokesman, Doctor Lamine-Debaghine stated, a few days later:

> "Elections are a domestic matter in which Algeria alone is concerned, to the exclusion of France and the United Nations. We demand prior and unconditional recognition of Algerian independence. No cease-fire can be contemplated before the proclamation of our independence . . ."

Neither party, at this stage, was approaching the problem of an Algerian settlement with any degree of realism: there was no way, by 1957, in which the word "free" elections could be used without inverted commas, and the French Government must by this time have realised that it was not able to give adequate guarantees of a fair electoral consultation, even if it had wanted to do so; likewise, the F.L.N. demands for "prior and unconditional independence" were totally devoid of realism: it was manifestly impossible for Ferhat Abbas to step straight into M. Lacoste's shoes without a long transitional period.

A repetition of the Ben Bella affair occurred sixteen months later with the French bombing of the Tunisian frontier village of Sakhiet Sidi Youssef. The raid came after a number of frontier incidents in which rebels had harassed French army units and strafed French spotter planes in the frontier area before returning to their Tunisian base. The Gaillard Government had grudgingly granted French forces in the area the "right of pursuit" into Tunisian territory, but had explicitly banned any air attacks on neighbouring Tunisia. Who was responsible for ordering the bombing of Sakhiet? Orders seem to have come from a relatively junior colonel at Bône air base, but, as in previous operations of this kind, he was "covered" by his superior officers, and by Premier Gaillard himself who placed responsibility for the civilian casualties on the shoulders of the Tunisians for harbouring rebels close to the frontier. Privately, members of the government admitted that they realised Bourguiba could not avoid behaving as he did, and of the 68 people killed at Sakhiet, few seem to have been Algerians.

The brutal bombing of Sakhiet focused world-wide attention on Algeria for the first time, and Tunisia used it to charge France with aggression before the Security Council. France filed a counter-charge, and a debate was only avoided because both the French and Tunisian Governments announced that they would accept United States and British "good offices".

The "good offices" of Robert D. Murphy, then U.S. Deputy Under-Secretary of State, and Harold Beeley, of the Foreign Office, continued for nearly a month. They were handicapped by French refusals to discuss any aspect of its Algerian policy, which was, after all, the main cause of Franco-Tunisian difficulties. What the "good offices" committee did establish was a series of proposals designed to bring French relations with Tunisia nearer to normal: it recommended the withdrawal of the 22,000 French troops still in Tunisia (and confined to barracks since Sakhiet), the neutral surveillance of French-operated military air bases in Tunisia, the negotiation of new agreements over the lease of the Bizerta naval base and a re-examination of the cases of those European "colons" expelled by the Tunisians. These common-sense recommendations were at first rejected by the Gaillard Government, and the Murphy–Beeley "mission" lingered on without much hope of success. But by April 12, after lengthy reconsideration of the matter, the Murphy–Beeley proposals were largely accepted as a basis for settlement between Tunisia and France. They did not, of course, touch on the main point at issue—the Algerian war—although there is no doubt that the Murphy–Beeley mission made it clear to the Gaillard Government that the danger of future Sakhiets would continue until some kind of an Algerian settlement was reached. By this time it was the conviction of the U.S. Government that the Algerian rebellion could not be ended by solely military means, and Mr. Murphy was forthright enough to say so, though not in public.

The "good offices" mission of Messrs. Murphy and Beeley came at a time when both France's army in Algeria (now increased to half a million men) and her Parliament were going through a major crisis. The cadres of the French army had been humiliated by the failure of the Suez expedition, and had put the blame fairly and squarely on the United States. The real reasons which compelled the U.S. to act as it did over Suez were ignored: encouraged by an irresponsible press and a latent French xenophobia, army officers saw in U.S. action over Suez only the expression of American territorial ambitions in the Middle East and in North Africa. Ever since the Algerian rebellion began, there had been a tendency to blame the United States (and to a lesser extent Britain) for French failures there; with Suez, senior French army officers developed a kind of anti-American frenzy: for a brief spell officer-cadets in French military schools were systematically taught a course in "American imperialism", and it was stated as an incontrovertible fact that the United States had designs on the newly-discovered Saharan oil deposits. There was no logic or semblance of continuity in the charges made: in one breath a senior French officer would accuse the United States of refusing to participate, alongside France, in the task of "Algerian pacification" whose result would determine whether North Africa would turn communist or stay in the Western bloc; in the next he would assert that the Algerian rebellion was a purely French affair.

Dispassionate argument was impossible with all but a fraction of army officers, who appeared to have accepted, as gospel, catch phrases like: "*ils veulent notre Sahara*" or "*L'Amérique essaie par tous les moyens de nous humilier*". French misconceptions concerning American policy were paralleled by misconceptions concerning the "American way of life". A surprisingly large number of French army officers in Algeria appeared to believe, at this time, that the fate of Algerian Moslems was preferable to that of Negroes in America. How deeply ingrained such prejudices were came to me during a talk with General Jacques Massu, the paratroop commander and police chief of the Algiers area. He had raised the issue of racial segregation in the United States, and said that American political leaders should seek to stamp out this injustice rather than attend to the imaginary grievances of North African Moslems. I replied that segregation was certainly distasteful, and should disappear, but that it did not seem that Negro resentment at segregation had led to a Negro nationalist movement. *"Encore faut-il,"* replied Massu, *"qu'un mouvement de ce genre ait la liberté de s'exprimer aux Etats Unis."* The "good offices" mission exasperated French suscepti- bilities still further. It must have been apparent, even at this time, to many French parliamentarians and senior officers that the Algerian rebellion could not be solely dealt with by military or even economic means. The French National Assembly had in fact adopted a *"loi cadre"* which would have given Algeria a single parliament and a measure of autonomy through increased local government, but no efforts had been made to implement this plan. The existence of the "good offices" mission underlined France's *"immobilisme"*: accurately reflecting the jingoist senti- ments of the French army, and of a part of French public opinion, the National Assembly brought down the Gaillard Government on April 16, thereby expressing its disapproval of the proposals made by the Murphy–Beeley mission.

For nearly a month the rebellion continued with some of the toughest fighting yet seen in Algeria while France remained in a political vacuum: in Tangiers, a meeting of the F.L.N., the Moroccan Istiq-lal and Tunisian Neo-Destour parties called for the formation of an Algerian government-in-exile, and com- mitted Tunisia and Morocco to the "total support" of the Algerian people "in the war of independence". Finally, as successive premier-designates groped for an elusive majority in the National Assembly, the F.L.N. announced the execution of three French soldiers in reprisal for the execution, in Algiers, of three terrorists (including a young chemistry student, Abderahmane Taleb, responsible for the manufacture—almost certainly under duress —of a number of explosives which had been used against civilians during the "battle of Algiers").

It is probable that the May 13 demonstrations in Algiers which led to the overthrow of the Fourth Republic would have occurred without the execution of these three French soldiers. For months politically-conscious French army officers and European civilians in Algiers had been plotting the overthrow of the Fourth Republic, though the actual seizure, by Pierre Lagaillarde and his students, of the Government-General building in Algiers took the main body of plotters by surprise before they were fully organised; Robert Lacoste, who stayed on as "caretaker" Minister for Algeria after the fall of the Gaillard Government, had openly hinted at the possibility of a "diplomatic Dien Bien Phu", and this irresponsible phrase was well calculated to fill army officers and civilians in Algeria with the gravest misgivings. By this time, Lacoste had to all intents and purposes ceased to act as a representative of the French Government in order to become the spokesman of "activist" French army officers. In an interview with an *Express* correspondent he said:

"What we want can be resumed in a single word: the tricolour. No privileges for the French inhabitants of Algeria, no return to the past, but France's honour. And any form of '*abandon*', any negotiation leading to it, is a blot on our honour."

Whether Lacoste realised it or not, language of this kind was a direct incitement to mutiny.

By May 13, 1958, tension had thus been built up—some of it deliberately—to such an extent that some explosion appeared inevitable. Lacoste was undoubtedly responsible for playing on the feelings of Algeria's French army cadres and Europeans; France itself had been without a government for almost a month —and this was the third Government crisis in the space of a year; the Premier-designate, Pierre Pflimlin, was known to favour a return to the possible good offices of Tunisia and Morocco which the arrest of Ben Bella had brought to nothing. The execution of the French soldiers provided the peg for the European demonstration in Algiers on May 13 which led to the seizure of the Government-General building, the establishment of "Committees of Public Safety" throughout Algeria and the collapse, within days, of the Fourth Republic itself.

The extraordinary circumstances in which the Government-General building was occupied by a comparatively small mob of European students led by Pierre Lagaillarde are well known. The ease with which the mob made its attack came as no surprise to those who had watched the French army in Algeria become increasingly contemptuous of civilian authority over the preceding years. Lacoste himself knew something of the European "activists" plans, and had conveniently left for France on May 10, meanwhile warning the authorities in Paris that "order might not be maintained" if European-led demonstrations started. (This, in itself, was an oblique form of encouragement to the rioters: on May 13 they acted in the knowledge that they would face minimum physical risks.) "Ultra" organisations, organised and strengthened by a number of political adventurers of various hues (some of whom later remained loyal to General de Gaulle, like Etienne Neuwirth, the assistant Mayor of Saint-Etienne, but most of whom turned against him, like the R.P.F. leader Roger Delbecque), operated untroubled by police investigation or the threat of expulsion. Finally, when the mob assault on the Government-General building came, the only troops likely to provide any genuine oppositon—the highly disciplined "Companies Républicaines de Securité"—were withdrawn on orders of a senior army officer after a brief scuffle with Lagaillarde's students. In their place came the heroes of the "battle of Algiers"—Colonel Maurice Trinquier's third *"régiment de parachutistes coloniaux"*—who took no steps to evict the mob from the Government-General building, but instead formed what was, to all intents and purposes, a guard of honour around it.[1]

As on February 6, 1956, the Moslems remained aloof and unconcerned when the European demonstrations first started, except for a small, docile group of Moslem ex-servicemen, mostly the aged veterans of the First World War, who took part in the march through the city which preceded the wreath-laying ceremonies in honour of the three executed French soldiers.

After their initial success, however, the organisers of the May

[1] Colonel Trinquier, sent back to France in disgrace after the January "barricades week", was later hired, while on extended leave, by the Katanga Government to reorganise Katanga's army and security services.

13 demonstration, both civilian and military, realised that they would only impress startled public opinion in France if, somehow, they managed to associate the Moslems in their movement too: and this, surprisingly, they succeeded in doing, not immediately, it is true, but three days later.

Since the arrival of thousands of Moslems on the "Forum" in front of the Government-General building and their participation in the mass demonstrations there was the most important step in the victory of the "ultra" elements in Algiers over the dying Fourth Republic in Paris, the reasons which led the Moslems to act in this fashion must be understood. Needless to say, Moslem behaviour appeared, at the time, baffling and incomprehensible. To explain Moslem docility and cooperation one has to go back at least a year to the period of the "battle of Algiers".

During and after the "battle of Algiers" the French army enjoyed, to all intents and purposes, every conceivable right over the Moslem population: the "paras" could, and did, arrest and imprison suspects for unlimited periods without charging them with specific offences; torture and summary executions were widespread; at the time of the arrest of the last members of the F.L.N. terrorist network in Algiers the Moslem population was thoroughly cowed, and it remained particularly terrified of the "para" regiments. A group of renegade F.L.N. ex-members, operating under the direct supervision of the "paras", kept the Moslem population of the Kasbah under constant supervision. (These *bleus de chauffe*, thus nicknamed because they wore workmen's blue jeans and overalls, were to maintain their activity right up to the end of 1960. Their leader, called "Ali-Loup", a former henchman of Ali-la-Pointe, finally lost his reason.) At another level, the officers of the *"Sections Administratives Urbaines"* also kept close watch on the Moslem population: it is impossible to explain the hold of the S.A.U. officers over the population under their charge without resorting to practical examples: an S.A.U. officer could, for instance, provide suitably docile Moslems in his area with housing, increased rations and jobs. Similarly, he could withhold the barest necessities of life from "trouble-makers", and of course see to their arrest and punishment.

Many of the F.L.N. leaders of 1956 and 1957 were dead or under arrest by May 1958. The Moslem population included a large number of unemployed, and a huge proportion of people living on the fringe of starvation. Finally, the S.A.U. officers (mostly humane, dedicated men) had worked hard to win the confidence of the Moslem population and a vast "psychological warfare" campaign had been in progress for at least a year to win the Moslems round to the notion that the French army was the Moslem's best friend. For all these reasons, when orders came for the Moslems to join their "brothers" at the Forum, and when army trucks came to take them there from the suburbs of Belcourt and Clos Salembier, few Moslems demurred. *"J'ai fait venir toutes mes femmes,"* one S.A.U. officer was heard to say, as if this was the most natural thing in the world. For the benefit of the world's assembled photographers and cameramen, Moslem women burned their veils and danced round the fire, though the effect was slightly spoiled by a paratrooper onlooker, who recognised, among the frenzied "newly emancipated" Moslem women, a number of prostitutes from the Kasbah's various "houses".

By May 16, when the Moslems first joined the Europeans on the Forum, the army officers caught up in the all-too-successful demonstration against the Fourth Republic realised that their only chance of extricating themselves from their dangerously ambiguous position was to obtain the return of General de Gaulle. In the wild, unreal atmosphere of Algiers immediately following May 13, the Europeans believed that General de Gaulle would put an end to the rebellion, restore *"L'Algérie Française"* and introduce a kind of settler Golden Age in which nationalist aspirations would be forgotten and their sympathisers banished into limbo. By May 16 the demands of the European demonstrators had crystallised around the cry: *"de Gaulle au pouvoir",* and this despite the fact that Gaullism had never, during and after the war, had more than a tiny following in Algeria itself.

Author and Ferhat Abbas in the latter's villa in Tunis (1960).

Author on operations with French paratroopers in Algeria (1957).

Algiers—1960.

Algiers—an engraving of 1830.

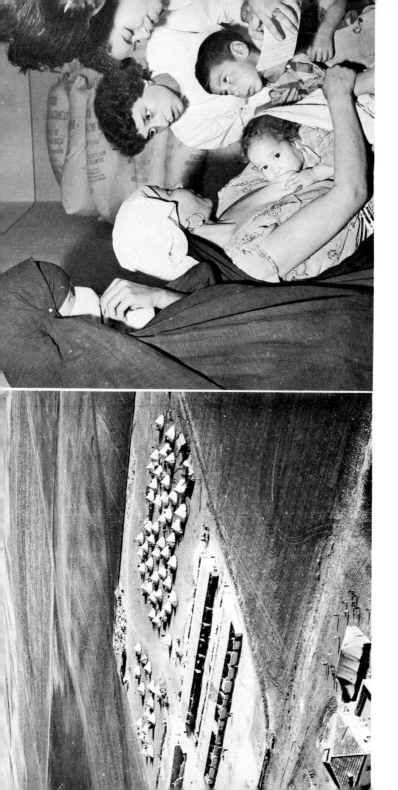

Moslem women social workers in remote Kabyle village.

Model "regroupment centres" of evacuated villagers.

F.L.N. troops in training on the Tunisian border.

A Kabyle village entirely destroyed by French Air Force bombing.

Robert Lacoste, Algeria Minister until May 1958, receiving the "cross of military valour" at a ceremony in Algiers only a few days before the May 13 insurrection broke out.

Demonstrators breaking into the "Gouvernement-Général" building in Algiers on
May 13, 1958.

Crowds—Moslem and European—massed outside the "Gouvernement-Général"
building on the "Forum" during the May 13–20 demonstrations.

The "Forum" during the wild May 1958 week.

Jacques Soustelle (*right*) and General Raoul Salan (*left of microphone*) on the balcony of the "Gouvernement-Général" building on May 17, 1958.

Jacques Soustelle and General Jacques Massu inside the "Gouvernement-Général" building on May 18, 1958.

General de Gaulle and Moslem schoolchildren near Bône, September 1958.

European women tearing down pro-de Gaulle banners displayed at Aïn Temouchent during de Gaulle's December 1960 visit.

General de Gaulle in Algeria during his visit of December 1960.

Study in frustration; enraged Europeans carrying "Algérie Française" banners being contained by Moslem militiamen during General de Gaulle's 1960 visit to Cherchell, Algeria.

Moslems staging pro-F.L.N. demonstration at Algiers Kasbah on December 10, 1960.

General de Gaulle greeting Kabyle peasants on his second visit to Algeria.

Pierre Lagaillarde surrendering at the barricades in January 1961.

At the hour of defeat the four generals gather to prepare a final announcement to the people. (*Left to right:* Edmond Jouhaud; Raoul Salan; Maurice Challe; André Zeller.)

Paratroopers of the First Foreign Paratroop Regiment, which spearheaded the short-lived "generals" insurrection, leaving their Algiers quarters for the Legion Headquarters of Sidi Bel Abbes after its collapse, where the regiment was disbanded. As they left, they tossed roses to the cheering Europeans who saw them off and kept up a steady chant of "Algérie Française".

The F.L.N. Delegation on the steps of the Hôtel du Parc at Évian before the opening of the Evian Conference on May 20, 1961.

The F.L.N. Delegation to the Évian Conference leaving their Geneva villa. (*Left to right:* Ahmed Boumendjel, Taieb Boulahrouf (half hidden), Dahlab Saad, Belkacem Krim, Ahmed Francis.)

For the Moslems, too, de Gaulle represented a vague hope. Very much more aware of world political developments than most Europeans realised, many Moslems knew that de Gaulle entertained good relations with King Mohammed V of Morocco and had privately branded his banishment in 1953 as a stupid mistake; they knew, too, that de Gaulle had had a "cordial" conversation with the Tunisian ambassador in Paris, Mohammed Masmoudi, at the latter's request, just after the Sakhiet bombing episode. De Gaulle was *"l'homme de Brazzaville"*. He was, just conceivably, in favour of a generous Algerian settlement. The wild enthusiasm displayed both by Europeans and Moslems during the first few months of de Gaulle's premiership resulted from the diametrically opposed hopes of the two communities: the Europeans hoped for a return to *"L'Algérie Française"*, the Moslems for a settlement between de Gaulle and the F.L.N. Disenchantment came slowly but surely to both parties, but on May 16 and on succeeding days only the enthusiasm was visible.

There was another reason for Moslem participation in the pro-de Gaulle demonstrations of May 16 and after: for years, relations between Europeans and Moslems had been not so much bad as non-existent: the two communities lived in two completely different worlds. Apart from a tiny middle class with Western patterns of consumption, the Moslem economic "circuit' was a closed one, based on an incomparably lower standard of living. Terrorism and counter-terrorism had led to mutual suspicion and growing mutual resentment. Suddenly, as the first Moslems, led by the *"bleus de chauffe"* and directed by their S.A.U. officers, arrived at the Forum, they were greeted by cheering, clapping Europeans who appeared to have forgotten their hostility, their resentment and their ingrained sense of racial superiority. The situation can be compared with the temporary "cure" of a seriously ill person during a hysterical prayer-meeting: the "chain of friendship" formed by oustretched European and Moslem hands outside the Government-General building did not in any profound way alter the natural antagonisms of the two

communities, and the opinion-makers among the Europeans were
quick to point out that the much-vaunted "integration" proposed
as a panacea for all Algeria's ills was to be mainly an "*integration
des âmes*": but for a very brief period the mingled hopes of both
Moslems and Europeans were stronger than the passions which
divided them.

CHAPTER TWELVE

THE ALGERIAN REBELLION AND THE FRENCH ARMY

THE European demonstrations of May 13, 1958, which brought General de Gaulle back to power, could not have occurred without the tacit consent, and in some cases the active encouragement, of certain elements in the French army. These same elements were to play a crucial role in the January insurrection during "Barricades week" in Algiers two years later, and much of de Gaulle's time, after returning to power, was spent countering these groups in the French army, which did their best to pursue a policy in complete contradiction to his own wishes and instructions. At the beginning of the rebellion, the French army was still an army in the service of the French Government, facing an unpleasant, almost impossible task: it rapidly became something else—a force no longer in the service of the State but seeking to supplant it, and equipped with a doctrine forged from years of warfare in Indo-China which, if carried to its logical conclusion, would have led to fascism not only in Algeria but in France as well.

Some of the reasons implicit in the French army's Algerian attitudes can be traced back to the period between the two world wars. The pre-war French army cadres were bitterly opposed to the social aspirations of the French working class, and regarded the advent of the Popular Front as an unmitigated calamity. The French defeat in 1940 was due at least in part to the lack of faith of the French army cadres in their own men and in their lack of conviction for the cause they were meant to defend. It was characteristic of a defeated country to cling to the trappings of glory: when it tried to find scapegoats for the 1940 defeat, France's Vichy Government turned on the politicians who had held office

during the Popular Front period, not on the soldiers who had
lost the war. At the Riom trial, the only soldier on trial was
General Gamelin, not because he had been a disastrous commander
in the field but because he had been Commander-in-Chief at the
time of the Popular Front. In a directive to the docile Vichy press
on the eve of the Riom trial, the government of the day instructed
editors that whatever happened "the honour of the French army
must be safeguarded".[1] The quest for "honour" took strange
forms—as when Marshal Pétain, in a letter to Hitler, requested
that France be allowed to take part in her own defence against
British aggression.

As the war progressed, General de Gaulle's tiny forces gradually
swelled, but opposing Gaullist and Vichy troops clashed both
at Dakar and in Syria. At the end of the war the leaders of
France's army were faced with immense difficulties: there was a
tiny group of men proud of its early allegiance to General de
Gaulle; there were the troops who rallied to de Gaulle much
later, after the latter had set up his "provisional Government" in
Algiers; there were diehard Pétainist officers who had changed
their allegiance only after the issue of the war, in Europe and the
Far East, was no longer in doubt; and there were the motley
"forces of the interior", including the pro-communist *Franc-
tireurs et partisans*" (F.T.P.), all of whom had to be welded into
a single army.

Inevitably, such difficulties left an indelible mark on the
French army. Those who had experienced its divisions and
upheavals resolved that it should never again be placed in a
position where it was liable to become divided against itself.
Despite the rapid healing of past wounds, the French army, in the
immediate post-war period, never quite lost an "inferiority complex" which had several causes: the humiliating memories of the
1940 "*débâcle*"; the fact that France's actual contribution to
military victory had been small in proportion to her size; the
feeling that, throughout the war, the majority of France's cadres,

---

[1] Pierre Mazé and Roger Genebrier, *Les grandes journées du procès de Riom* (Paris,
la Jeune Parque, 1945).

apart from the happy few who rallied immediately to de Gaulle, had somehow lost control of their destinies, and had been the puppets of the pre-war and Vichy politicians as well as of their new Anglo-American allies; post-war French dependence on U.S. and British arms and equipment was also deeply resented.

Such feelings explain, to some extent, the spendidly lavish shows put on by the French Occupation forces in Germany immediately after the war. They explain, too, the eagerness with which France's post-war army involved itself in a war in Indo-China.

The Indo-China war provided the French army with a new traumatic experience. It was a war fought against increasingly well armed and well-organised nationalists of communists inspiration, over seven years, in a climate of general indifference in France itself. It certainly succeeded, as nothing else could have done, in cementing the unity of the French regular army, but only at the expense of turning it into a "band of brothers" isolated from the French nation as a whole. Since the French expeditionary force in Indo-China was confined to regulars and volunteers, the nation itself did not feel seriously involved. Since American aid, in the latter stages at least, more than paid for the cost of the war, there was not even the sense of financial involvement. It was only after the catastrophe of Dien Bien Phu that France was jolted into consciousness of the war. By that time the French cause in Indo-China—which at the very best of times had had only the slenderest chance of success—was doomed.

The theme of treason is dear to a defeated army: and it was easy, as well as convenient, to adopt the myth of an Indo-China defeat brought about by communists, leftists, Mendès-France and the French opposition press. The regular army's hatred for politicians showed itself in no uncertain form in May 1954, just before the Mendès-France Government came to power: at a ceremony commemorating the end of the Second World War in Europe, several regular French army officers, in civilian clothes, publicly and with immunity slapped, kicked and man-handled two French Cabinet Ministers.

While France had been enjoying the comforts of peace and had blandly accepted the scandals of the "*Quatrième*", the French army in Indo-China felt that it, and it alone, had been living real history and taken the full shock of communist aggression. The experience of Indo-China left the French regular army with an abiding contempt for the politicians of the Fourth Republic, who had given them an impossible task while denying them the means of success. Regular officers drew bitter conclusions from the end of the Indo-China war: the first was that promises, in politics, meant nothing. The army, acting in the light of public statements made by a whole succession of governments, had pledged itself to protect the loyal, pro-French Vietnamese minorities, many of whom had been enrolled on the French side during the war. These had been left to their fate. Another conclusion, drawn from the hasty way in which the United States began replacing France as an economic and political bulwark in the anti-communist part of partitioned Indo-China, was the suspicion that within the free world itself the United States had a vested interest in supplanting France in her traditional "spheres of influence". These thoughts hardened into obsessions with the proclamation of Tunisian and Moroccan independence, which France's regular army saw in simple, black and white terms: the French tricolour was being hauled down, the French empire was rapidly and tragically shrinking. There were additional, less high-minded reasons for anger: in the underpaid French army, occupied Germany, Tunisia and Morocco had been the last bastions of gracious living, and the dangers of Indo-China had been partly compensated for by generous field allowances.

But by far the most important conclusion drawn by France's regular army from its Indo-China experience was the conviction that war, in the atomic age, was permanent. The balance of terror which paralysed the great world powers left the field open for "revolutionary wars" launched by the Soviet Union by remote control at chosen weak points. French war theorists went so far as to assert that limited wars were the only type of military conflict which remained possible outside instantaneous atomic annihilation. When the Algerian insurrection broke out, it could be interpreted easily enough in accordance with this strategic theory. And if this theory were true, it seemed legitimate to demand Western solidarity on the Algerian front as well, in the name of defence against communism. After all, Lenin had predicted that Bolshevism would reach Europe by a gigantic flanking movement through Africa and the Middle East.

Lacking any authoritative political leadership during this period, the French army was left to its own devices to define a strategy which implied a policy as well: basing itself on its Indo-China experiences, the army decided that its objective, in the common interests of the West, was to wage war on international communism whatever its forms. Any retreat, any armistice, any compromise strengthened the enemy; if necessary, the army was prepared to save the nation from itself.

Rather than approach the problem of the growth of nationalism in the twentieth century from a rational point of view, it was easy for the French army doctrinaires to carry their reasoning one stage further: that nationalism, whatever form it might take, was bound to serve the communist cause. The following Manichean proposition was stated, time and time again: in an under-developed country, independence = neutralism, neutralism = satellisation by the communist bloc. Such reasoning led the editors of the official *"Bulletin Militaire d'Information"* to publish a special issue containing a survey of all past revolutions in the last fifty years, from the original Bolshevik revolution of 1917 to the Algerian rebellion, and including studies of the Spanish Civil War, the growth of Indian nationalist agitation, the war-time revolt in Iran, and the growth of Tunisian, Moroccan and Indonesian nationalism. The similar characteristics of these widely differing historical events were codified and stressed, their differences deliberately or unconsciously ignored. This doctrine also gave credence to the existence of a hidden criminal conspiracy within Western society to destroy itself: just as, during and after the Indo-China war, it became widely accepted in French army circles that the war was lost in the Paris "salons" and in the offices of the Left-wing opposition press, so it gradually became widely accepted, in the French army at least, that the F.L.N. drew most of its strength from outside Algeria, from facilities offered it in Tunisia and Morocco and also from the sympathies of irresponsible or downright wicked "liberals" in France itself.

In the course of its contact with the Vietminh communists, the French army had learnt not only the necessity of waging war to the bitter end but also how to wage it. France's regular army had been beaten by a semi-clandestine army of partisans; like all armies, it carefully dissected the reasons for its defeat. The lesson learnt was that the best army in the world is not worth anything if it is not backed up by political action. To the communist revolutionary faith must be opposed a contrary faith of comparable dynamism. Alongside traditional military weapons other techniques of "mobilising the masses" and of manipulating opinion must also be used. Some French army officers had seen these techniques employed in Indo-China while in captivity. After the end of the Indo-China war, a new branch of the General Staff was created: the office of "Psychological Action". The Algerian rebellion enabled the French army to put such theories into practice.

"I am a communist without doctrine," one of the French army's well-known exponents of "revolutionary warfare" told an Associated Press correspondent in 1958. His statement was symptomatic of the blanks implicit in such a theory: the Vietminh partisans were provided with a ready-made dogma, communism. The Algerian rebels had their slogan: independence. Democracy implies not blind adherence to a single slogan but a whole diversity of ideas and of the right of people to have them. Even the most single-minded French army exponent of "revolutionary warfare" recognised that the French democratic traditions could not be ignored. After casting around for a slogan which would not run directly counter to this tradition, the French army came up with the slogan of "integration". Also, though it did not emphasise this aspect of its policy except to answer charges of brutality, the French army gradually assumed the enemy's methods. "What we have to do," said Colonel Trinquier in an interview with an Associated Press correspondent in September 1958, "is to organise the population from top to bottom. You can call me a fascist if you like, but our aim is to make the population docile and everyone's actions must be controlled." Any means—including torture, brain washing or obsessive propaganda—were justified to achieve this end. Jean-Marie Doménach, the editor of the left-wing Catholic review *Espirit*, summed up the situation[1] as follows:

"Their 'war of ideas' required a single idea, fixed and clear. From this position the army arrived somewhat experimentally at political action. Its chiefs sensed that the old principles of patriotism and discipline were not enough to set up against 'subversive warfare'; and in order to fulfil their mission they demanded that the state define a policy and hold to it. As the state was weak and divided, the army naturally substituted itself for the state; in its ten years of continuous combat it had worked out a coherent conception of permanent interests and of the objectives of guerilla war."

Up to May 13, 1958, the state itself seemed to accept, and even to encourage this transition: the Resident-General in Algeria, Robert Lacoste, himself delegated full administrative and police powers to General Massu by administrative decree; the government had approved the establishment of the "Psychological Warfare" bureau, as well as the setting-up of secret police detachments within the army called D.O.P. (*Détachements Operationnels de Protection*). The S.A.S. and S.A.U. officers not only acted as teachers, road builders and administrators: they became political propagandists as well. Some 130 years after the conquest, the French army seemed to be still acting in the spirit of Marshal Bugeaud, who had once written, in his Memoirs, that "the army is no less necessary to develop than it is to preserve our Algerian heritage. It is and will remain for a long time the only serious task

[1] Jean-Marie Doménach, "The French Army in Politics", Foreign Affairs, January 1961.

force capable of transforming the country, of opening it up to African and French commercial channels". Shortly after the fall of the Fourth Republic, the Delegate-General appointed by General de Gaulle, Paul Delouvrier, told me: "There are two political forces in Algeria today. There is the F.L.N. And there is the French army."

When the European uprising came on May 13, 1958, the French army was powerful enough to channel the revolt towards "integration" and Franco-Moslem "fraternisation". This in itself was a considerable achievement, though—in the light of subsequent European uprisings—one cannot but feel that it would have been a far better thing if the army had overcome its reluctance to act against the European mob then instead of waiting for it to gather strength for another two years; by acting as an arbiter between Europeans and Moslems, between Paris and Algiers, the army did not claim to be the state, but acted as though it were itself the state, or at any rate its provisional replacement during a moment of crisis. This fact was underlined by France's top serving officer, General Paul Ély, in an important editorial entitled "L'armée dans la nation," published in the *Revue Militaire d'Information* shortly after May 13. Ély admits that the army "assumed, alone and on its own initiative, responsibilities which should normally be shared". But he goes on to explain that this occurred during an exceptional period, at a time when a power vacuum existed both in Paris and in Algiers, and adds that the army was the only "unifying factor between a rebellious Algeria and a leaderless France". The army, according to Ély, did not foment the events of May 13, but once they had occurred it was determined to "channel the movement to keep it in the national interest". In any case, he adds, the army was only a few days ahead of public opinion, since Parliament, and later a national referendum, legally ratified, by a huge majority, the army's own choice of General de Gaulle.

General Ély's apology is, to a certain extent, a valid one: the army sought neither a "putsch" nor a "pronunciamento", and acted only to the extent that it felt certain of being followed by the overwhelming majority of French public opinion. Nevertheless, for three weeks, the army took the place of the government and by skilful pressure obliged it to give way. Through the events of May 13, 1958, the army imagined that it had acquired a kind of *de facto* power to intervene in crises when the government admitted that it was unable to maintain national unity. It was reluctant to surrender this power to anyone—even to General de Gaulle. And much of the subsequent history of the Algerian rebellion must be seen in terms of France's struggle not only against the rebels but against its own army in Algeria.

General de Gaulle's battle against the French army in Algeria almost immediately centred around the army's slogan destined to counter the nationalists' cry for independence—integration. As General de Gaulle correctly surmised, the "integration" offer came several years too late, and the last-minute adherence to this slogan of the Europeans who had previously bitterly opposed it made it even more suspect to the Moslems. But for months after de Gaulle's return to power, the army went on painting "integrationist" slogans on walls, pavements and even road surfaces: *"L'Algérie c'est la France"*, *"De Dunkerque à Tamanrasset, 70 millions de Français"*, *"La Méditerranée traverse la France comme la Seine traverse Paris"*, these and other catch-phrases abounded wherever the French army was active. General de Gaulle was careful to avoid making any statements which could be interpreted as approval of "integration", though once, carried away by the enthusiastic shouting around him (in Mostaganem), he did end a speech, during his first visit to Algeria after resuming power, with the words *"Vive l'Algérie Française"*. When he announced, on September 16, 1959, that he was prepared to grant the Algerians "self-determination" there was consternation among the majority of French army officers. "We won't have our men killed," said one French officer, "in order that the Algerians may be given the right to vote F.L.N." Aware of the considerable latent opposition to him, de Gaulle, over the space of two years after resuming power, had more than a thousand officers transferred out of Algeria; the army's "pyschological warfare" budget was drastically cut and the army gradually deprived of its political powers. Meanwhile, the rebellion continued and the F.L.N. proved, in a number of ways, that it was still a force to be reckoned with in Algeria. Somewhat naturally, many French officers blamed de Gaulle's new policy for the continuing existence of the F.L.N. "If only we had been able to put 'integration' to the test," one of them told me recently. "The F.L.N. was already on the wane at the time of the May 13 uprising, and it suffered a tremendous blow from the Franco-Moslem fraternisation which took place a few days later." (Such charges were current in 1960 and 1961. Needless to say, they too were the product of wishful thinking: according to the French High Command's own figures, the F.L.N.'s activity did not slacken at all throughout May and June 1958.)

Characteristically, General de Gaulle chose to wear the "integrationist" elements in the French army down: he did not engage in any frontal attacks. Officers of doubtful loyalty were posted out of Algeria by small groups; local commanders were told to pay less attention to politics, and more to waging war on the rebels; General Raoul Salan, later to be posted out of Algeria, too, and to become a violent if somewhat extreme opponent of de Gaulle's Algerian policy, was rapped over the knuckles as early as June 1958 for allowing the Algerian "Committee of Public Safety" to appear to dictate integrationist policy to de Gaulle.

> "On the subject of the offensive and untimely incident caused by the peremptory motion of the Algiers Committee of Public Safety," de Gaulle replied, "I remind you that this Committee has no other right and no other role than to express under your control the opinion of its members."

By October 9 General de Gaulle ordered all officers to resign from the remaining Algerian "Committees of Public Safety". No efforts were spared to restore the primacy of civilian over military authority in Algeria: de Gaulle's representative in Algeria, Paul Delouvrier, whose title was "Delegate-General", was given overall responsibility over the Algerian Commander-in-Chief who succeeded General Salan, General Maurice Challe. Officers who had held civilian responsibilities (as prefects, in areas where prefects loyal to the Fourth Republic had been removed by the European insurgents around May 13, 1958) were made to give up their civilian duties: prefects and "*sous-prefets*" from France were sent to Algeria in increasing numbers to resume civilian control. Similarly, S.A.S. officers were told to reduce the emphasis previously placed on "*L'Algérie Française*", and the practice, common under Lacoste, of allowing local commanders to put pressure on their troops to write letters home full of integrationist propaganda was dropped.[1]

De Gaulle was at first only partly successful in bringing the army to heel, and the first referendum campaign in Algeria led to a positive orgy of "integrationist" slogans. On January 15, 1960, in an interview with a German journalist, Massu himself publicly attacked de Gaulle's Algerian policy, adding darkly: "So far it (the army) has not shown its power . . . At the right moment it can impose its will." Later that year, France's only living marshal, Alphonse Juin, and General Salan, the former Algerian Commander-in-Chief, also publicly and violently attacked de Gaulle.

In the European insurrection which followed Massu's removal from Algeria, many French officers teetered on the edge of rebellion. The army "*incertitude complaisante*", to use de Gaulle's own words, was punished by further postings and the public trial of Colonel Jean Gardes[2] along with the civilian plotters of the January 24 insurrection, commonly known as "barricades week". The trial itself turned very largely into a trial of the French army officers who had failed to carry out orders on January 24, though none except Gardes were charged with any offence. Not till de Gaulle's visit to Algeria in December 1960, when the French army

[1] Lacoste had, in a directive to French army commanders, urged troops to "correct, in their letters home, French misconceptions about Algeria". This naturally led the most rabid doctrinaires in the French army to carry out their own private indoctrination of their troops, and relatives of Frenchmen serving in Algeria began receiving curious letters drafted more or less as political manifestoes.

[2] At the trial, Colonel Gardes disclosed that he had initiated and planned Ben Bella's "kidnapping" while Intelligence Officer in Morocco in 1956.

in Algeria behaved loyally despite every conceivable kind of provocation, could it be said to be under control, and in April 1961 De Gaulle had to weather yet another army upheaval: the short-lived Algerian "generals' insurrection" led by retired Generals Challe and Salan which threatened, more than at any time since the 'commune', to bring France to the brink of civil war.

To some extent, the French army's incursion into politics sprang from long-standing tolerance of "politically-minded" officers: both General Jacques Faure, and Colonel Auguste Broizat, were allowed to stand as parliamentary right-wing candidates; beaten, they resumed their place on the active list. Both Broizat and Faure were doctrinaire devotees of "permanent war". But the politically-minded in the French army were not all of this hue: some were believers in a form of "patriotic socialism", and—in close contact with Moslem poverty—had acquired a bitter contempt for the Europeans in Algeria. Most of them, however, knew that France, in a period of economic expansion and prosperity, would not tolerate a military dictatorship. Faced with the prospect of dividing the army against itself, and of possible civil war in which some regulars, paratroopers and Foreign Legion units might side with the "integrationists" while the overwhelming mass of conscripts would continue to obey those officers who obeyed de Gaulle, the "activists" in the French army wisely decided that the risks were too great: and after de Gaulle's immense personal success in the January 8, 1961, referendum, giving him full powers to settle the Algerian rebellion as he saw fit, and the failure of the four-day "generals' insurrection", they stood no chance of imposing their views on France.

CHAPTER THIRTEEN

GENERAL DE GAULLE STEPS IN

THE May 13 1961 "revolution" was, above all things, a spectacle an
pageant: it was singularly bloodless, its casualties being, in order
of importance, a *"Companies Républicaines de Securité"* (C.R.S.)
guard who suffered severe concussion when a typewriter, thrown
out of a *"Gouvernement-Général"* window, hit him on the head, a
woman typist who was manhandled by the rioters, and Thomas
Brady, the indomitable *New York Times* Bureau Chief in North
Africa, who was hit over the head by a "C.R.S." guard on the
Forum[1] who took him for a rioting European. The American
Cultural Centre, the "locale" of the U.S.I.A.[2], was of course
smashed and looted, though nothing like as badly as it was to be
during the later "barricades" week in January 1960. Partly the
bloodlessness was due to the gentle way in which the army
channelled the uprising along lines acceptable to it. According to
one usually reliable source, General Massu—who was not aware
of the combination of the "Algérie Française" and Gaullist plotters
machinations—rang up Felix Gaillard, while the latter was still
technically premier, and asked him whether the army should open
fire on the rioters. He was given, according to this informant, a
categoric "no". By the evening of May 13, the Forum presented
a strange sight: there were hundreds of thousands of torn up
scraps of paper littering the courtyard of the *"Gouvernement-
Général"* building and the Forum—for the rioters had looted the
files, part of the G.G. archives and library; dozens of cars belonging to government officials had been smashed; tens of thousands
of Europeans, in their shirt-sleeves or in summer dresses, remained
massed on the Forum all night, while on the first-floor balcony,
illuminated and decked out with the tricolour flag, as well as with

[1] Square in front of the *"Gouvernement-Général"* building.
[2] United States Information Agency.

147

a battery of microphones, a succession of announcements and speeches were made—mostly by army officers (including General Massu), and by European leaders of various "patriotic" groups. The premature announcement of the arrival of Soustelle sent thousands of Europeans rushing out to Algiers airport. There was, needless to say, no curfew that night, and sleep was impossible: throughout the night, excited and exultant Europeans drove their cars through the Algiers streets, sounding off the familiar three short, two long "Al-gé-rie Fran—çaise" blasts on their horns. There was even dancing on the Forum, in which the off-duty paratroopers joined. The tall, superbly turned out paratroopers of the "Troisième Régiment de Parachutistes Coloniaux", were greatly admired by the Europeans. The regiment had played a leading part in the "battle of Algiers", and wore the distinctive visored forage cap of Colonel Bigeard's own design, which singled them out from all other "para" units. They had been on duty since the very beginning of the May 13 uprising, and had replaced the C.R.S. and gendarmerie unit which had defended the G.G. building from the mob for a short time by tear-gas. The "paras" made no effort to prevent the rioters, led by the then student leader Pierre Lagaillarde, dressed in parachute officers uniform, from breaking into the building. Once the place had been occupied and looted, they gradually restored some sort of order. But the "para" cordon round the occupied building—as it was perhaps meant to be—symbolised the army's ambiguous position: it did not prevent the rioters from going in and out of the building as they pleased. It merely showed that the army was, in some obscure and not yet fully realised way, "*engagé*" alongside the European rioters.

General Massu's press conference, on the day after May 13, showed clearly that he, at least, had had no prior knowledge of the imminent riot, and had been forced to cope with the situation in the absence of all orders. Prudent as ever, General Raoul Salan, the Algerian C.-in-C., had disappeared for the first few moments of the riot, and Massu, as commander of the Algiers area as well as the man invested with full civilian as well as military police powers, was left in embarrassed charge. "I was harpooned by a bunch of fellows," he told newspapermen. "I tried to convince them that their demonstration was, to say the least, misplaced. But there was no loudspeaker to make myself heard . . ." It was then that the ringleaders proposed that Massu should join in their "Committee of Public Safety". At that moment General Salan arrived. The ringleaders repeated their demand. Massu looked enquiringly at Salan. Salan, inscrutable as ever, looked back. "General Salan did not say anything," Massu continued. "I had only a few seconds in which to reflect. I decided to accept in order to control the action of the committee . . ." I asked General Massu: "Did you know any of the ringleaders by sight or by name?" He replied: "I knew none of them by name or by sight, except for Lagaillarde, whom I had met on a couple of occasions. He was wearing his reservist's para uniform and I told him to change."

Massu, straightforward soldier that he was, had no inkling of the impact of his decision to join (in fact to head) the "Committee of Public Safety". The announcement was greeted by a huge roar of delight by the crowd outside the Government building, on the Forum: in Paris, where the Pflimlin Ministry was being invested, deputies were in touch with the events in Algeria by the "Agence France-Presse" despatches. Fearing a full-scale "coup d'état", the National Assembly invested the Pflimlin Government, and the powerful French communist bloc in the Assembly abstained. Had the communists voted against him, Pflimlin would have been beaten. As it was, he had an uneasy majority (274 to 129 against, with 137 abstentions). But such distinctions were to be short-lived: as the hours went by, it became obvious that no Pflimlin-appointed minister would ever have sufficient authority even to land at Algiers airport without being manhandled, and that the army would do nothing to protect him. Army and settler distrust of Pflimlin had been stimulated by reports that he was in favour of negotiations with the F.L.N., though Pflimlin himself had angrily denied this. Asked whether he would obey a Pflimlin-appointed Algeria Minister, General Massu answered cryptically: "He'd have to get here first."

Though Massu, from the start, made it clear that he joined the

"Committee of Public Safety" in order to control it, his subordinates immediately began acting as though a military régime were about to begin in Algeria: the prefect of Grande Kabylie, who resolutely decided to remain loyal to "republican institutions", and ordered his gendarmerie to hold out, by force if necessary, against the paratroopers, was placed under army arrest, along with a group of French journalists (including Eugène Mannoni, of *Le Monde*) whose "loyalty" was "suspect". The rioters, with a paratrooper guard, took over the studios of "*Radio Alger*" and began using it as a violent, if chaotic, means of stating the rioters' case. Three French lawyers, who had defended F.L.N. members before military courts, were arrested as they boarded a ship back to France and held under arrest for over a fortnight. A group of high-ranking French officials, who refused to cooperate with the paratroopers and the rioters, were placed under house arrest or flown out of the country.

The gradual realisation, by the newly invested Prime Minister, by nearly all French political leaders (including socialist leader Guy Mollet) and President Coty himself that the return to power of General de Gaulle was inevitable is part of French, rather than Algerian, history. As early as May 15 General de Gaulle had issued a short statement which had increased the determination of the Algerian army leaders and Europeans to stand firm.

> "The degradation of the state," it read, "leads infallibly to the estrangement of the associated peoples, the distress of the army in action, national dislocation, the loss of independence. For twelve years, France, beset by problems too harsh for the régime of parties, has been caught in a disastrous process.
>
> Not so long ago, the country from its depths put its trust in me to guide all of it to its salvation. Today, in the face of the trials that again are mounting toward it, it should know that I am ready to assume the powers of the Republic."

In a crowded press conference on May 19, de Gaulle re-stated that "the moment seemed to me to have come when it would be possible for me once again to be directly useful to France," adding that, "when someone assumes the powers of the Republic, it can only be because the Republic will itself have delegated them." And this, of course, after the "seizure" of Corsica by the Algerian "Committee of Public Safety" on May 24, and a huge anti-fascist counter-demonstration in Paris on May 28, is what eventually happened: on June 1 General de Gaulle was invested as Premier by the National Assembly (329 to 224), having demanded, and obtained, full powers for a six-month period and the right to prepare, and submit to popular approval through a referendum, constitutional changes which would give France a strong executive and put an end to "government by parliament". Until he was safely and legally invested as premier, General de Gaulle gave no hint as to his Algerian policy: a few initiates suspected that de Gaulle might not give satisfaction to the boisterous and triumphant army leaders and Europeans in Algeria. Just how quickly their adulation was to turn to hatred only de Gaulle himself could know.

The politicians of the Fourth Republic knew, once they had handed over to General de Gaulle, that things were going to be different. Even the army officers and European civilians who had clamoured for de Gaulle's return felt some slight apprehension. De Gaulle's methods, it became obvious, represented a clean break with the past: whereas the Governments of the Fourth Republic had been talkative, even garrulous, de Gaulle not only made his ministers the humble *"exécutants"* of his own policy but withheld from his own Cabinet all but the most essential and immediate necessary guidance for its application. Historians of the future will probably argue at length on the extent to which General de Gaulle deliberately moved towards the acceptance of some kind of Algerian independence and the extent to which he was, as it were, pushed. Any analysis of events in Algeria from June 1958 onwards involves a somewhat tedious reference to de Gaulle's own pronouncements: nowhere else is his Algerian policy defined, and in his speeches it appears like the Seine itself, full of meandering loops followed by a long spurt forward. (It

is significant that when the F.L.N.'s first negotiators arrived for
talks at Melun, in June 1960, the first thing they did was to sit
down with French delegates and attempt to force the latter into
an interpretation of de Gaulle's recent speeches which would give
them grounds for believing that de Gaulle favoured direct
negotiations. And when these same French officials, at Melun,
interpreted de Gaulle's statements in the most restrictive way, the
F.L.N. envoys returned to Tunis to carry on the rebellion.)

De Gaulle's statements on Algeria were placed under the sign
of ambiguity from his very first cryptic utterance on his first—and
only fully triumphant—tour of Algeria just after resuming power
in June 1958. "*Je vous ai compris*" he bellowed to the huge crowd
of Moslems and Europeans massed on the Forum below. The
phrase had a reassuring ring to it. But before long, in Belcourt
and Bab el Oued, it became a deadly insult.

On his first Algiers speech, de Gaulle announced that

"from this day forward, France considers that in the whole of
Algeria there is only one category of inhabitants, that there are
only Frenchmen in the full sense, with the same rights and the
same duties";

—a sop to the 'integrationists', but then went straight on to say:

"this means that opportunities must be opened that, for many,
have until now been closed. This means that a livelihood must
be given to those who have not had it. This means that the
dignity of those who have been deprived of it must now be
recognised. This means that a country must be given to those
who may have thought they had no country."

The slightly disappointed Europeans noticed that de Gaulle
consistently refused to shout "long live French Algeria" (although,
on this initial tour of Algeria, this cry did escape him once, in
Mostaganem). De Gaulle, in his Algiers speech, had announced
that the Moslems would vote to elect representatives to the
National Assembly in a single electoral college, adding, "With
these representatives, we shall see how to accomplish the rest."

This was the first clear hint to the "ultras" that de Gaulle would not feel bound by their initial support. At this stage, most Europeans in Algeria still believed in the magic of slogans: if chanted long enough, they were bound to lead to the desired end. De Gaulle was in power, the hated and vacillating Fourth Republic overthrown, "*L'Algérie Française*" seemed a reality and all their remaining problems would soon be over. "*Le reste—quel reste?*" one leading European settler asked me shortly after the speech. "Everything has already been done." General de Gaulle might at this stage appeal to the over-excited crowds and use language which they endorsed, but in private—and after being briefed by operational commanders in the field, after sensing that Moslem support stemmed from their longing to see him make peace with the rebels—he acted quite differently. An over-eager, inexperienced aide asked de Gaulle for his impressions, on this first Algerian trip, only to get a cold stare back and the ominous words: "*L'Afrique est foutue, et l'Algérie avec.*" In the "djebel" the F.L.N. guerillas remained active, and its underground organisation in France had begun a series of terrorist raids on police stations, oil storage tanks and railway lines.

The one-day referendum in France by which de Gaulle sought to remove any stigma of illegality in his return to power was, for security reasons, a three-day affair in Algeria. The referendum was organised and controlled by the French army, and they did their job well: the expensive propaganda machine of the "*cinquieme bureau*" covered walls, roads and even rooftops with "Algérie Française" slogans. The F.L.N. in Tunis ordered a boycott, then—realising that this might expose Moslems in Algeria to needless dangers—added that conditions were such in Algeria that no electoral consultations could have any validity. 79·9 per cent of all registered voters cast a vote, and of these 96·7 per cent replied "yes" to de Gaulle. As one who watched the referendum in Algeria at first hand, I can bear testimony that no direct force was used on the population—there was no need for that. Those who did not vote knew that a proscribed list would be made, and that punishment might come in any one of a hundred different ways.

The purple (for most Moslems, an inauspicious colour) "No" ballots were ostentatiously thrown away. For months afterwards, Jean Rigaux, France's wittiest cabaret satirist, brought the house down with the story of the Moslems in a remote village setting out to vote at a polling station in the Sahara a hundred miles away. The N.C.O. in charge explains that they are off to vote for de Gaulle, hands round white and purple ballots, and explains that on arrival, each Moslem is to put the white ballot in an envelope and slip it into the urn. Bolder than the rest, one Moslem asks him: and what is this purple ballot for? Oh, that, replies the N.C.O., that entitles you to a seat on the bus back.

Inside the polling stations the Moslems' vote was expeditiously handled by the French army and French civilian volunteers: not the least surprising thing was that despite the Moslems' relative inexperience in voting matters (Moslem women were voting for the first time) only a tiny fraction of votes (39,726 out of 3,751,522 cast) were "spoiled"—a much smaller percentage than in any subsequent polling figures.

De Gaulle made no immediate comment on his referendum triumph. It came from him, a few days later, in Constantine, and carried a sting which caused the members of the Constantine "Committee of Public Safety" to walk off their special grandstand seats in disgust: after announcing the main headings of the "Constantine Plan" to increase wages, create 400,000 new jobs and turn Algeria into an industrialised country, de Gaulle paused, under the still strong Constantine sun, and said:

"What will be the political consequences of this evolution which calls for very extensive and prolonged efforts? I believe it is quite useless to freeze in advance, in words, that which, in any event, is going to take shape, little by little, as it is undertaken. But in any case, two things are certain as of now:

"In two months Algeria will elect her representatives under the same conditions as will metropolitan France. But at least two-thirds of her representatives will have to be Moslem citizens.

"The other refers to the future. The future of Algeria will in any event—because that is the nature of things—be built on a double foundation: her personality and her close solidarity with metropolitan France.

"In any case, it is absolutely essential that this fruitful transformation be accomplished . . . this transformation, this immense political, economic, social and cultural task—who could effect this transformation if not France? Now it happens that France has the will and the means to do so. It also happens that the vote of the Algerians has just proved that they desire this transformation and that it should be carried out with France.

"Therefore, turning to those who are prolonging a fratricidal conflict, who are organising lamentable attacks in metropolitan France, or who are spreading—through the chancelleries, through underground dens, by means of the radios and newspapers of certain foreign capitals—vilifications of France, to those I say: why kill? We must enable people to live. Why destroy? our duty is to build. Why hate? we must co-operate.

"Stop this absurd fighting and you will see at once a new blossoming of hope all over the land. You will see the prisons emptying; you will see the opening up of a future big enough for everybody, and for yourselves in particular. . . . Long live the Republic, long live Algeria and long live France."

No European settler could deny that this first statement of long-term policy—with no emphasis on "integration" but instead a deliberate accent on change, an undisguised appeal to the F.L.N. and no reference whatever to the European minority—ran completely counter to the "spirit of May 13". Their fears were increased by a further statement of de Gaulle's, made during a Press conference on October 23, 1958, which contained his memorable reference to a "peace of the brave". In answer to a reporter's question about the attitude of France towards possible F.L.N. peace overtures, de Gaulle began his answer by referring to the F.L.N.'s increased plight in the field ("the forces of law and order are little by little gaining control") and by a perhaps unfortunate reference to the "decisive demonstration that took place on September 28" (by this time, few people—in metropolitan France at any rate—were unaware of the peculiar conditions in which the Algerian referendum had been conducted). "However", de Gaulle continued,

"I say unequivocally that, as for most of them, the men of the insurrection have fought courageously. Let the peace of the brave come, and I am sure that all hatred will fade away and disappear. What does this mean? simply this: wherever they are organised for combat, their leaders need only enter into contact with the French command. The old warrior's procedure, long used when one wanted to silence the guns, was to wave the white flag of truce. And I answer that, in that case, the combatants would be received and treated honourably.

"As for the external organisation of which we were just speaking, which, from the outside, strives to direct the struggle, I repeat openly what I have already made known. If delegates were designated to come and negotiate with the authorities the end of hostilities, they would only have to address themselves to the French Embassy in Tunis or in Rabat. Either one would ensure their transportation to metropolitan France. There, they would be assured of complete safety, and I guarantee them the freedom to depart. Some say: but what would be the political conditions that the French Government would be willing to discuss? I reply: the political destiny of Algeria is Algeria itself . . .

"In any case a vast physical and spiritual transformation is under way in Algeria. France, because it is her duty and because she alone is capable of doing it—France is bringing about this transformation. As and when developments occur, political solutions will take shape. I believe, as I have already said, that future solutions will be based—because that is the nature of things—upon the courageous personality of Algeria and upon its close association with metropolitan France. I believe also that this ensemble, completed by the Sahara, will link itself, for the common progress, with the free states of Morocco and Tunisia . . ."

The "peace of the brave" and the "white flag of truce" aroused indignation among F.L.N. leaders in Tunis, who complained that this was yet another call to military surrender, although couched in dignified, high-flown language. But for the French army, and for the European settlers, de Gaulle's references to "courage" among F.L.N. rebels caused further bitterness. General de Gaulle had timed this particular offer well: it was only with considerable effort that the F.L.N. was managing, after the heavy reverses in the field and the consequences on morale of the failure of the "Battle of Algiers", to hold its troops and sympathisers together. On the French army side, de Gaulle's "purge" had already begun: some of those most closely connected with the regional (and ephemeral) "Committees of Public Safety" were being posted out of Algeria, or at any rate out of the big cities. General Raoul Salan, who had played a major role in Algeria by swinging his support to de Gaulle after forty-eight hours' deliberation, was sent into gilded retreat as Military Governor of Paris. (He was, later, to become the chief army spokesman against de Gaulle's Algerian policy, a slightly ridiculous figure, who, after settling in retirement in Algiers against de Gaulle's wishes, was finally banned from going there and left instead for Spain, where he whiled away many months in angry idleness before joining Challe in the "Generals' insurrection" in Algiers on April 22, 1961.) Within the French High Command in Algiers angry mutterings could be heard: the continuing rebellion was being blamed on de Gaulle's refusal to support a policy of "integration". "If only he had cried 'Algérie Française'", one French colonel in charge of psychological warfare told me—as though this would, by some miraculous stroke, have ended the Tunis-based F.L.N. leaders' will to continue the struggle for independence.

A pragmatist, General de Gaulle would doubtless have exploited to the full any F.L.N. willingness to take up the offer of a "peace of the brave". But he met with no such response, and, in his next public appearance (a Press conference on March 25, 1959, some six months later), de Gaulle answered tartly, when a reporter asked him how the situation in Algeria had developed since his offer of the "peace of the brave":

> "There have been 130 years of vicissitudes in Algeria. . . . I doubt that anyone has ever been able to imagine that peace and prosperity would come all of a sudden to a torn Algeria, or that all that was necessary, at the height of a persistent fever, was to shout down one slogan with other slogans in order that all the internal and external causes of the present war should disappear as if by magic."

In the meantime general elections had taken place, and had resulted in the return to the National Assembly of a group of Algerian deputies of disappointing calibre: some, like Lagaillarde, were Europeans brought into prominence by the May 13 uprising; a sprinkling were courageous Moslems who really believed that de Gaulle was the only person in the world who could bring the conflict to a satisfactory conclusion. Others were the docile Moslem counterparts of such men as Lagaillarde—men who had, very often at the risk of their lives, thrown in their lot with France but who could in no ways be deemed representative of Algeria. After de Gaulle's Constantine speech, in October 1958, the French Army had begun to have serious doubts about the wisdom of General de Gaulle's Algerian policy, and many officers, somewhat naïvely, believed that a solid "Algérie Française" group of Moslem deputies in the National Assembly would, somehow, influence his course of action. This, of course, grossly underestimated de Gaulle's contempt for individuals, especially since he himself was known to be somewhat disappointed in the deputies elected from Algeria, and would have preferred in their stead a group of moderate or even out-and-out nationalists.

So, with the rebellion still active, despite the good generalship of the new Commander-in-Chief, Maurice Challe, and the newtone given to the "Délégation Générale" by the appointment of Paul Delouvrier, one of France's most brilliant economists and civil servants, as de Gaulle's chief representative in Algeria, a new move was called for: and on September 16, 1959, in a nation-wide radio and TV address, de Gaulle advanced one huge step along the road to an Algerian settlement. After a survey of the various political changes which had come about in Algeria since his return to power—Parliamentary, Senate and Municipal elections (under new regulations Moslems were given seats on municipal councils commensurate with their numbers, and for the first time in Algeria there were more Moslem than European mayors)—and after recalling that Algeria, with a galloping birthrate, was above all a "human problem", de Gaulle made his historic "self-determination" proposition. This part of his speech, in the light of later events, deserves to be quoted in full:

"Thanks to the progress of pacification, to democracy, and to social advancement, we can now look forward to the day when the men and women who live in Algeria will be in a position to decide their own destiny, once and for all, freely and in the full knowledge of what is at stake. Taking into account all these factors—those of the Algerian situation, those inherent in the national and the international situation—I deem it necessary that recourse to self-determination be here and now proclaimed. In the name of France and of the Republic, by virtue of the power granted to me by the Constitution to consult its citizens —if only God lets me live and the people listen to me—I pledge myself to ask the Algerians, on the one hand, in their twelve Departments, what, when all is said and done, they wish to be; and, on the other hand, all Frenchmen, to endorse that choice.

"The question, obviously, will be put to the Algerians as individuals. For since the beginning of the world there has never been any Algerian unity, far less any Algerian sovereignty. The Carthaginians, the Romans, the Vandals, the Byzantines, the Syrian Arabs, the Cordova Arabs, the Turks, the French have, one after the other, penetrated the country without there being—at any time, under any shape or form—an Algerian

State. As for the time of the elections, I will decide upon it in due course, at the latest four years after the actual restoration of peace; that is to say, once a situation has been established whereby not more than 200 persons a year will lose their lives, either in ambushes or isolated attacks. The ensuing period of time will be devoted to resuming normal existence, to emptying the camps and prisons, to permitting the return of exiles, to restoring the free play of individual and public liberties and to enabling the population to become fully aware of what is at stake. I would like to invite, here and now, observers from all over the world, to attend, without hindrance, the final culmination of this process.

"But what will this political destiny finally be, for the men and women of Algeria who will choose it, once peace is restored? Everyone knows that in theory it is possible to imagine three solutions. Since it is in the interest of all concerned—and especially of France—that the question be answered without ambiguity, the three conceivable solutions will be put to the vote:

either—secession, where some believe independence would be found. France would then leave the Algerians who had expressed their wish to become separated from her. They would organise, without her, the territory in which they live, the resources which they have at their disposal, the government which they desire. I am convinced personally that such an outcome would be incredible and disastrous. Algeria being what it is at the present time, and the world what we know it to be, secession would carry in its wake the most appalling poverty, frightful political chaos, widespread slaughter, and soon after, the warlike dictatorship of the communists. But this demon must be exorcised, and this must be done by the Algerians themselves. If it should appear through some inconceivable misfortune that such is indeed their will, France would undoubtedly stop devoting so much of value and so many billions of francs, to a cause shorn of any hope. It goes without saying that on this assumption, those Algerians, regardless of origin, who might wish to remain French would do so in any case, and that France would arrange, if need be, for their regrouping and resettlement. On the other hand, everything would be arranged so that the operation of oil wells, the handling and shipping of Saharan oil—which is the result of French efforts and which is of interest to the whole Western world—would be ensured in any event.

or—out-and-out identification with France, such as implied in equality of rights: Algerians can accede to all political, administrative and judicial functions of the state and have free access to the public service. They would benefit, as regards salaries, wages, social security, education and vocational training, from all measures provided for in metropolitan France: they would live and work wherever they saw fit, throughout the territory of the Republic; in other words, they would be living, from every point of view, regardless of their religion or the community to which they belonged, by and large on the same footing and at the same level as other citizens, and become part and parcel of the French people who would then, in effect, spread from Dunkirk to Tamanrasset.

or—the government of Algerians, backed up by French help and in close relationship with her, as regards the economy, education, defence and foreign relations. In that case, the internal régime of Algeria should be of the federal type, so that the various communities—French, Arab, Kabyle, Mozabite—who live together in the country would find guarantees for their own way of life and a framework for co-operation.

"But since for a year now it has been settled that—through the institution of equal rights, the single college and the emergence of a majority of Moslem representatives—the political future of Algerians is to depend on Algerians; since it has been officially and solemnly emphasised that, once peace has been restored, the Algerians will let it be known what fate they want for themselves, to the exclusion of any other, and that all of them, whatever their programme may be, whatever they might have done, wherever they come from, will take part, if they wish to do so, in this vote: what then could be the meaning of rebellion?

"If those who lead it claim for all Algerians the right to self-determination, all paths are wide open. If the insurgents fear that in stopping the combat they will be turned over to justice, then it is entirely up to them to settle with the authorities the conditions for their unhindered return, as I suggested when I offered the peace of the brave. If the men who represent the political organisation of the insurrection intend not to be excluded from the debate, or later from the polls, or finally from the institutions which will determine the fate of Algeria and ensure its political life, I proclaim that they will have the same place as all the others—no more, no less—a hearing, a share, a place which will be granted them by the votes of the citizens. Why then, should the odious strife and the fratricidal murders, which are still drenching the Algerian soil with blood, continue?

"Unless it be the work of a group of ambitious agitators, determined to establish by brute force and terror their totalitarian dictatorship and believing that they will one day obtain from the Republic the privilege of discussing with it the fate of Algeria, thus building up these agitators into an Algerian Government. There is not a chance that France would lend herself to anything so arbitrary. The future of Algerians rests with Algerians, not as forced on them by knife and machine-gun, but according to the will which they will legitimately express through universal suffrage. With them and for them, France will see to the freedom of their choice . . ."

It is impossible to underestimate the importance of de Gaulle's September 16, 1959, address: whatever had gone before was forgotten; ever since this speech and in one form or another, the offer—and the deliberate or unconscious ambiguities it contained —have been at the heart of all discussions and speculations on Algeria. For de Gaulle deliberately sought to advance towards a solution by conceding a right which the nationalists themselves had been advocating: the right to "*autodetermination*" had been sought, in the past, both by Messali Hadj's and Ferhat Abbas's parties. The offer put paid, once and for all, to the long-cherished notion of an "Algérie Française". The reference—even a negative reference—to an "Algerian state" was in itself a hint that such a state might one day be tolerated; de Gaulle's implicit preference for an "associated" Algeria, a "Government of Algerians by Algerians", his insistence that those taking part in the rebellion would not be excluded from playing a part in a future Algeria, came as the first realistic approach to the Algerian problem since the outbreak of the rebellion.

Had such an offer been made in the first three years of the rebellion, it is virtually certain that it would have been immediately accepted by the rebel leaders. Now, however, they required further enlightenment. (In subsequent exchanges between the F.L.N. and the French Government, the rebels sought to clarify the "conditions of self-determination". For so doing, they came under severe criticism in France and elsewhere. It should be recalled that the very word "elections" had long been suspect to the F.L.N., and that the 1958 referendum and general elections, both heavily stage-managed by the French army, had done nothing to allay such suspicions. De Gaulle's willingness to allow "observers" in to witness an eventual referendum was another piece of ambiguity. Did he mean international observers with some official status, or did he merely mean the press?) On the French side, there was an immediate outcry: as an "ultra" spokesman was to say, in one of the numerous "balcony" broadcasts during the European uprising in the last week of January 1960:

"What's all this nonsense about self-determination? If no one takes the Moslems to the polls, they will stay at home. If the army takes them, they will vote for France. If the F.L.N. takes them, they will vote for independence . . ."

In the French army in Algeria, a distinctly rebellious spirit could now be detected: one of General de Gaulle's boldest commitments was to let the F.L.N. play a part in an Algeria of the future, and to invite them to take part in peaceful political organisation. But would the French Army, hardened by years of guerilla warfare, and obsessed by its "revolutionary warfare" theories, really allow self-confessed F.L.N. sympathisers to campaign for independence? I asked this question to dozens of French army officers in the months that followed de Gaulle's address. Nearly all made the same remark that General Massu had once made, referring to a Pflimlin-designated minister: "They'd have to get here first." There was no doubt, at this stage, that de Gaulle's offer could not be fairly implemented, and that de Gaulle must first face, and overcome, the by now violently anti-de Gaulle European and French army factions in Algeria.

CHAPTER FOURTEEN

THE SHOWDOWN:
"BARRICADES WEEK" AND AFTER

THE 1958 "revolution" had been peaceful and good-natured. The showdown of "Barricades week" in January 1960 was not. Long before it occurred—and owing to the fact that, as an old friend of de Gaulle's *"Délégué-Général"* in Algiers, Paul Delouvrier, I was privy to some of his innermost thoughts and fears—I had realised that a growing conflict was opposing him to a group of senior French army officers in key Algerian posts. Some of these officers had been transferred, and Delouvrier's own relations with the Algerian Commander-in-Chief, Air Force General Maurice Challe, were excellent. With General Jacques Massu, the Algiers *"super-préfet"* and overall operational commander, he was barely on speaking terms. By January 1960 Massu had become the spiritual leader of the growing faction in the French army which was utterly opposed to General de Gaulle's Algerian policy of "self-determination". He was also one of the last of the senior officers of the "May 13" uprising still in an Algerian command. With General Massu, Delouvrier's staff was at loggerheads over a number of points, some of which involved Delouvrier's own status as de Gaulle's delegate, theoretically responsible not only for civil affairs but for overall military matters too. One of the issues opposing them was that of military justice and security: Massu wanted to put into practice a rough and ready kind of military justice (including speedy trials and public executions) to stamp out terrorism; Delouvrier's interpretation of de Gaulle's policy led him, more and more, to adopt a liberal policy towards political detainees, and General Massu did not hide his anger at Delouvrier's decision to cut down the number of Algerians detained in camps and to check the army's natural propensity for

165

arresting suspects on flimsy grounds. Increasingly, General Massu came to ignore or impede Delouvrier's specific instructions, and encouraged others, including civilian officials, to follow his lead. Before January 1960 Delouvrier had already asked de Gaulle for General Massu's transfer. But Massu's own Gaullist record (he was a member of the exclusive "Order of Liberation" given only to resistance heroes and de Gaulle's closest Free French companions) seemed to be guarantee enough that he would not enter into open conflict with de Gaulle. "I knew," Delouvrier told me later, "that we were in for trouble the day General Massu's transfer out of Algeria was announced. I had no idea what kind of trouble."

The situation on the eve of the January 24 uprising could, to a certain extent, be compared with that which existed just before the uprising of May 13, 1958. The "plotters" were more discreet, and thus perhaps more effective; and of course there was none of the helplessness and lack of direction which so characterised the last days of the Fourth Republic. There were, however, a number of minority groups actively seeking de Gaulle's downfall as the only possible way out of "self-determination". In Paris the "Algérie Française" deputies had entered into close relations with disgruntled politicians of the Fourth Republic such as ex-premier Georges Bidault and André Morice, extreme right-wing leader Jean-Baptiste Biaggi and General André Zeller, the French Army Chief of Staff recalled to duty after May 1958.[1] In Algeria European "activist" groups had re-formed, after May 13, into a number of associations of which the most powerful was the "Front National Français" headed by Algiers café-owner Joseph Ortiz. As the head of the French army's "cinquième bureau" in Algiers Colonel Jean Gardes had the task, among other things, of keeping the army finger on the local political pulse. A crusading anti-communist, Gardes found himself drawn more and more towards the various European leaders of "Algérie Française" factions. In close contact with Gardes, most local European "activist" leaders

[1] Zeller was, later, to join with Challe, Salan and Jouhaud, in the April 22, 1961 "Generals' insurrection".

in Algiers came to the conclusion that Gardes' bitter opposition
to de Gaulle's Algerian policy and his evident sympathy for their
own cause was representative of the French army officers' thinking
in Algeria as a whole. The Algiers district security chief (with
overall responsibility over the Algiers civilian police and security
forces) was Massu's subordinate of the "Battle of Algiers" days,
Colonel Godard. He too shared most of Colonel Gardes' views
(and was, in 1961. to play a prominent part in the "Generals'
insurrection").

The immediate cause of the January 1960 Algiers uprising,
known later as "Barricades week", was General Massu's abrupt
recall to Paris following the publication, in the West German *Sud
Deutscher Zeitung*, on January 18, of an interview with the paper's
chief correspondent, Ulrich Kempsky, in which Massu voiced particularly bitter criticism of de Gaulle, implying that the majority
of French officers in Algeria would not obey him. The real cause,
of course, went back to de Gaulle's "self-determination" address:
"self-determination" for Algeria had been approved and ratified
by a huge majority in the National Assembly, and de Gaulle had,
in private, sought to reassure French army leaders by telling
General Challe that he had no intention either of negotiating anything but cease-fire terms with F.L.N. leaders or of withdrawing
the French army from Algeria. By this time, however, many
officers believed that de Gaulle had merely said this to keep the
French army officers quiet. "For me," Massu told a friend after
September 16, "Algeria comes before de Gaulle."

A week after the Massu interview a huge European rally was
staged in Algiers to protest against his recall. It rapidly got out of
hand, and as a company of "Gendarmerie Nationale" began to
disperse the crowd someone opened fire: while the gendarmerie
company crawled for cover, fire continued from the rooftops for
a full twenty minutes. Individual troopers of the gendarmerie
may or may not have fired back .(At the subsequent "barricades"
trial, their officers and N.C.O.s claimed that none of their men
had.) When the shooting finally died down, 24 people—mostly
gendarmerie officers and men—had been killed and 160 (including

140 gendarmerie men) wounded; the barricades in the Rue Michelet which it had been the gendarmerie's purpose to clear were immediately strengthened by thousands of armed civilians and territorials, and Algiers remained in a state of siege for a full week, ending with the flight of F.N.F. leader Joseph Ortiz and the surrender of Pierre Lagaillarde, who had also set up a fortified camp in the Algiers University building.

It is almost impossible to give an adequate account of Algiers at the time of "Barricades week": it soon became apparent that the rioters were far better prepared for a showdown than anyone in the *Délégation-Générale* had suspected; almost to a man, the *"Unités Territoriales"* (able-bodied Europeans under sixty who took turns to do guards and other chores to relieve the French army for more active duties) mustered under "activist" leaders with their uniforms and weapons, and most of Ortiz' avowedly fascist F.N.F. movement consisted—at the barricades—of uniformed territorials.[1] During and after the firing, scenes of incredible brutality were witnessed by the gendarmerie survivors: at least one wounded gendarmerie trooper was killed in cold blood by maddened European youths; others were paraded up and down lifts in neighbouring buildings. European women were seen pouring shot after shot down on to the trapped security squad from the windows of the buildings surrounding the War Memorial.

What actually occurred has never been fully revealed. But months later, at the closing stage of a trial whose military judges attempted to assess the responsibilities of those involved in the events and in Algiers over "Barricades week", some interesting details came to light.

Belatedly, General Challe seems to have realised, on January 23, that the next twenty-four hours might lead to an armed European

[1] Only in Oran did the then Oran Zone army commander, General Fernand Gambiez, take the elementary precaution of guarding U.T. armouries effectively to prevent weapons from being used by rioters.

Throughout "Barricades week", Ortiz led the insurrection from his headquarters from a large flat, recently acquired by the "Interfédération des Unités Territorials" which overlooked the "Plateau des Glières". It was from one of these balconies that the first shots were fired on January 24.

civilian uprising in Algiers, and that armed insurgents might occupy the University Building. Challe asked a number of senior officers, including the commanders of the regiments of the Tenth Parachute Division quartered in Algiers, the point-blank question: "Will you, if so ordered, fire on the insurgents?" Several replied that they would not, under any circumstances. With no other adequate troops at his disposal, General Challe decided to keep the Tenth Parachute Division in reserve, and let the highly disciplined "Gendarmerie Nationale" handle the mob if possible. When it became apparent that the rioters were beginning to entrench themselves, behind barricades, in the Rue Michelet, the general in charge of Algiers area, Germain Costes, ordered a gendarmerie company to charge the mob and tear down the barricades. At the same time, he ordered two parachute regiments, the "1er Régiment de Chasseurs Parachutistes", whose commanding officer was Colonel Auguste Broizat, and the "1er Régiment Etranger Parachutiste", whose commanding officer was Colonel Henri Dufour, to advance on the barricades from the rear.

At the trial, Colonel Jean Debrosse, the commander of the gendarmerie in Algiers, angrily told the court how his company charged down the steps leading to the War Memorial and promptly ran into enfilade fire, while the two parachute regiments which should have been there to break up the rioters from the rear did not show up until the shooting was over, despite the fact that they were waiting in reserve a mere 300 yards away. Colonel Broizat (who had already told General Challe he would refuse to open fire on rioters) gave the court no satisfactory explanation for his delay, and Colonel Dufour was equally vague.[1]

When Premier Debré flew to Algiers after the firing to meet army colonels, and attempt to reason with them, one of the

[1] Broizat's account in court was as follows: "I learn that orders have been received to clear the 'Plateau des Glières'. I reply: this is incredible, appalling. I am told: you must proceed by Boulevards Baudin and Péguy. Note that I am not instructed to clear the streets, merely to progress down them. I do not attempt to clear Boulevard Péguy, which is full of demonstrators, but plan to move down Boulevard Baudin, which is empty. While I am issuing orders to that effect, firing breaks out . . ." After the firing, Broizat told the court: "I told General Challe: 'You have proclaimed a state of siege, but you are incapable of enforcing it, and you know it'."

colonels threatened to kick his backside. Colonel Broizat, giving evidence at the trial, said he told Debré that . . . "there could be no question of using force, that we would have nothing to do with a new Budapest, that the aim of the President of the Republic should not be to have Frenchmen fire on each other, and that personally I would refuse to execute any order to clear the barricades by force." In his evidence, Colonel Dufour merely said he told Debré: "It is a political problem. It needs a political solution . . ."

Probably the most complete account of the shooting—and of the astonishing behaviour of the officers of the Tenth Parachute Division, who, with Ortiz and the rioters themselves cannot escape moral responsibility for what occurred—came, during the trial, from the then Algiers Area Commander, General Germain Costes, whose statement makes further comment on the state of mind of the Tenth Paratroop Division officers unnecessary.

> "Algiers was against self-determination," said Costes, "guided by a throughly orchestrated opposition movement. By whom? first by the local press, particularly *L'Echo d'Alger*, by student groups, ex-servicemen's organisations, by deputies, mayors and councillors. Some published statements were a direct incitement to murder . . ."
>
> By January 24, he went on, "it was necessary to envisage the possibility of opening fire on the mob. Will you accept? I was asked by General Challe. I replied, Yes. Gentlemen, does a uniformed servant of the state have the right to discuss the law and obedience to the law? . . . In Algiers at the time the only concept of the forces of law and order was to be tough on the Arabs . . ."

By mid-afternoon on January 24, General Costes said,

> "I realised that the European insurgents were not citizens but revolutionary outlaws. I knew that Algiers wanted to impose its will on Paris. I could not accept such blackmail. In such a situation I was like a bound Gulliver with only one free arm:

the gendarmerie. . . . Let us examine the circumstances of the gendarmerie charge: did I summon up all available means— tanks and bombs? No . . . the situation was not without risk, but I could not imagine that Frenchmen were ready to open fire on their own army with machine guns. To hide themselves in the dark to get themselves a gendarme[1], as the phrase was at the time . . ."

Asked by the Court to comment on the Parachute Regiments' delays, General Costes replied: "I had no illusions about them."

The Court: "Were you aware of this delay?"

General Costes: "Yes."

The Court: "Did you delay the operation?"

General Costes: "What use would it have been?"

Lagaillarde's Defence Counsel: "You still ordered the gendarmes to charge?"

General Costes: "I repeat that I had no illusions as to the paratroopers' will to arrive on time . . . Colonels Dufour and Broizat may have had their difficulties. But it seems to me that certain testimonies in this court reveal an extraordinary state of affairs for an army. They show that for some officers an order is not an order but a basis for discussion."

Defence Counsel: "You were faced by a peaceful crowd of women and children, no threats, only a few cries, and you used fifteen squadrons of gendarmerie?"

General Costes: " 'Maître', that is a lie: let me explain further: there are two trials going on in this courtroom. One concerns the events of January 24. The other is a trial of falsehood. I now realise what is meant by the phrase: 'a conspiracy of silence', a conspiracy of people suddenly struck dumb, of people who have suddenly lost their memory, a conspiracy of bold liars . . ."

Defence Counsel: "Whom do you accuse?"

General Costes: "A whole world, sir. This trial is empty, spineless, devoid of content . . ."

Alone of the accused in dock, *Echo d'Alger* director Alain de

---

[1] "*Se payer un gendarme.*"

Serigny chose to cross-examine General Costes and asked him why, if they were that dangerous, he had never banned general notices from Ortiz's "*Front National Français*". With a withering glance at de Serigny, General Costes said pointedly: "Because, at the time, I was myself under orders of General Massu"—the inference being that he had tried to get them banned and failed. (The Military Court, it should be noted, acquitted the only accused army officer on trial, Colonel Jean Gardes. Colonel Dufour spent three months under close arrest for taking to the "Maquis" for a brief spell with his regimental flag when posted out of Algeria but was persuaded to return and later given a command in West Germany; no charges of any kind were ever laid against Colonel Broizat.)

From the shooting on the evening of January 24 until the following Friday (January 29) several thousand rioters occupied the central part of Algiers (including the University) bringing the life of the town to a standstill. To say that they had barricaded themselves inside this perimeter would not be strictly accurate: for the first few days, at least, the insurgents, by the hundred, in uniform and with their rifles slung over their soldiers, came and went as they pleased under the noses of the "neutral" and obviously sympathetic parachute regiments surrounding the "camp retranché". Municipal ambulances and private cars came and went, bringing in food and drink, weapons and ammunition. Many of the insurgents, for the first few days at least, slept at home: I watched them return to the "camp retranché" in the early morning, and drift away again at night. The paratroopers openly fraternised with the insurgents, and even mingled with them in front of the barricades. A tricolour flag in front of the main barricade was raised in the morning and taken down at night, and during the flag-raising ceremonies the paratroopers sprang to attention and saluted. A whole procession of army officers, of whom Colonel Gardes was the most prominent, found their way into Ortiz's headquarters. Such was the passive coalition against him that Delouvrier's staff could not even cut off water, gas and electricity within the perimeter of the "camp retranché".

The aim of Ortiz and Lagaillarde, in setting up such a "camp retranché", was to force the army to take sides: the insurgent leaders knew the state of mind of a number of officers mostly in the Tenth Parachute Division. They knew that there was little physical risk involved, since the army would in all probability refuse to fire, refuse—in the words of one officer, to "stage another Budapest". They hoped that the army's deliberate unwillingness to clear the barricades would snowball into a full-scale army "coup" against de Gaulle, leading to the latter's downfall and the installation of a military régime, first in Algeria then in France. They thought that, before such a "coup" could become effective, de Gaulle would bow to their demands and proclaim "*L'Algérie à jamais Française*". But de Gaulle was not Guy Mollet, and the Tenth Parachute Division was not the whole of the French army. But there was, during the first few days of "Barricades week", the same kind of atmosphere and to a certain extent the same kind of situation as that which had existed at the time of the insurrection on May 13, 1958. Then, the "paras" had stepped in, nominally to restore law and order, but in effect to enable the rioters to operate without interference, and the "Gouvernement-Général" building, guarded by paratroopers with almost ceremonial deference, had become a kind of shrine where tens of thousands of Europeans went to worship. After the shooting on January 24, 1960, paratroopers put on a similar kind of show around the barricades, and tens of thousands of Europeans massed for hours on the "Plateau des Glières", encouraged by the inflammatory speeches, the shouted slogans and the military music broadcast from dawn to dusk from the balcony outside Ortiz's headquarters.

Intoxication was mutual: the insurgents, from within the barricades, were given a tremendous fillip by the evident support of the great majority of the European population of Algiers; while the onlookers came to believe, as they watched the harmonious relationship between the insurgents and the paratroopers, that the whole of the French army was really on their side and that de Gaulle's downfall or moral surrender was imminent.

The January insurrection was broken by three successive events:

on the fourth day of the barricades, Delouvrier, in an impassioned, sentimental speech deliberately keyed to the European population of Algiers appealed to them to have faith in de Gaulle, and announced that he and the Algerian Commander-in-Chief, General Challe, were leaving Algiers for a headquarters "where they would be able to exercise command". Delouvrier's decision to move to the French air force camp of Reghaïa, about eighteen miles east, was prompted partly by the "passive resistance" of a number of local officials and army officers. It also served as a warning to the rest of the army—and to public opinion in France, which deplored the insurrection and would have rallied to de Gaulle in case of a real showdown—that at least part of the armed forces in Algeria were ready in the event of a civil war.

The second dampener came when the activists, who remembered that their full success had only come with "fraternisation", attempted to get the Moslems to demonstrate in their favour too. That they should have tried at all showed their almost incredible lack of awareness of Moslem opinion: a long-announced and oft-delayed procession finally got under way: it consisted of the European members of various ex-servicemen's organisations, wearing their decorations and carrying flags. With them walked, or rather limped, a pathetic assortment of elderly Moslem veterans, mostly maimed, and mostly of first world war vintage. Two were so old they had almost to be carried by the European organisers of the procession.

The third, and without doubt the most effective, instrument with which the insurrection was broken was de Gaulle's own voice. I happened to be inside the barricades when his January 29 broadcast came through. The loudspeakers were turned off, and a hush settled over the whole "camp retranché" as de Gaulle, firmly and inexorably, announced that he would not be swayed by any consideration into altering his "self-determination" policy. This, one of his finest speeches, including as it did a stigmatisation of certain army elements' "accommodating uncertainty"[1] had an immediate effect on the insurgents and on the army alike: as

[1] See Appendix A.

soon as the speech ended, I watched men and women break down and cry with impotent rage; within hours, the Tenth Parachute Division cut off all contacts with the insurgents, and next day they allowed themselves to be relieved. The relieving force, units of the 25th Parachute Division which had seen hard service on the Tunisian frontier and had no sentimental ties with Algiers, backed by non-paratroop conscript units, did what the Tenth Parachute Division units should have done in the first place: a strict cordon was placed all around the "camp retranché". All roads leading to the "Plateau des Glières" were blocked off by army trucks, and the army prepared to keep up the blockade for days, even weeks. On Sunday night the great exodus from the barricades started, and by noon on Monday Lagaillarde and his hard core of "irreductibles" had surrendered.

For the insurgents, defeat came as soon as it was obvious that the French army was not going to turn against de Gaulle, but was at long last obeying government orders. Since the whole point of the "camp retranché" had been to force the army into challenging de Gaulle's authority, there was no sense in prolonging the "barricades" once it had become clear that they had failed. In the weeks that followed there were bitter recriminations from European "activists" who accused French army officers of having betrayed them.

The failure of the January 24 insurrection had important consequences in Algeria: "activist" and "ultra" organisations were disrupted or banned, the territorials were at long last disbanded, their main "activist" leaders were forced to flee or were arrested. The European inhabitants of Algiers, disrupted by the general strike, demoralised by the army's apparent "betrayal", suffered a severe hangover from which they never fully recovered. For the first time they had challenged Paris, and authority had refused to bow to their demands. Some of the army's "accommodating uncertainty" was punished by an increased spate of postings and a number of disciplinary measures. The Moslems had shown that they could no longer be used as docile instruments of army or "activist" policy. Finally, the failure of the insurrection strengthened General de Gaulle not only in France but on the international plane: one of the principal arguments put forward by F.L.N. leaders in Tunis against negotiations was that de Gaulle, like his predecessors of the Fourth Republic, would be unable to keep control of events and that policy would in fact be dictated, as in the past, by the European settlers and the army. After the failure of the "barricades" they could no longer hold this view.

CHAPTER FIFTEEN

THE HARD ROAD TO PEACE

THE failure of "Barricades week" left General de Gaulle in a stronger position than at any time since his return to power. But then, as later, he was to display a contempt for the time factor in politics which was to delay preparations for an Algerian settlement for over a year. Looking back on the course of events since 1958, it is obvious that the turning-point came on September 16, 1959, with de Gaulle's first reference to Algerian "self-determination". Yet the Algerian war was to drag on for at least two more years before the F.L.N. and a French Government Delegation met face to face. Each step forward was accompanied by a half-step back. And if, as far as Algeria's Europeans were concerned, de Gaulle seemed to be practising the "politique de l'artichaut" (the phrase first coined by Lagaillarde implying that as every leaf was pulled away, de Gaulle's "politique d'abandon" was revealed with increasing clarity), in the eyes of the F.L.N. each "positive" statement on Algeria was accompanied by unacceptable qualifications. And each time deadlock seemed to have been reached, the F.L.N. turned with increasing assurance to the communist bloc.

Perhaps—for only General de Gaulle could tell—this was France's deliberate policy. The unsatisfactory behaviour of some French army units during the "barricades" uprising showed that the authority of the state had not been entirely restored; Algeria-born officials, at all levels of the Algerian administration, could still not be counted on to carry out official instructions in the proper spirit. Perhaps de Gaulle was hoping to make his policy more acceptable as time went on, and proceeded deliberately by cautious stages. But in retrospect, it is obvious that in getting his own way over Algeria, General de Gaulle relied not only on patience, good judgement and an inexorable will, but also on a fair amount of sheer luck: General de Gaulle did not carry out a thorough purge of army elements until almost too late: though hundreds of officers were sent out of Algeria, none save Colonel Gardes were put on trial (and since Gardes was acquitted, it could not be said that an example was made of him), none were dismissed from the army for their attitude during the "barricades" insurrection. Many languished in the comparative idleness of garrison life, or awaited postings which never came. Far from forgetting their old habits, they intensified their plotting. Before direct negotiations with the F.L.N. began, General de Gaulle faced, and triumphed over a totally unexpected revolt of once-trusted generals and colonels. Luckily, the generals' insurrection was short-lived, and collapsed because the plotters failed to gain a moral or material foothold in France itself, and were faced with the insubordination of all French army conscripts in Algeria and a number of loyal officers. It was a good thing for de Gaulle that the generals' insurrection was over by the time the French and F.L.N. delegations actually met at Évian. But the fact that such an insurrection ever got going at all showed how tenuous was de Gaulle's authority over certain army elements, and how he had been wrong to treat past insubordination with comparative leniency.

Immediately after "Barricades week", de Gaulle inspected a number of French Army units in Algeria, leaving officers there with the impression that negotiations would be indefinitely delayed until the last uniformed rebels had been put out of action. A communiqué, after the Algerian visit, announced that de Gaulle had told army officers that "nothing could be decided by the Algerians . . . as long as the fighting and the outrages continued". This dampener was interpreted, in Tunis, as meaning that de Gaulle was prepared to see the war drag on endlessly, and Algerian emissaries left Tunis for Peking with further promises of increased Chinese aid.

Then came de Gaulle's radio and TV address on June 14, 1960, a lyrical, balanced, moving survey of France's place in the world, with a message, right at its very end, designed to correct F.L.N. apprehensions:

> "Once again," said de Gaulle, "I turn in the name of France to the leaders of the insurrection. I say to them that we are waiting for them here, in order to seek with them an honourable end to the fighting that is still going on, to settle what is to become of the weapons, to ensure the fate of those fighting . . ."

The F.L.N. "government" responded by despatching a small team of negotiators, headed by Maître Ahmed Boumendjel, to France for preparatory talks prior to a full-scale conference. Hopes were high on both sides, but it soon became clear that the Melun conference would end in deadlock. Perhaps de Gaulle had never expected the F.L.N. to initiate talks so soon. In any event, much of the time in Melun was spent by the F.L.N. and French officials in futile discussions on the meaning of de Gaulle's latest speech. Rightly or wrongly, and perhaps to de Gaulle's own intense annoyance, the French officials at Melun interpreted the speech in its most restrictive sense. That, and the fact that Boumendjel was told that an F.L.N. Delegation to France would be kept virtually incommunicado, without direct access to the press, caused the talks to be broken off.

The consequences of the Melun failure were serious, for the Algerian Moslems did not hide their bitter disappointment. As de Gaulle explained in a series of short speeches while on a tour of Normandy, failure was due to F.L.N. reluctance to "leave the knives in the cloakroom" before sitting down to talks. From the F.L.N. point of view, this was putting the cart before the horse: for a number of reasons the rebels could only agree to a negotiated cease-fire. The F.L.N.'s general impression, therefore, was that its earlier assessment of de Gaulle's attitude had been a correct one. In a series of defiant speeches and editorials, F.L.N. spokesmen announced that after Melun they could no longer put their trust in bilateral talks with France but must seek, instead, United Nations arbitration. As always when their peace hopes were dashed, F.L.N. leaders turned anew to the communist bloc: at the October 1960 ceremonies commemorating the tenth year of the Communist Chinese Revolution, Ferhat Abbas stood as an honoured guest at Mao Tse-tung's right side.

The failure of Melun also had repercussions on the administration in Algeria: after Melun, the Algerian Delegate-General, Paul Delouvrier, had suggested that de Gaulle should of his own accord propose a unilateral truce, and offer to renew preparatory talks through Tunisian and Moroccan good offices. De Gaulle did not follow Delouvrier's advice, and before the end of the year an important government reshuffle had taken place: Louis Joxe, the former Education Minister, a career diplomat of great and varied experience, was appointed Algeria Minister. Under him, but dealing solely with administrative and security matters, the French government appointed Jean Morin, a career "prefect". Delouvrier, it was widely thought at the time, owed his removal from office at least in part to his emotional speech to the Algiers Europeans during "Barricades week". But there was at least one additional reason: as Delegate-General, with considerable responsibilities but no cabinet prerogatives, Delouvrier was constantly under pressure from a number of ministers who attempted to interfere in Algerian affairs. Some members of the Premier's office (though not M. Debré himself) had attempted to influence Algerian policy in a manner which Delouvrier considered to be contrary to the spirit of de Gaulle's general instructions. (It came as no surprise, for instance, to learn that two of the generals who played an active part in the abortive "generals' insurrection" of April 1961 had served for a considerable time on M. Debré's personal staff.) From Louis Joxe's appointment onwards, it was understood that the Prime Minister's office was to have no say whatsoever in Algerian affairs—this, in fact, was believed to have been the sole condition posed by Joxe before his nomination.

It was four months before General de Gaulle seized the initiative again in Algeria. His speech of November 4, 1960, contained a further offer which it was difficult for the F.L.N. to ignore.

"The Algeria of tomorrow," said de Gaulle, "as self-determination will decide, can be built either with France or against her. France—I state it once again—will not oppose the solution, whatever it may be, which will be determined by the vote. If this were to be a hostile break, we would certainly not persist in remaining by force alongside people who would reject us, or in allowing efforts and billions which are needed elsewhere to be swallowed up in an endless and hopeless undertaking. We would leave Algeria to herself, while taking, of course, the measures necessary in order to safeguard on the one hand those of the Algerians who would like to remain French, on the other hand our interests there. But if—and I believe this with all my heart and with all my mind—it is to be a matter of an Algeria in which the communities of Moslem and French origin co-operate, with the desired guarantees, of an Algeria which would choose to be united with France for economic, technical, educational and defence matters—which is only commonsense—then we would furnish to her material and human development the powerful and fraternal assistance which we alone are able to give her . . ."

After proposing talks with "the leaders of the external organisation of the rebellion . . . in good faith and without restrictions", de Gaulle went on:

"But the rebel chiefs, who have lived outside of Algeria for six years and who—if we are to believe them—will continue to do so for a long time to come, claim to be the Government of the Algerian Republic, a Republic which will one day exist, but which has never yet existed. In this capacity . . . they claim that they will have the murdering stopped only if, to begin with, they alone determined with us the terms of the future Referendum . . . as if they were the representatives of all Algeria. It would then all take place as if they had been appointed beforehand, and appointed by me, as the rulers of Algeria . . . Consequently their arrival in Algiers under such conditions would render self-determination a meaningless formality and, even if they do not wish it, throw the territory into terrible chaos. . . .

"That is why, without abandoning the hope that one day commonsense will finally prevail, and that general negotiations will be opened after the fighting and acts of terrorism have ceased, we are going, with the Algerians of Algeria, to continue along the road to an Algerian Algeria, while waiting for Algeria herself to be able, by her vote, and if she so wishes, to turn the *de facto* situation into a *de jure* situation . . . in the final analysis the responsibility for Algeria's affairs will, at all levels, be assumed by the Algerians."

By this time there was no doubt, in the minds of most informed Frenchmen, as to the nationalist sentiments of the overwhelming majority of Algerian Moslems. The December riots were to show that if a "third force" might emerge after independence, it could have no real existence for as long as the fighting continued. French military successes, it was now proved, did not mean the eradication of nationalism. "We have pacified the country so well," a French captain wrote about this time in a report to his commanding officer, "that the 'fellagha' have almost disappeared. Nowadays, almost no one joins the guerillas. It is more practical to stay put and campaign for independence in a thousand legal ways."

Such was the situation when de Gaulle decided to test his popularity with the Moslems by appearing in Algeria in person. Activist-led European demonstrations against de Gaulle had continued throughout the autumn, and there were massive demonstrations around November 11. But despite the newly-formed "Front de l'Algérie Française" (F.A.F.) claiming half a million members, including 200,000 Moslems, the Europeans were still smarting from the failure of their January 1960 insurrection. They were, however, intent on making their feelings known: no sooner had de Gaulle set foot on Algerian soil than Europeans began demonstrating against him. The Rue Michelet, in Algiers, became a writhing mass of demonstrators and security troops. A car was overturned and burnt, and security squads moved in with armoured cars and tear-gas under a hail of paving-stones and bottles. For three days the riots continued in Algiers while in the rest of Algeria relative calm prevailed—though wherever he went de Gaulle was confronted with crowds of hostile Europeans, whose cries were mostly drowned by the numerically superior Moslems' cries of "Algérie Algérienne" and "Vive de Gaulle".

At Aïn Temouchent and Orléansville, Europeans and Moslems came to blows. Elsewhere, bloodshed was avoided only by the skilful and determined use of troops and gendarmerie.

Then, on the night of December 9, while de Gaulle was still in Orléansville, tragedy began in earnest: a small group of Europeans began attacking Moslems in the mixed Algiers suburb of Belcourt: their original, and preposterous, aim had been to get some Moslems to demonstrate on their side. Almost immediately fighting broke out. Moslems retaliated by stabbing Europeans, and set a large store on fire.

This, it soon appeared, was merely the first stage in a series of Moslem chain reactions: the following morning, under the eyes of Europeans and security troops, Moslems all over Algiers staged huge openly pro-F.L.N. demonstrations. The banned green and white flag, with red star and crescent—the F.L.N.'s official emblem—appeared by magic all over town. The Kasbah was soon a mass of demonstrators, chanting, "Abbas au pouvoir." Within hours the demonstrations had been taken in hand by F.L.N. underground agents. They were to go on for several days. In sporadic fighting some 100 Moslems were killed—mostly by Europeans indulging in individual reprisals. One French paratroop unit also opened fire on some demonstrators, while Europeans screamed encouragement from their windows. Several Europeans were stabbed or butchered to death by the Moslems, and at least one pro-French Moslem was killed. In Bône, for the first time in the history of Algeria, a French army unit opened fire on demonstrating Europeans, killing two French youths.

The pro-F.L.N. demonstrations could of course have been put

down by French security troops, but only at immense cost in Moslem life. Their task was unbelievably delicate: on the one hand, the appearance of the F.L.N. flag in the streets of Algiers was an almost direct incitement to open fire. On the other hand, they knew that de Gaulle would not sanction the use of methods which had brought the Kasbah to its knees in 1957: far from denying the existence of Algerian nationalist feeling, de Gaulle had accepted it as an incontrovertible fact: the Moslems themselves knew this too, and this made them bolder than they otherwise would have been. On that fateful Sunday morning, I watched a scene, at Belcourt, which summed up the situation: a Moslem came careening round a corner on a motorcycle, tied to which was an enormous F.L.N. flag. A gendarmerie captain told him to put it away. "Pourquoi? On ne fait pas de mal," he replied. "Le Général de Gaulle a dit: Algérie Algérienne. On est Algériens, non?"

De Gaulle's critics, who put the blame for the demonstrations on his shoulders, could not or would not admit that the "fraternisation" of May 1958 had occurred in very special circumstances and that Moslem attitudes, up to the time of these riots, had largely been dictated by fear. To be sure de Gaulle's determination to allow the Moslems to express themselves politically had itself made these demonstrations possible. As de Gaulle himself somewhat cynically remarked on returning to Paris, they had "cleared the air".

They also, perhaps more than any other single event, revealed a state of affairs which, it was realised in France, could not continue indefinitely, and prepared French public opinion for drastic changes. On January 8, 1961, a Referendum held in France and Algeria gave General de Gaulle wide powers to act: the Referendum itself took the form of an oblique question (whether France agreed to widespread reorganisation in Algeria while awaiting Algerian self-determination which would come later), but it was widely understood as giving de Gaulle a free hand to negotiate with the F.L.N., as approving the establishment of "The Algeria of tomorrow" in which "the Algerians will conduct their own affairs, and it will be up to them alone to found a state with its own government, its own institutions and its own laws"[1].

The Referendum was a success for de Gaulle, though his large majority fell short of his 1958 plebiscite: most of the Europeans in Algeria, naturally enough, voted against him, and a large minority of Moslems either voted "no" or abstained. There was also a higher proportion of Moslem spoiled votes than at any time since voting had become an established tradition in Algeria—a sure sign that voting conditions were fairer.

Almost immediately after the Referendum, secret talks between F.L.N. and French emissaries directly mandated by de Gaulle began, leading, on March 15, to the official announcement of impending talks between France and the F.L.N. at Évian. Before talks got under way, however, two hurdles had to be cleared: the first concerned F.L.N. suspicions that de Gaulle would try and turn the Évian Conference into a round-table conference of all interested parties, including the rival minority nationalist movement, the M.N.A. The second was the brief, but threatening, Generals' insurrection of April 22.

For F.L.N. leaders, the M.N.A. was not merely a rival organisation: it was a deeply distrusted "counter-revolutionary movement" headed by a man whom they had once revered but now hated—partly because he had refused to take the lead when direct action was being planned, partly because his vanity precluded any progress towards independence which did not stem from his own will. Moreover, French authorities had used M.N.A. members as convenient pawns in the struggle against the F.L.N. They had made much of the spectacular "ralliement" of M.N.A. men, particularly after the brutal F.L.N. massacre of some three hundred Moslems at Kasbah Mechta in 1958—a village which was in an area under local M.N.A. control—and had also used them as informers. To be sure, there was an M.N.A. "maquis" in Algeria, but its effectiveness was negligible. In France things were different: living in relative freedom at Chantilly, under heavy protection from his own bodyguard and French security troops,

[1] Broadcast and televised speech by General de Gaulle, December 20, 1960.

Messali Hadj continued to attract a large proportion of Algerian workers in France.

It was a chance phrase of Louis Joxe (chosen to head the French Delegation at Évian)—"I will talk to the M.N.A. as I will talk to the F.L.N."—which led to a temporary breakdown before the Évian Conference had actually begun. Joxe had meant, of course, that he would consult all different expressions of opinion in Algeria—Europeans, pro-French Moslems, M.N.A.—as the talks with the F.L.N. progressed. The F.L.N. took this to mean that the Évian Conference might be duplicated by another conference elsewhere with M.N.A. leaders: not until secret assurances to the contrary had been given (and until the F.L.N. began realising that by drawing attention to the M.N.A. it was in fact according it a welcome and unexpected publicity) did the conference start. There was probably a further reason for delay. Faced with the immediate prospect of meeting a highly competent French delegation across a conference table, the F.L.N. leaders developed a bad attack of stage fright. Like schoolboys cramming for an exam, they welcomed an additional delay to acquire a working knowledge of the files they intended to bring with them to Évian.

Then, shortly after a blunt press conference by General de Gaulle in which he threatened to leave Algeria high and dry without aid or assistance should "secession" be the F.L.N.'s aim, the generals' insurrection once more brought France to the brink of chaos: it occurred out of the blue, and was skilfully planned by a small group of officers, mostly known "activists" removed from their Algeria commands or retired. It was led by General Maurice Challe—Algeria's commander-in-chief from 1958 to 1960 and one of the few French generals in Algeria to have acquired the respect and devotion of regimental officers of the crack paratroop and Foreign Legion units in Algeria. It benefited not only from the support of a large number of career officers in Algeria, but from the vocal, unequivocal support of the Europeans of Algeria who suddenly felt that despite the threats of de Gaulle's "self determination" some kind of miracle was at hand.

Some of the details of the insurrection will probably never be fully known: was the Algiers insurrection all part of a plan to murder de Gaulle and get French army units in West Germany to march on Paris? Did the insurgent generals really expect the whole of the French forces in Algeria to rally to their cause? Were paratroop landings in France really contemplated? The fact remains that from the very start of the insurrection, the generals (André Zeller, a retired chief of staff and prominent right-wing polemist, Raoul Salan, the former commander-in-chief who had been living in Madrid after his expulsion from Algiers, Challe and Jean Jouhaud, a retired Algeria-born Air Force commander) not only faced a mounting series of defeats and obstructions but also started falling out among themselves. Challe's plan, he was to claim later at his trial, was to prove to France that the Algerian war could be won by proven "tough" methods and the massive recruitment of local Europeans. (Throughout his trial he was to minimise his role in attempting to overthrow de Gaulle, though, as the proclamations of the general's junta proved during the insurrection, this was their aim too.) The conscripts rebelled against the insurgent officers and both the French Navy and nearly all of the Air Force remained loyal to de Gaulle. At the end of their heady four days, during which normal life in France was brought to a standstill as Frenchmen prepared for a possible civil war, the generals were left with the crumbling remains of an initial 17,500 men—mostly paratroopers and Foreign Legion units. Of these some 3,000 men remained loyal to Challe to the last, returning to their barracks when Challe decided to surrender. (Zeller gave himself up a few days after the insurrection's collapse. Jouhaud and Salan went into hiding.)

Although General de Gaulle affected to consider the generals' insurrection as an "odious and stupid pronunciamento . . . (which) will not in any way impede France's forward march"[1] he was badly shaken by the suddenness of the insurrection and the ramifications of the plot not only in the army but in the higher ranks of the administration. The Air Force chief of staff (later imprisoned and cashiered) had, it was discovered,

[1] Broadcast and televised speech on May 8, 1961.

himself helped smuggle General Challe into Algiers. A number of generals and colonels indulged in fence-sitting until it was apparent that de Gaulle would win. Some senior staff members of Ministries and of the French administration had responded in lukewarm fashion to de Gaulle's appeals for help during the crisis: in fact, it could be said that de Gaulle was saved on this occasion by the trade unions (including the communist-led C.G.T.), the conscripts in Algeria and the information media (including the peripheral radio stations "Radio Luxembourg" and "Europe Numero Un").

The consequence of the insurrection was an overhaul, long overdue, of French army cadres and the promotion to key posts of officers whose loyalty was not in doubt. One reason for de Gaulle's reluctance to carry out such a drastic overhaul earlier stemmed, almost certainly, from his own reluctance, as a once regular officer, to divide the French army. It had been de Gaulle's fate, as a patriot and statesman, to cause Frenchmen to fire on Frenchmen (in Syria during the second world war) and to purge the army, at war's end, of a large number of officers who had remained loyal to Pétain until too late. Now the Algerian question had divided the French army once more, and de Gaulle was forced to place some 200 officers under close arrest and dissolve some of France's finest fighting units, including the famed "Premier Régiment Etranger Parachutiste" of the Foreign Legion which had been fighting practically non-stop in Indo-China and Algeria since 1952.

The Europeans of Algeria, who had not been given prior warning of the insurrection, were demoralised by its sudden failure. Long before the insurrection occurred, the extremist "Organisation Armée Secrète" (O.A.S.) had begun its own terrorist campaign against de Gaulle: more than one hundred and fifty plastic bombs went off in France and Algeria during March and April (one of them killing the gaullist Mayor of Évian, Camille Blanc). Shortly before surrendering, Challe had distributed some ten thousand sub-machine guns and pistols—contents of the entire police armoury of Algiers—to the Europeans' extremist organisations there. Inevitably retribution came in the form of house-to-house searches, prolonged curfews and the banning of three of Algiers' four dailies which had sided with Challe.

Inevitably, the Europeans felt they were being victimised, and developed a bitter hatred for the conscript troops who had "betrayed" Challe. Enormous troop concentrations (28,000 men in Algiers, 20,000 in Oran) were needed to prevent further "activist" outbreaks. With the paratrooper units and the Foreign Legion undergoing drastic reorganisation, and large numbers of troops tied up in "internal security" duties, it was difficult to keep up full-scale operations against the F.L.N. guerillas. The scene was set, in fact, for some kind of a truce. From the F.L.N. point of view, the generals' insurrection had brought home the reality of French opposition to any peaceful Algerian settlement, and made the G.P.R.A. more amenable to immediate negotiations. On May 18, an F.L.N. delegation, headed by "Foreign Minister" Belkacem Krim, landed in Geneva. Two days later, Swiss army helicopters made their first flight across Lake Léman to Évian, bearing the F.L.N. negotiators to the first of many meetings with the French Delegation at Évian's heavily guarded Hôtel du Parc.

The choice of Krim was a good one: as one of the "historic" leaders of the rebellion, his prestige was high with the guerillas. Krim was known to favour negotiations with France and to have persuaded some of the more reluctant members of the G.P.R.A. to take up the French offer. He therefore had a vested interest in their success. Other members of the F.L.N. delegation included "Finance Minister" Ahmed Francis, a former doctor who had run the F.L.N.'s finances successfully since 1957, Saad Dahlab, a prominent ex-terrorist and secretary-general of Krim's "foreign ministry", and Maître Ahmed Boumendjel, who had led the abortive F.L.N. mission to Melun in 1960.

As the conference started, and with an eye on international public opinion, General de Gaulle announced a series of liberal measures in Algeria: the transfer of Ben Bella and other imprisoned F.L.N. personalities to a comfortable mansion near

Saumur, where they remained under house arrest; a unilateral cease-fire; the release of some 6,000 Moslem political prisoners; and the dispersal of a number of Moslem "regroupment centres".

In an opening address at Evian, M. Joxe announced these measures and in a general survey of the Algerian problem attempted to define French aims: a cease-fire to restore "normal" conditions in Algeria, to be followed by a mutually agreed referendum on the choice between "francisation", association or independence. In his reply, Krim stressed the "national integrity" of Algeria and the "unity" of its population. In later statements to M. Joxe and to the press he denounced the unilateral cease-fire as "premature from a military, psychological and political point of view". "The French Government," said Krim, "has constantly sought to have us stage a cease-fire before beginning negotiations, and this is one of the constant factors in French policy."

Such statements revealed the weight of F.L.N. obsessions with the past, with the "peace of the brave" of 1958 and the so obviously unacceptable proposals of Guy Mollet in 1956. It was difficult for the F.L.N. to realise that circumstances had changed and that France was now resigned to a sovereign Algeria.

But there was another reason for F.L.N. intransigence—however unfavourably its reactions were interpreted in the eyes of international public opinion: a guerilla army, unlike a regular army, has no traditional structures. Its combativity, its discipline and morale to a large extent depend on the pressures to which it is subjected by the regular forces against which it is pitted. Should these regular forces renounce all offensive action, there must be an almost overwhelming temptation to set aside one's weapons and leave one's mountain hideouts. There is no doubt that if the French unilateral cease-fire decision was made partly for humanitarian reasons, and to impress the Algerian Moslem population, it resulted also from the desire to "soften up" the remaining guerilla bands. These reacted, at first, by increasing their operations against the French army now on the defensive. But there could be no doubt that in the long run it would be difficult for guerilla commanders to keep their men in hand.

On the timing of a cease-fire, on the Sahara, on the question of French bases in Algeria and on the status of Algeria's Europeans once Algeria had become a sovereign state there was a huge gulf between the French and F.L.N. points of view, as expressed during the first few days of the Évian Conference. The F.L.N., as a question of fundamental principle, would not even envisage discussing a cease-fire otherwise than as a result of a wide political settlement. The F.L.N. insisted that the Sahara was part of Algeria, rejected any form of partition or double nationality for the European minority. Finally, on the question of association with France, the F.L.N. wished to postpone discussions until independence had been achieved. It sought, at Évian, to confine the talks to guarantees of "real" Algerian self-determination, which, their spokesmen repeatedly stressed, in F.L.N. eyes could only result in independence.

After weeks of exploratory "statements of principle", the Évian conference broke up—almost certainly at General de Gaulle's behest—to convene again at the Château de Lugrin, a few miles South of Évian, in July. This time both sides went some small way towards a settlement: they produced rival agendas to determine the points at issue. As in practically all post-war conferences of crucial importance, the order of the points listed for discussion on the agendas was as important as the points themselves: and the talks were further broken off—this time by the F.L.N.—when the French Delegation refused to accept the F.L.N.'s agenda listing the "national unity and integrity of Algerian territory" as the first item for discussion.

The F.L.N. decision to break off the Lugrin talks caused dismay among the Algerian Moslems in Algeria as well as in France, where there was mounting impatience at the slow progress made towards peace. It could be explained on several counts: the

F.L.N.'s long-delayed meeting of the C.N.R.A. was due in Tripoli, and no member of the F.L.N.'s provisional government was big enough to force a major decision on the F.L.N. in the knowledge that he might be blamed later for doing so without consulting the F.L.N.'s "Parliament"; there was, as it turned out, dissatisfaction with F.L.N. leadership which led, in Tripoli, to Ferhat Abbas's replacement as "Premier" by the younger, little-known Youssef ben Khedda; the Franco-Tunisian crisis over Bizerte was at its height, and there was something odd about the F.L.N. sitting down to major talks with France at the very moment when French troops were fighting Tunisians in Bizerte amid Tunisian charges of atrocities; finally, the F.L.N. felt at this stage that by breaking off the talks it would give General de Gaulle a further opportunity to concede some ground over the Saharan questions. (Among those French officials who claimed to be in touch with current *Élysées* thinking, it had long been claimed that General de Gaulle's preoccupations with French sovereign rights over the Sahara stemmed more from a concern for the French military atomic base of Reggane, south of Colomb Bechar, than for Saharan oil supplies. The Berlin crisis—also nearing its peak in July 1961—by bringing the Western powers closer together and in a backhand way, when Soviet tests started, demonstrating the relative futility of French tests—paradoxically made Reggane's future less important. And General de Gaulle was himself, after the breaking-off of talks at Lugrin, to revise his attitude over the Sahara in a televised speech and concede Algerian sovereignty there).

The change in leadership from Abbas to Ben Khedda was an important one. Born in 1923, Ben Khedda had—unlike Abbas— been a leading terrorist during the 1956–57 "battle of Algiers" and had survived scores of narrow escapes. He had been opposed to the establishment of the "provisional government" in exile, claiming that leadership should remain in Algeria where the risks were being taken. His appointment was a return to the "fundamental principles" of the F.L.N. as defined at the 1956 Soummam Conference. Vested with more powers than Ferhat

Abbas had enjoyed, Ben Khedda was given a freer hand to end the war, on the understanding—unlikely to be contravened—that increasing attention be paid to socialist planning, to agrarian reform, and to the "political education" of the Algerian masses.

But the F.L.N.'s move to the left should not be seen—at this stage at least—as a move towards communism: a devout Moslem, Ben Khedda had himself, as an underground leader, been responsible for the "liquidation" of a small rival communist cell; Ben Khedda, and his new "Foreign Minister", Saad Dahlab, were perfectly aware of the wiles of Soviet strategy, of the inherent opportunism displayed towards newly independent countries or areas still under colonial rule. The change in leadership from Abbas to Ben Khedda confirmed a trend—it did not imply a reversal of policy. There were other reasons, including the bad state of Abbas's own health (he had suffered spells of dizziness and migraine ever since a serious automobile accident in Morocco in 1957) to justify a change in leadership. Abbas had always been more of an arbiter than a leader, never anxious for personal power, often requesting to be allowed to resign. From 1956 to 1960, the F.L.N., leading a clandestine, worried existence, needed the respectable well-known figure of Ferhat Abbas, who had sat on the benches of the French National Assembly, had cultivated a wide range of French politicians, and was patently the reverse of a revolutionary leader. As time went on, and as the F.L.N. received increasing support and was treated with increasing consideration throughout the world, this "front" became less necessary. Another possible reason had to do with internal Algerian politics—already an important factor despite the F.L.N.'s still-clandestine structure: Abbas had been the leader of the pre-rebellion "U.D.M.A.", the more moderate of the two Algerian nationalist movements. Most of the rest of the senior leaders of the F.L.N.—including Ben Khedda—stemmed from the more violent "M.T.L.D." whose leader, Messali Hadj, had refused to lead an overt rebellion against French rule. The members of the M.T.L.D. who had broken away from Messali Hadj and organised the rebellion called themselves—before setting up the F.L.N—the "centralists", and they were in a majority both in the "C.N.R.A." and in the "provisional Government" itself: it was significant that the changes in leadership at Tripoli involved not only Abbas but his brother-in-law, Ahmed Francis, the G.P.R.A.'s Finance Minister, also a former "U.D.M.A." man. Another conjecture, less high-minded, was that Ferhat Abbas, the moderate, grand old man of Algerian nationalism, had become too popular for the likings of some of the younger F.L.N. leaders: in December 1960, and then again on July 4, 1961, when the F.L.N. called for a general strike to demonstrate its hold over the Algerian Moslems, their rallying cry had been "Vive Ferhat Abbas". This (once totally unexpected) triumph of Abbas may have increased the younger generations' wish to replace him as "premier". Should Ferhat Abbas return to Algeria as Premier, they are said to have argued, his popularity would be so great that their own revolutionary aims—with which Abbas was known to be at variance—might suffer.

One of the stumbling-blocks towards a peace settlement had been the F.L.N.'s insistence on "collegiate" methods, which in turn had led to endless fruitless discussions: the C.N.R.A., at its Tripoli meeting, also urged speedier action on the part of the F.L.N.'s "Government", and this—together with Ben Khedda's increased powers—led to renewed hopes of a speedy negotiation. There were signs, after two temporary failures, that both sides now agreed that negotiations should be conducted completely in secret until substantial agreement had been reached: and late in 1961 French and F.L.N. officials met again, but this time without publicity of any kind, in Switzerland. While preliminary contacts were taking place, there was no official change in French Government policy: if agreement with the F.L.N. failed, General de Gaulle was still determined to set up some kind of "Algerian executive", without the F.L.N., to prepare the way for independence, and in a later press conference he announced the possibility of earmarking a *"force publique"* of 50,000 men—presumably Algerian troops and militiamen—

as a nucleus of such an Executive's military and security arm. Nobody in Algeria believed that a transition government could last more than a few weeks, or even that Algerians would be found to staff it.

Meanwhile a peaceful settlement between France and the F.L.N. was becoming increasingly urgent: the "Secret Army Organisation", the O.A.S., led by ex-general Raoul Salan and a small group of army officers who had gone underground after the failure of the "Generals' Insurrection" of April 1961, had gathered considerable support and was responsible for some twenty or thirty daily plastic-bomb explosions throughout Algeria. The O.A.S. had broadcast four times on Algiers Radio and TV networks (previously sabotaged) and was getting funds from just about every European resident in Algeria. It claimed to be about to go into action with "an army of 100,000 men" to stake out its own claims to an "Algérie Francaise". It was proving difficult for skilled security officers to winkle out the leaders of the O.A.S., protected by a whole network of complicities reaching up into high places in the Algerian Administration itself, and several police officers were murdered by the O.A.S. There was a double danger: of a renewed "putsch" by still-discontented elements in the French Army and of a real civil war sparked off by the O.A.S. against France as an ultimate enemy but against the Algerian Moslems as an immediate target. And it was doubtful whether even General de Gaulle's magic could save France again if both were to occur at once.

There were some signs that this was understood by the F.L.N.'s leaders in Tunis, and that they realised the full threat represented by the O.A.S. But as each day passed without a settlement, it brought the eventuality of a full-scale clash between Europeans and Moslems in Algeria ever nearer; it was difficult, in the winter of 1961, to see how a settlement could occur without something along the lines of the religious and race massacres in 1947 which preceded and accompanied Indian partition: In Algiers and Oran, in October 1961, there was almost daily rioting, and racial hatred had never been at a higher pitch. Violence might lead to temporary partition and thus provide the French Government with an immediate *de facto* solution. But in the long run, partition—while spelling the ruin of an independent Algeria—would lead to endless violence in the French-held enclaves of Oran and Algiers, where the Moslems were in a small majority and among the most vocal and determined supporters of an independent Algeria. On the seventh anniversary of the outbreak of the Algerian rebellion (November 1, 1954) and three years after coming to power, General de Gaulle was faced with a test of almost inhuman severity: how to reconcile France's interests in Algeria (and the protection of her one million strong minority there) with independence in the teeth of an intransigent, aggressive F.L.N., a French army whose officer cadres had been profoundly shocked by the abortive army insurrection and its aftermath, and a European minority hysterical with fear and determined to cause bloodshed rather than submit to change.

CHAPTER SIXTEEN

THE ALGERIAN ECONOMY
AND THE REBELLION

THE traveller landing in Algiers or Oran for the first time invariably feels surprise at the sight of a huge airport, modern factories, vast housing projects, solidly prosperous residential areas and relentless traffic jams. Both towns are surrounded by tidy vineyards and orange groves of various sizes, and both are active, humming commercial centres. Those visitors who have seen only Algiers and Oran, and the rich farmland surrounding them, will almost certainly come away with the feeling that, after all, Algeria may well be France, especially if they avoid the "bidonvilles" (shanty-towns) in both cities and regard the Algiers Kasbah, not as one of the most overcrowded slums in the world, but as a picturesque reminder of things past. In Oran and Algiers, in the prosperous farm country in the Oranais and Algérois, it is indeed difficult to imagine that one is in Africa.

But such a superficial look is deceptive: the fertile Mitidja plain around Algiers is a mere fifty miles long and ten miles wide; despite the pace and the glitter of towns like Algiers and Oran and the evident prosperity of most of their inhabitants, despite Algeria's 25,000 miles of good roads and 3,000 miles of railways it is a desperately poor country. Nearly half of its total surface consists of utterly barren mountains or deserts, and of its total arable surface of 13 million hectares, only some seven million are actually under cultivation. Algeria is a country where highly developed living standards exist side by side with the most primitive standards of the world's most under-developed countries, and like all under-developed countries (which in a sense it is) Algeria suffers from an appallingly high birthrate. The European birthrate in Algeria is increasing at a normal "western" rate. The Moslem rate is more than ten times as high. From 1955 to 1960—and despite the rebellion—the excess of Moslem births over deaths was around 220,000 a year, and this rate is expected to rise even higher at least for the next ten years. By 1965 Algeria's total population will have reached between 11 and 12 million. By 1970 it will reach 15 to 16 million.

French colonisation—and the major western scientific discoveries of the nineteenth and early twentieth centuries—were in part responsible for this huge increase: at the time of the French conquest, the total Moslem population was about three and a half million. Malaria, bubonic and pneumonic plague, smallpox, cholera and typhoid have entirely disappeared; antibiotics have reduced the enormous incidence of venereal disease, and penicillin, among the poorer Moslems of Algeria, is referred to as "the drug which enables one to have children".

But while the *"présence Française"* made this population rise possible, it was not realised, until far too late, that the increased Algerian birthrate would result in new, almost insoluble problems. Only after the rebellion began did the French Government try and remedy the situation after decades of indifference and neglect. In 1954 a group of senior French officials and economists, under Roland Maspétiol, carried out an extensive economic and social survey of Algeria. Their findings[1] came as a serious shock to the French Government. In 1954, according to the Maspétiol report, 90 per cent of Algeria's wealth was in the hands of ten per cent of its inhabitants; nearly one million Moslems were totally or partially unemployed, and two more millions seriously underemployed; the average yearly income per head of the rural Moslem population stood at about 16 pounds sterling, and for another 1,600,000 Moslems living in towns the annual per capita income was about 45 pounds sterling. Eighty per cent of all Moslem children did not go to school at all. The report stressed French achievements in road building, urban development and public health, but, taking account of the changing value of the

[1] *Groupe d'Etudes des Relations Financières entre la Metropole et l'Algérie:* rapport général Algérie, Imprimerie Officielle, 1955.

franc, it estimated that France was spending on Algeria, in 1953, about the same amount yearly as she had spent in 1913. Though the report did not specifically say so, it confirmed the suspicion held by some sociologists that in 1954 about three-quarters of the Moslem population was illiterate in Arabic, and about 90 per cent illiterate in French. The galloping birthrate over the last twenty years, together with no rise in local agricultural resources, had resulted in the dramatic "pauperisation" of a large part of Algeria's rural population.

There is no easy way out of Algeria poverty: to be sure the discrepancy between the value of Moslem-owned and European-owned land is great and some kind of land reform necessary, but this in itself would not make Algeria richer or more truly self-supporting. In 1954 six and a half million Moslems owned and farmed some 615,000 small farms of a total surface of 4,750,000 hectares. The European *colons* (some 120,000 including dependants) owned and farmed about 22,000 farms of various sizes of a total surface of 2,350,000 hectares. Whereas the yearly revenue per Moslem farm was about one hundred pounds sterling a year, per European farm it was of about two thousand eight hundred pounds a year: in size the average European farm was thirty times as big as the average Moslem farm. In revenue it was forty-eight times as valuable. However absurd this might seem to those who are used to western standards it was—and is—more profitable in many cases for a Moslem to be a landless agricultural worker than to be an owner-farmer; and though Algerian Moslems do not drink wine, and though most of the wine sold by French *colons* to France goes to swell a surplus which is turned into alcohol at immense cost, the total wage bill of Moslems who work on vineyards in Algeria represents more than half the total revenue all Moslems get from working on the land either as farmers or as labourers. This argument is naturally used by those who have a vested interest against the break-up of large estates. It did not prevent a government agency, the *"Caisse d'Accession à la Propriété et à l'Exploitation rurale"* (CAPER) from buying up part of the land which owners of Algeria's largest estates were willing to sell and distributing it to landless Moslem agricultural labourers: but the work of the "CAPER" proved, by its failures as well as its few successes, that it was not sufficient just to take away land from a vast European-owned estate and give it out, in plots, to a number of Algerian farmers. Rather, it pointed the way to the need for the setting-up of vast agricultural co-operatives, so that the benefits of farming on a large scale could be retained.

In 1955, out of Algeria's total Moslem population, 570,000 had "stable" jobs in industry, commerce or in administration; another 200,000 were "regularly" employed in agriculture; the rest were casual workers or unemployed. Thus, some three to five million Moslems lived off those who were able to find work—for in Algeria, as in other under-developed countries, as a defence mechanism against starvation, those who work unhesitatingly contribute towards keeping alive those who do not.

Hence the growing exodus to France, since 1947, of Algerians in search of work: between 1951 and the end of 1954 some 600,000 Algerian immigrants left Algeria for France. Though most of them aimed at returning to Algeria, they began settling in France at the rate of 25,000 a year. In 1955 Algerians sent 35 billion francs in savings to their families in Algeria. Today the four to five hundred thousand Algerian workers in France bring in as much, from their wages, as one third of the entire agricultural labour force in Algeria.

The Algerian rebellion was to have an immense effect on Algeria's economy. In its earliest phase it led to a boom in the towns. As French reservists began arriving in Algeria in large numbers in 1956, drawing allowances far in excess of conscript troops, they spent freely in Algeria's shops, restaurants and bars. Soft drinks factories and breweries were the first to benefit from Algeria's "war boom". When French forces in Algeria began totalling half a million men, their spending power became noticeable, and the boom spread to farmers and middle men who provided the army with food and wine. The influx of large numbers of officers with their families, of officials, of oil engineers and executives (as the oil discoveries in the Sahara took shape) led to a rapid rise in property values and to a building boom.

Though the "war boom" led to the unforeseen and speedy prosperity of a number of Europeans in Algeria it benefited a number of Moslems too. Algiers absorbed some 300,000 Moslem refugees from the countryside seeking comparative safety in the city, and manage d to provide most of them with jobs. Spending on consumer goods spiralled: one French car firm, which sold 3,000 cars a year in Algiers in 1954, was selling 14,500 in 1959 and close on 20,000 in 1960. Total Algiers taxes, collected in 1954, amounted to 91,048 million francs; in 1959 they amounted to 241,500 million francs. Between 1956 and 1957, bank deposits in Algiers banks doubled.

The boom was transformed, and given a more permanent character, by General de Gaulle's pledge, on September 16, 1958, to grant massive aid to Algeria in the social, economic and educational fields, a pledge later embodied in the "Constantine Plan". The idea of increased financial aid for Algeria was not in itself new: the Maspétiol report had outlined two possible plans, and the French Government had opted for one of the suggested alternatives: investment, for seven successive years, at the rate of 15 billion francs a year, to be stabilised and continued on a semi-permanent basis after that period. Both Soustelle and Lacoste had pressed for increased financial aid, and some had been granted: but the administration in Algeria until 1958 lacked the necessary administrative and economic talent to put a really massive aid plan into operation. The Constantine Plan had been preceded by aid of various kinds: tax rebates had been granted to French firms willing to invest in Algeria, and sums distributed to farmers at low interest rates (but most of these funds were granted to European *colons*, not to Moslem landowners). According to a report put out by the Constantine Plan authorities themselves, the index of industrial production had risen in Algeria by 33 per cent between 1950 and 1954 and by 39 per cent between 1954 and 1958. But—as the report itself admitted—"the benefits . . . have

almost entirely gone to the large ports (Algiers, Oran, Bône) and
to the already most favoured urban social groups".

General de Gaulle's main promise, embodied in his "Constantine Plan" speech of October 1958, was to provide Algerians
with 100,000 new jobs in the next five years and to wipe out
illiteracy. The financial backbone of the Constantine Plan (to
be spread over five years from 1958 to 1963) was a 2,000 billion
franc fund to be spent partly on essential infrastructure (roads,
factory plants, housing estates and power stations) partly as loans
to firms willing to invest in Algeria. It was, in fact, an expanded
and speeded-up version of the Maspétiol suggestion for increased
aid.

The success of the Constantine Planners in attracting investors
(including a handful of non-French firms such as Unilever) to a
large extent accounts for the present building boom on the out-
skirts of Algiers, Oran and Bône. So far, some 450 firms have
obtained loans and made detailed investment plans, and—only
three years after de Gaulle's Constantine speech—the face of urban
Algeria has undergone considerable change. Among the firms
whose investment plans have been approved are food and canning
plants, textile, clothing and leather works, as well as assembly
plants for the Berliet truck firm and the Renault car works. The
number of jobs provided has fallen short of de Gaulle's bold
promise. In all some 35,000 new jobs have been created as a direct
consequence of Constantine Plan investment, but the planners
claim that for every new job directly provided through new
investment two more have been created indirectly through the
growth of private trade, building and various services. The
planners are also confident that firms will continue to settle in
Algeria at the rate of between 100 and 200 a year.

But the Constantine Plan has also shown inherent shortcomings:
general poverty in Algeria, and the rural masses' sense of neglect
at the hands of the French administration were at least partly
responsible for the outbreak of the rebellion in 1954; so far, the
Constantine Plan has had little effect on the most under-privileged,
poverty-stricken section of the Moslem population, which is also

the most numerous. Despite increased financial aid for those investors willing to go outside the comparatively "safe" and already booming Algiers, Oran and Bône areas few have been found to take the risk of going farther afield. Since the Constantine Plan began taking effect, the countryside has not benefited along with the already partly industrialised urban areas and the gulf between town and country is increasing.

As time went on, the Constantine Plan authorities recognised this. It became their policy, not to create new industrial areas in the remote mountains and deserts far from the coast, but to draw the population away from those areas by promises of new jobs elsewhere.

Since Algiers, Oran and Bône have more or less reached their limits of expansion (and this despite the growing "bidonvilles" in all three towns) the planners began encouraging investors to establish new plants in "satellite towns". Near Algiers massive public investment went into the development of Rouïba, Reghaïa and Blida—all within a thirty-mile radius of Algiers, and in Sainte Barbe du Tlelat, near Oran. Plans are afoot for the setting-up of other "decentralised" industrial towns at Arzew, Mostaganem, Sidi Bel Abbes, Relizane, Duzerville and Kroubs. Arzew, near Oran, is being planned as an important chemical industry centre (using natural gas from the Hassi R'mel deposit in the Sahara, which reached Arzew by the end of 1961). Duzerville will be the centre of Algeria's at present non-existent steel industry, using iron ore from the nearby Ouenza iron ore mines and energy from the Hassi R'mel gas deposits (reaching Bône by 1963). With natural gas from the Sahara fixed at 3·15 (old) francs per cubic metre, planners claim that industrialists in Algeria will, eventually, become competitive with Common Market countries in Europe. By 1965 they hope that Algeria will outgrow its local needs and find markets outside Algeria as well. They hope, too, that by 1963, Algeria's revenue from Saharan oil will be sufficient to reduce some of the pressure of public investment: instead of relying on funds earmarked out of the French budget, Algeria would use some of its own oil revenue for loans to new industries and for additional infrastructure. Moreover, the Constantine Plan is not designed to end abruptly in 1963, but to be continued by two more five-year plans. The planners themselves, led by former Algerian Delegate-General Paul Delouvrier, embarked on the scheme without any political "parti pris", and claim that it is valid whatever Algeria's political future may be. Delouvrier said to me recently: "Of course, the Constantine Plan will not stamp out poverty in Algeria. But at least it points the way to continuous progress. Without it, the consequences of Algeria's staggering birthrate are too terrifying to be considered."

But despite the Constantine planners' praiseworthy lack of political prejudice and their speedy implementation of the investment loans, the Plan contains drawbacks which seem insoluble for as long as Algeria's political future remains unsolved and even once its political future is clearer. To survive, Algeria's growing industries will need some form of Customs protection—at any rate at first—from French-made goods which at present enter Algeria without any discrimination. Such protection could conceivably be applied by mutual agreement after Algerian independence. In the industrial field, the Constantine Plan is an ingenious mixture of liberalism and state direction, of the kind which proved highly successful in setting post-war France on her feet and was applied, with equal success, by the European Coal and Steel Community's Executive to the coal and steel industries of the Common Market countries.

But more than half Algeria's total population is engaged in agriculture, and Constantine Plan methods are irrelevant in a country, like Algeria, where modern and archaic agricultural methods exist side by side. To be sure, the Europeans' immeasurably better-kept estates provide employment for Algeria's landless Moslem labourers, and it would be economic folly to try and transform the present 450,000 hectares used for wine-growing into wheatfields: it would take 6 million new hectares to make Algeria self-supporting in wheat, and such land is just not available. It is economically sound to put industrialisation first—as is the case in the "satellite" countries of the communist bloc—in the hope that agriculture will "catch up" later; it is economically unsound to redistribute land in small plots to individual farmers, when it should be exploited as a large unit. In any case, the European *colons* do not, as a rule, possess huge estates which would make redistribution a valid palliative (only about 300 *colons* own large estates, and of these only ten—mostly registered as companies—have estates of over 1,000 hectares). Yet the concentration of valuable landed property into the hands of a comparatively small proportion of Europeans (for the number of European landowners—as distinct from their dependants—is only about 20,000) provides additional political and social problems. One way of safeguarding the interests of the present *colons* would be to devote part of the Constantine Plan to land reclamation: but after two years' study, the planners became convinced that the costs of such a programme would be out of proportion to its results. The harsh truth is that there is no readily available land for reclamation.

The alternative—which the Constantine planners are putting into practice—consists in drawing away the Moslem rural masses to new jobs in the towns—to new towns, if need be—in the hope that little by little the under-employed, underfed Moslem millions who eke out a bare living on the land will gradually become thinned out in numbers and able to carry out some kind of qualitative agricultural reform themselves.

To cut across complicated income categories, Constantine planners have divided Algeria's total population in three categories: those whose living standards can be compared to those of an average industrialised western country; those enjoying what they call a "Mediterranean" living standard comparable to that enjoyed by the average person in Greece, Portugal, Spain or Southern Italy; and those with the recognisable "under-developed" status comparable to the backward rural masses of Egypt and India. As of 1961, a mere 12 per cent of Algeria's total population (including, of course, most of its European minority) came into the first category; 26 per cent (including the remaining portion of the European minority) came into the second, "Mediterranean",

category; and 62 per cent—all Moslems—in the third. The aim
of the Constantine Plan is to move as many people out of the
third category into the second, and—eventually—from the second
into the first.

But even if the planners' most favourable calculations come true,
the effect of the Constantine Plan will to a certain extent be offset
by the galloping birthrate. By 1970—and taking the increased
population into account—the pattern, they say, will be as follows:

> "Industrialised"   23 per cent
> "Mediterranean"   34 per cent
> "Under-developed" 43 per cent

Since the population, by 1970, will have reached between 15 to
16 millions, the actual numbers of "under-developed" will in
fact be the same as in 1961.

This in turn raises a series of problems which are political and
social rather than economic: assuming that considerable change
has occurred in the political field, and that Algeria has become,
by 1970, fully independent, how will an all-Algerian Government
deal with its own poor? At present, Algeria is in the forefront of
countries attempting the "breakthrough" from an under-developed
to an industrialised state, and this breakthrough is being carried
out without the hideous stresses which resulted, in the Soviet
Union in the twenties, in the deaths through starvation of millions
of people. Algeria's present rate of growth is probably the fastest
of all under-developed countries in the world—including the
satellite countries of the communist bloc. But this growth is
based on a combination of favourable circumstances: the presence
of one million "productive" Europeans, the existence of foreign
aid on a large scale, the Saharan oil and natural gas riches, the
existence of a large-scale investments programme.

Should the Europeans leave in large numbers, or French aid be
cut off, or should an independent Algerian government use its oil
revenues for other purposes than investment in essential projects,
the whole Algerian drive towards progress will collapse. In Algeria,
as elsewhere, the real difficulty will consist in equating what is

economically necessary with what is politically feasible. Future political pressure towards land redistribution, for instance, may become irresistible; but land reform in itself will not solve Algeria's poverty, and the amount of wheat which could be planted in the place of vineyards would not go very far towards making Algeria agriculturally self-supporting, while it would place one third of the agricultural labour force—and that part of it which is most profitably employed—out of work; the problem of protecting Algeria's growing industries may call for Customs protection: but this in turn would have repercussions on Algeria politically and economically, since Algeria imports (mostly from France) more than five times what she exports; on the world market, Algeria has little chance of selling her wine or fruit—and the dilatory way in which communist bloc countries have treated Tunisian and Moroccan exporters shows that there would be no certainty of even politically-orientated exports. Whatever Algeria's political future may be, it would be folly for her to sever her economic ties with France. But again, the severance may come as a result of political ill-feeling. The influx of hundreds of thousands of Moslems to the towns, and their impatience at the contrast between Moslem poverty and European prosperity, is bound to have political repercussions, especially after a long, bitter nationalist struggle. There will be an almost overwhelming temptation, for a newly independent Algerian government, to "take it out of the Europeans". And the massive exodus of Europeans from Algeria would, in itself, be sufficient to put an end to its chances of ever becoming an "industrialised" or even a "Mediterranean" country. Should the Europeans leave as a result of ill-treatment or discrimination against them, an easy retaliatory measure would be the expulsion of the Algerian workers at present in France, whose savings are keeping some three million Algerians alive. In short, should anything occur which would compromise Franco-Algerian relations, the country will almost certainly be plunged into the kind of desperate poverty and chaos from which it will be unlikely ever to recover.

Fortunately the example of Tunisia and Morocco is at hand to

show that evil memories fade: in 1953 Moroccan nationalist
agitation took on an undeniable anti-French character, and the
last few months preceding independence in Morocco saw the
French army engaged in a full-scale war in the Riff mountains;
for two years Tunisian "fellaghas" skirmished with French troops
in Southern Tunisia and bomb outrages were a daily occurrence
in most towns. Yet, a few years after independence, and whatever
the political instability of Morocco may be, none of the French
settlers in Morocco feel threatened or discriminated against; and
any reasons for occasional uneasiness between the two communities in Tunisia and Morocco are bound to vanish with the
end of the Algerian war. Tunisia and Morocco have set an example
which any future independent Algerian Government may profitably follow. It can only be hoped that despite the far more serious
damage done to the fabric of the two communities in Algeria,
such a pattern will be repeated. It will be a test of Algerian
maturity, and its only way of overcoming an otherwise hopeless
struggle against poverty.

The chapter may profitably be concluded with a discussion of
developments in the Sahara area. Algeria's "Territoires du Sud"
were, until 1957, separated from Algeria proper by a dotted line
(to denote that this area was under military control), but on all
maps up to that date there were no other distinctions made. The
frontier delimitation between Algeria proper and the Sahara was
an administrative one, and the boundaries between specifically
French, Moroccan and Tunisian southern territories were hazy in
the extreme: since independence, Tunisia has protested at the
arbitrary way in which its southern frontier has been fixed, and
has (half-heartedly, it must be admitted) asked for some of the
territory back. The Moroccan Government has, undoubtedly for
demagogic reasons, laid claim to a huge chunk of the Sahara
(including all territory up to the river Senegal) on vague historical
grounds. Some of the difficulties over frontiers stem from the
lackadaisical way in which frontiers were established when Algeria
was uncontested French territory and both Morocco and Tunisia
were protectorates. Since all three southern areas were under

effective French control, why bother to define frontier limits further, and with whom?

By 1956 both Tunisia and Morocco were independent, and by 1957 was established the *"Organisations Communes des Régions Sahariennes"* (O.C.R.S.), a development agency with special powers, as well as a French Saharan Ministry. Four Saharan deputies (three Moslems and one European) were returned to the French National Assembly in the 1958 general elections. The May 13 "revolution" sought as much to emphasise French sovereignty over the Sahara ("Tous Français de Dunkerque à Tamanrasset") as it did to proclaim "L'Algérie Française". "Committees of Public Safety" were formed all over the Sahara, including the Hassi Messaoud oil centre, and Colomb Bechar, and telegrams of support for the May 13 insurgents flowed in from all over the Sahara.

A neglected part of the world until the first major oil discoveries were made in 1956, the Sahara was, by tradition, the home of a certain type of French officer: the "blédard", the "méhariste", was the subject of a large number of French·films between the wars; popular novels (including Pierre Benoit's wildly romantic, incredibly inaccurate fantasy *"L'Atlantide"*) gave Frenchmen an idealised, wholly distorted image of the Sahara. The conquest of the Sahara had been a genuine epic. But improved communications, the increased efficiency of specially adapted trucks and jeeps, the decline of the camel as a means of transport, the fact that service in the Sahara was a bar rather than a help to promotion in the regular French army, the feeling of isolation from the rest of the world, contributed to make it a boring place; colourful, perhaps, if one was a tourist flying from oasis to oasis, but oppressive, fly-blown and above all provincial: in the oases and small towns of the Sahara, each new arrival was scrutinised and criticised, gossip was rife and petty hatreds vicious and enduring: the oases had all the drawbacks of small garrison towns.

Oil discoveries turned the Sahara, almost overnight, into a quite different place. The oil prospectors, engineers and contractors who

turned up in increasing numbers from 1956 onwards had no time
for the sleepy ways of the few European civilians (small shopkeepers, small contractors and hotelkeepers) or the routine-bound
French army there. For years the French army units in the Sahara
had worn the baggy trousers (sarouel) and huge flat thonged
sandals (naïl) of the local inhabitants: the oilmen went out in the
midday Saharan sun in khaki shorts and shirts, bush hats and
tennis shoes. Rather then deal with the slow local tradespeople,
the oil companies brought in their own personnel: contractors,
hotel managers and oil engineers from all over the world.

The policy of the French military administration in the Sahara
had been worthy but intensely conservative: military patrols kept
a constant watch on the Saharan nomads, reporting—and supervising—all tribe and camel flock movements; as in Algeria, the
French army officers worked through local tribal chieftains. While
they sought to improve the lot of the desperately poor Saharan
population (whose total strength is under one million), dug
wells and encouraged camel breeding selection, they were handicapped in a number of ways: in the first place the Saharan budget
prior to the oil discoveries—was pathetically small. Secondly, the
military administration had a vested interest in maintaining the
power of the Saharan nomad chiefs, most of whom owned
valuable date palms and exploited their workers to the hilt (prior
to 1956, a common wage for a whole day's date-picking was 100
old francs).

Oil discoveries had a profound impact on Sahara's social
structure: when the extent of Saharan oil was confirmed, labour
was needed—and needed quickly. Recruiters took what was
available. From oases from all over the Sahara, nomads who had
never seen an aeroplane before were enrolled into a decently paid,
housed and clothed labour force, and flown to Hassi Messaoud or
Edjeleh. Others were hired by road-building and pipe-line contractors. Saharan nomads began earning hitherto undreamed-of
sums. In Ouargla's, in the 'thirties, poverty had been such that the
French army had had to distribute wheat regularly to prevent
part of the population from dying of starvation. By 1959,

Ouargla's tiny hole-in-the-wall shops were selling radios and bicycles, refrigerators and even washing machines. Significantly, the chief beneficiaries of this new wealth were not the aristocratic Reguibat, Chamba or Touareg tribesmen, but the "*harratin*", the dark-skinned former slaves whose traditional role had been that of tending the oases while their masters roamed the desert. Comparatively few Touareg or Reguibat tribesmen benefited from the Sahara's silent social and economic revolution. The Chamba tribesmen (who provided the bulk of the French army's militia and "méharistes") suffered less. But all over the Sahara wealth passed from the hands of the aristocratic camel-owning tribesmen into the hands of the "*harratin*", who started buying up date palm trees belonging to their former masters. From 1957 onwards, the owners of date palms found it difficult to obtain sufficient manpower for the date harvest.

With the development of Saharan oil riches, the decline of the camel became accelerated. One single Berliet truck could carry the equivalent load of several hundred camels, and in the wake of oil development came the development of Sahara's roads. Such was the plight of the Reguibat tribesmen (traditionally the Sahara's most important camel dealers) that the French Saharan Ministry, in 1958, actually toyed with the idea of setting up a camel meat-canning plant at Tindouf. (Whoever has tasted camel meat will realise how desperate a step this was.) The aristocratic Saharan tribesmen refused to change their ways, despising education of any kind, while the "*harratin*" took full advantage of the newly opened schools set up after General de Gaulle's return to power. They hoped against hope that their traditional way of life would remain as it had been before 1956, and with them many members of the French army in the Sahara deplored their decline and the rise of the "*harratin*".

It could not be said that either "*harratin*" or camel-owning nomads had any firm political or national beliefs: there were innumerable feuds between tribes, or within the same tribe, but an efficient French camel corps militia had put down all attempts at inter-tribal fighting; there was a considerable amount of petty crime, mostly camel stealing; there were, occasionally, clashes between Reguibat tribesmen on the French side of the border and Moroccan "army of liberation" tribesmen in Southern Morocco, along the ill-defined and disputed Moroccan frontier. But the Saharan nomads—like nomads everywhere—had little conception of frontiers: the Touareg wandered out of French-owned Hoggar and into the (later independent) ex-French Niger and Sudan, returning to the Hoggar as the spirit moved them; the Reguibat in the west roamed over French, Moroccan and Spanish portions of the Sahara without passports or any feeling that they were moving from one country to another. Even after the oil discoveries had started transforming the face of the Sahara, its nomadic and semi-nomadic inhabitants, by and large, remained uninterested in the political turmoil to their north.

Only the Mozabites, the tiny (about 60,000) dissident Moslem minority who live in the "five towns" around Ghardaïa and travel north as traders and shopkeepers, could be said to have any political awareness. And they were by no means all favourable to the F.L.N.

When the rebellion began, on November 1, 1954, its leaders had not even considered appointing a rebel guerilla leader for the Saharan zone. The Saharan population was looked down on, by most Algerians, as being backward and primitive. Only in 1956 was an F.L.N. leader appointed for the "Southern Zone", and F.L.N. attempts to bring the rebellion to the desert never achieved very much: a few isolated acts of sabotage (including the destruction of the Laghouat power station) occurred in 1957; a company of 'Chamba' "*méharistes*" mutinied, near Timimoun, also in 1957, attacked an oil prospectors' convoy, and were finally wiped out by a French paratroop regiment specially parachuted into action in the Sahara (one of two occasions during the rebellion when troops were parachuted operationally); one oil train from Hassi Messaoud to Bougie was blown up in 1958. But by and large F.L.N. action in the Sahara was a failure. Distances were too great, and since the Sahara was under constant air patrol, any unusual activity was quickly detected.

The F.L.N.'s decision to assert its sovereignty over the Sahara stemmed first and foremost from fears that, even if independence were achieved, a French-controlled and militarily-occupied Sahara[1] would in some way remain a constant threat to Algerian independence, a barrier between Algeria and its southern African neighbours. There were other reasons for Algerian stubbornness: the F.L.N.'s realisation that, if the rebellion ended, the Algerian "war boom" and prosperity wave would end too, and that an independent Algeria would in all probability have to cope with increased poverty. The Sahara, in French and Algerian eyes, had been, since the oil discoveries, a symbol of potential wealth: no F.L.N. leader wished to leave himself open to the charge of having thrown away such a precious asset.

Figures of the Sahara's oil and natural gas reserves are certainly impressive: at a conservative estimate, recuperable reserves of oil amount to 700 million tons, natural gas to 750 billion cubic metres. Output—a mere eight and a half million tons in 1960—is expected to rise to 18 or 20 million tons of oil in 1962, and may reach 40 to 50 million tons by 1965. Saharan oil (from both the Hassi Messaoud and Edjeleh oilfield farther south) is "light sweet crude", highly suitable for car and airplane consumption, not at all suitable for breaking down into "black" components—fuel and diesel oil. But the world has been witnessing, since 1959, a distinct glut in petroleum products, particularly of the "sweet crude" variety. France's own requirements (20 million tons in 1958, steadily rising to an estimated 36 million tons by 1965) are to a certain extent covered by long-standing contracts. France can refine any Saharan output up to 20 million tons and absorb present Saharan production into its own consumption easily. But—assuming that France will continue to handle Saharan oil output under any circumstances—the French Government will perforce have to seek exchange agreements with other oil producers, both for the refining of massive quantities of Saharan oil and for the exchange of "white" for "black" products.

[1] There was talk, in 1961, of moving the headquarters of the French Foreign Legion from Sidi bel Abbès in Algeria to some Saharan base.

There is no doubt about France's tremendous achievement in developing the Sahara oilfields—ranking as thirteenth or four-teenth biggest in the world—in a very short space of time and under considerable geographic and climatic difficulties. Not the least ser-vice which the Saharan oil finds have rendered France is that it has turned French companies connected with the oil industry into some of the world's most efficient and most competitive enter-prises. The Saharan oilfields have been developed at enormous expense: and the French Government has been careful—some non-French oilmen claim that it has been over-careful—to see to it that at every stage of the process from prospection to production French interests are safeguarded.

French funds (private or public) amount to 78 or 79 per cent of all funds invested in Saharan oil development. French companies have not been allowed to sell their operating rights to non-French companies, though foreign companies have been allowed in on an "association" and "minority partner" basis with French com-panies. The S.N. R.E.P.A.L., and the C.F.P.A., which operate at Hassi Messaoud, are 100 per cent French: 40·51 per cent of the R.E.P.A.L.'s shares are held by the French state, and 40·51 per cent by the "Gouvernement Général de l'Algérie", the rest of the shares being in private, but exclusively French, hands; the C.F.P.A. is a subsidiary of the large French "Companie Française des Pétroles" (C.F.P.), and 85 per cent of *its* shares are owned by the C.F.P., the rest being in French investors' hands. At Edjeleh, the C.R.E.P.S. (Companie pour la Recherche et l'Exploitation du Pétrole au Sahara) is owned by a majority group of French public and private holding companies, with 35 per cent participation by Royal Dutch Shell. All leases, prospection allocations, etc., have been jointly decided by the "O.C.R.S." and the French Trade and Industry Ministry. And though a number of United States firms (among them Esso, Sinclair, Phillips G.G. and City Service) have all started drilling in the Sahara on permits delivered by the French Government and the O.C.R.S., they know that if they strike oil, they will be forced to go into partnership with a French company holding a majority interest. Then there is the question of an "economic price" for Saharan oil: the oil is being extracted at enormous expense. Drilling costs in the Sahara are fantastic, and none of the productive wells in the Hassi Messaoud area are less than 3,000 metres deep. The 500 miles of underground pipeline—through desert and arid mountain areas—were also exceedingly costly. It is estimated that on the world market, Saharan oil may sell for $2·66 per metric barrel—which is more expensive than either Kuwait, Saudi Arabian or Venezuelan oil —and that even this price might conceal a discreet French government subsidy.

Seen in this light, Saharan oil is a good deal less attractive than it first seemed to be, in 1957: and France's huge investment and operations there are unlikely to be duplicated by any other power. Nor does there appear to be any alternative market for Saharan oil other than the French market. (After Suez, the French government was determined never to be caught napping again and decided to build up its oil reserves in the Sahara even at prohibitive cost.) One of the main reasons, apart from self-sufficiency, for Saharan oil development was that France spends 300 million dollars annually on oil imports (mostly from the U.S.) and that even expensive Saharan oil will save valuable foreign currency.

The natural gas reserves in the Sahara may play an even more important part in the Algerian and French economies than Saharan oil: the gas pipelines (from Hassi R'mel to the coast) will be finished by 1962. Gas pipelines will eventually reach not only Arzew, near Oran, but Algiers and Bône as well. The use of natural gas is a key factor in the "Constantine Plan" for Algeria's industrialisation.

But here again there are difficulties, caused this time by the very size of the natural gas deposits: to restrict the use of the Sahara's natural gas to Algeria's nascent industries is like using a power-station to keep a bicycle lamp alight. Any economic use of the natural gas resources commands that not only Algeria (and its Tunisian and Moroccan neighbours) benefits from the gas reserves, but also Europe as well: for years plans have been made for the exploitation of Saharan gas in Europe, either through an underwater pipeline somewhere between the Algerian and the Spanish coast, or through the establishment of a large methane tanker fleet feeding the gas into a specially built pipeline going through France and West Germany.

This means that not only Saharan oil, but also its natural gas, cannot really be exploited without full French participation. F.L.N. leaders realise that there is the danger of seeing the oilfields close down and the work on the gas pipelines abandoned if agreement is not reached. As far back as 1957, the F.L.N. warned, from Tunis, that all oil agreements made between the French Government and French or foreign oil companies would be "invalid". But common-sense requires the F.L.N. to reach agreement with France: revenue from oil—which will increasingly contribute to investment for Algeria's industrial development—will almost certainly trickle to nothing if France decides to cut its losses in the Sahara; and without natural gas, Algeria has no hope of achieving any degree of industrialisation.

There is another problem which will remain insoluble unless agreement is reached, and heavy concessions made by the F.L.N. to maintain, and guarantee the maintenance, of French interests in the Sahara. That is the future of the Saharan population itself. If the F.L.N. were to require a referendum in the Sahara to decide whether or not it should remain in Algerian hands, it is by no means certain that the F.L.N. would obtain a majority. And if there is no working agreement with France not only will there be no oil revenue. and no natural gas, but there will be hideous poverty among the Saharan inhabitants. Already, the oil companies in the Sahara have laid off a sizeable proportion of the Saharan labour force they maintained in 1958 and 1959. This labour force is being recruited, and used, on other development projects (the natural gas pipeline, road building, housing projects in the main Saharan oases). Should France withdraw from the Sahara, this labour force will find itself, from one day to the next, without any jobs at all. No oasis dweller who has sampled the relatively high wages paid for unskilled labour by the oil and public works companies will be content to return to the miserable pittance he earned by seasonal date-pickings; and—with a growing network of serviceable roads—the camel will soon be nothing more than an object of curiosity. Unless the F.L.N. comes to terms with France, it will face, in the Sahara, a hideously insoluble "human problem".

CHAPTER SEVENTEEN

A SUMMING UP

FOR close on seven years French public opinion was blinded, in its attitude towards the Algerian problem, by political passions and French nationalist slogans. Such passions are not yet dead—as a glance at any of the pamphlets put out by M. Soustelle at the time of the January 8 referendum can testify—but they have lost much of their force. The reactions of French public opinion, from the outbreak of the rebellion onwards, can be summarised as follows: first, anger and incomprehension after generations of history-books had instilled into most Frenchmen the notion that "L'Algérie, c'est la France"; then, a period of aggressive emotional nationalism which reached its peak at the time of the Suez Expedition of 1956; then a gradual, muddled disenchantment with the parliamentary régime of the Fourth Republic and growing disappointment at the continuing strength of the rebellion, which prompted many Frenchmen at the time to underwrite the May 13 "insurrection" in 1958 for reasons which had nothing to do with General de Gaulle; then a fairly long period of apathy, during which General de Gaulle, as France's father-figure, was entrusted with sole responsibility for France's affairs, including the conduct of the war in Algeria; finally, a growing realisation of the complex issues at stake in Algeria, a gradual rejection of the easy slogans and catchphrases behind which the protagonists of "la manière forte" had attempted to clothe their policies, a growing impatience both at the intransigeance of the European inhabitants of Algeria and their political mentors, an increased longing for an end to the war and the realisation that French loss of sovereignty in Algeria need not necessarily mean the end of France as a major power. Ever since the rebellion started, it had always seemed to me that the Algerian problem was capable of

no solution which did not have the approval of French public
opinion as a whole. From the beginning of the rebellion French
public opinion was baffled and often deliberately led astray: for
a time, during and after the Suez expedition, it seemed that the
fabric of French democracy itself was about to be destroyed. The
ease with which men like Mendès-France and Bourguiba became
identified, in the eyes of public opinion, with absolute evil, the
irrational and successful appeals to hatred, the emergence of a
number of "Poujadist" and other extreme nationalist supporters
with their all-too-familiar totalitarian paraphernalia, the irrational
swing towards General de Gaulle in 1958—all provided grounds
for alarm. That a certain part of the French army, disillusioned
by failures in Indo-China, Tunisia and Morocco, should incline
towards a totalitarian ideal was not surprising. That this tiny
military element, backed by embittered and ambitious politicians,
should find an echo in French public opinion as a whole became,
for a short spell, both surprising and frightening. Happily, the
man plebiscited into assuming power in June 1958 seems to have
been aware, from the first, of this dangerous state of affairs. Not
the least service General de Gaulle rendered France, in the first
four years of office, was that of educating a French public opinion
dazed by years of facile arguments, slogans and specious propaganda. For the first time, a Frenchman with unquestioned
authority, whose entire career incarnated those virtues which any
civilised nation respects above all things—disinterestedness
courage, intelligence and humanity—was able to state, obstinately
and with growing bluntness, the harsh facts underlying the
Algerian problem. Who else would have dared the scathing
reference to "ce problème pendant depuis cent trente ans"? Who
else would have held out against the army and civilian extremists
in Algiers in January 1960 and again in April 1961, restoring the
authority of the state in Algeria and reducing the importance of
the vocal European extremist minority there to its true propor-
tions? De Gaulle's tactics, his cautious timing, his passion for
secrecy may have prolonged the Algerian war and contributed to
needlessly protracted uncertainty among the European minority

in Algeria, whose reactions were inspired by fear bordering on
despair—the fear of a sick person whose doctor refuses to divulge
the extent of his illness—but none can question de Gaulle's success
in the deliberate "demystification" of the Algerian problem.

Rather than attempt to plot the course of France's future policy
in Algeria and predict the outcome of negotiations with the
Algerian nationalists, I should like to examine a number of issues
which have, in the past, been obscured by passion and prejudice.
An examination of this kind may not provide an immediate
pointer towards the way events may be shaping, nor can it, in
many cases, give any clear-cut answer. But it can contribute to the
better understanding of events on the fast-moving Algerian
scene.

(1) *The European Minority*

As was said at the beginning of this book, the presence of a large
European minority is at the heart of the Algerian problem. The
reason is not only that this minority, for years, made the most of
its economic power and politicial influence to block necessary
reforms: something has already been said of the complex origins
of Algeria's European population. Its violence, the tenacity with
which it opposed any proposals which would have led to change
in time to prevent bloodshed were among the direct causes of the
rebellion. But the demonstrations of May 13, 1958, and the later
"barricades" insurrection of January 1960, showed that more than
an economically powerful, influential minority was involved:
these demonstrations, which continued for days, with the support
of the overwhelming mass of Europeans in Algeria, showed that
the Europeans in Algeria possessed a kind of corporate consciousness: beneath the braggadocio, the absurd threats, the absolute
refusal to consider anything but their own predicament—in a
vacuum, as it were, for the existence of France and of the Moslem
majority was totally ignored—a sociologist could detect a whole
range of psychological problems affecting close on a million
people.

Something has already been said of the ambivalent attitude of Algeria's Europeans to France: as was pointed out in a remarkable study, the Europeans "do not want to be protected by France: they want to be loved"[1]. Whatever his origins, the Frenchman in Algeria craved love and total understanding from "la Métropole" and was bitterly hurt when it was withheld. At home only in Algeria, he desperately wanted to be "accepted" by France. It was not enough for France to sympathise with him or attempt to solve his problem: total involvement predicament, was required, and anything short of this was equated with treason.

But Algeria is not France, as any prolonged visit there will prove. On the other hand, nowhere in the world have the trappings of France been more self-consciously imported, down to the very names of a number of towns and villages (Chateaudun-du-Rummel, La Robertsau) and the hideous little "mairies" and village squares which are like tawdry imitations of the real thing. In France—even in those areas where there is a good deal of social conflict—there is a kind of inner strength and harmony in diversity which is an important part of the French national heritage. In Algeria the hidden structure was lacking: apart from the family, there is a vacuum. To be sure the different French political parties existed in Algeria, but—as any electioneer there knows—they meant nothing: politics in Algeria were almost exclusively concerned with personalities, and the wildly fluctuating membership of this or that party or group shows that Algeria's Europeans—a huge mass of floating voters—could turn to almost any platform—communist, Gaullist or just plain fascist—which they thought would best defend their interests. This political vacuum also showed itself in the proliferation of thousands of different associations, from the powerful ex-servicemen's organisations to the "association of players of 'boules'" or of Algeria's Bretons, Auvergnats, Alsatians or Corsicans, harmless in themselves, no doubt, but dangerous when these groups—welded together by a demagogue—assumed a political role. For

[1] Pierre Nora, *Les Français d'Algérie*, Paris Julliard, 1961.

then their only uniting factor was the thirst for violence, their only field of action the street.

Before the rebellion a noticeable characteristic of Algeria's Europeans was their tendency to forget the very existence of the Moslems among them. Was this some kind of defence mechanism, caused by an unconscious fear that the Moslems might one day become conscious of their numerical strength? Since the rebellion this feeling of insecurity has increased, and unscrupulous "activist" leaders have played on Europeans' feelings with remarkable efficacy: "ils nous prendront tout" became a familiar cry. And "ils" meant not only the Moslems, but the Americans ("thirsting after our Saharan oil"), the Russians, the big French financial interests ("they will always find a way of making a deal with the Arabs"). One of the corporate characteristics of Algeria's Europeans was their remarkable egocentricity.

Insecurity cut across class distinctions: for the comparatively small wealthy minority there was the gnawing fear that a misguided government might put an end to most of its economic privileges; but the further down one went in the social scale, among Algeria's Europeans, the greater the fear of the Moslem masses, ready to step into unskilled jobs and deprive even the poorest Europeans of their living. A demonstration in Algeria, therefore, became a "pretext to love or to hate together"[1]. The psychological factors bringing a crowd together were far more powerful than the social differences which might have kept them apart, and the mechanic from Bab el Oued, at the Algiers "barricades" of January 1960, was in total agreement with the sports-car driving Algiers University playboy undergraduate.

Small wonder that the Europeans, by nature ready to submit to a corporate, authoritarian form of government, turned to the French army in Algeria for leadership and sought to impose a form of military government. Small wonder, too, that no government was ever able to "reassure" the European community about its future (the nearest Algeria's Europeans ever came to peace of mind was during the Vichy régime). Like individuals whose

[1] Nora, *Les Français d'Algérie.*

frustrations are so severe that they lead to neurosis, Algeria's Europeans sought refuge in a dream-world of their own—a dream-world which reached the peak of absurdity just after the May 13 insurrection of 1958. It was a world where, despite all evidence to the contrary, it was believed that "*L'Algérie restera à jamais Française*" and a "renovated France" would be led to salvation by trusted army leaders; a world where all Arabs would become "good Arabs" "qui ne cherchent qu'à s'entendre avec nous", where Europeans and Moslems, hand in hand, would seek out the hated "fellagha" and destroy the very last of them. "Tous tranquilles comme avant," I heard an army general bellow through a microphone in a remote village south of Blida, without realising how absurd this statement sounded to a Moslem audience, however much it might make sense to the Europeans.

General de Gaulle has been blamed for his apparent delay in tackling the Algerian problem, and a number of Frenchmen have criticised him for wasting the first two years after his return to power, without realising themselves the extent of their own psychological change during this period. It would have been relatively easy to maintain, in Algeria, the hold over the Moslem population which existed in May 1958. It would have been possible to prevent by force the Moslem demonstrations of December 1960. Instead, General de Gaulle tackled the problem of the European minority from the beginning—sometimes obliquely, sometimes head-on. The Moslems gradually realised that they could speak their minds without fearing instant or long-term reprisals, and gradually gained confidence. Disgruntled army officers and enraged Europeans blamed the nationalist "explosion" on December 10, 1960, on de Gaulle's failure to support the theory of "integration" and his decision to reduce the power of the various army "psychological warfare" services. It was obvious, on the contrary, that the Moslems were expressing their real feelings for the first time, and that—for the first time since the "battle of Algiers"—conditions were such that they could give vent to their feelings without the fear of reprisals. The man responsible for this remarkable psychological change was, of course, de Gaulle himself[1] at the cost, of course, of the Europeans' bitter and lasting hatred.

Once the European community realised that it had definitely failed in its attempt to swing the French army against de Gaulle, it began taking more realistic stock of the situation. The change which Europeans saw could not but fill them with foreboding. In the first place, there was the widespread belief that, as a consequence of de Gaulle's and metropolitan France's betrayal, they were about to be handed over to cut-throats and murderers. It seemed inconceivable to them that the French army contingent in Algeria should ever be reduced. There was the sudden fear that, in an independent Algeria, they might be transformed from a privileged minority into a persecuted one. General de Gaulle attempted to explain, in speech after speech, that the Europeans alone did not represent Algeria, that their presence on Algerian soil—in some cases for five of six generations—could not block the rights and aspirations of an Algerian majority.[2]

As France gradually emerged from its own nationalist fog, and as the Europeans themselves woke up to imminent change ahead, the question of the future of Algeria's European community began to preoccupy French officials for the first time.

In Tunis the F.L.N. had defined its policy as far back as 1959. Broadly speaking, the F.L.N. did not wish for a massive European exodus, though there was a strong feeling that it would be necessary to seek the departure of a minority of Frenchmen. As Ramdane Abbane once said, reflecting the feelings of the F.L.N. as a whole: "Que les patrons de bistrots s'en aillent." But the F.L.N. claimed that it had no objections to key jobs, including administrative posts, remaining in the hands of Europeans until Algerians were sufficiently trained to take over. This transition

---

[1] This was the theme of a number of de Gaulle's speeches during his visit to Algeria in December 1960. At Tlemcen, for instance, de Gaulle said: "Algériens, l'avenir est entre vos mains, l'Algérie est à vous—à vous tous autant que vous êtes. Et puisque la communauté musulmane, algérienne, est ici la plus nombreuse, je lui dis, à cette communauté musulmane, que c'est à elle qu'il appartient d'assumer les responsabilités qui correspondent à sa valeur et à son importance . . ."

[2] See de Gaulle's address to French officers at Blida on December 9, 1960—Appendix B

period varied from one F.L.N. leader to another, but in any case went from three years to a generation.

For the permanently residing European minority, the F.L.N. proposed two alternatives: Algerian nationality or the retention of French nationality. Those Europeans who chose to remain French would be granted a special statute by charter. Those opting for Algerian nationality would be granted full political rights—including the right to form a political party, of being elected to parliament, of holding government office—"A solution", as one F.L.N. leader told me, "comparable to that of Lebanon or Cyprus."

On paper this offer looked attractive, even surprisingly liberal, but—understandably—it failed to allay the fears of the one million European minority. In the first place, the F.L.N. adopted an unrealistic attitude towards Algeria's 130,000 European Jewish minority, which considered itself as French as any of Algeria's other European residents. In doctrinaire fashion, F.L.N. leaders in Tunis maintained that all of Algeria's Jews should be regarded as Algerians.

In the second place, the alternative devised by the F.L.N. did not make any specific mention of guarantees. "The guarantee of the Algerian government," said one F.L.N. spokesman in Tunis, "should be good enough." While it was perfectly true that a large number of the European community in Algeria was rooted in Algerian soil and might adopt Algerian citizenship if this was the price to pay for remaining in Algeria, the overriding fear of Algeria's European community was that it would become a helpless minority—rather like the Arab minority in present-day Israel—and that though on paper democratic safeguards might appear to exist (in the form of local and national representation), in fact it might eventually not only be despoiled of its property but also be completely cut off from France—be refused, for example, permission to return to France (hence the pathetic rush on passport applications in 1961 from a large number of Europeans in Algeria who had not previously left the country, "to prove", as one of them said to me, "if need be, that we are French").

Even Algeria's most "liberal" Europeans required something more substantial in the way of guarantees. It was suggested[1] that Frenchmen in Algeria might be given some modified form of double citizenship, or, failing that, certain specific guarantees (including special courts for all non-criminal jurisdiction and guarantees against eventual economic discrimination), or even the status of "privileged foreigners" under diplomatic protection. From talks with F.L.N. leaders it seemed unlikely that they would agree to anything which would perpetuate European privileges in any form—in which case the exodus of Europeans from Algeria cannot fail to be massive, affecting perhaps as much as half the total European population. But F.L.N. leaders, as time goes on, may well be led to modify their somewhat intransigent attitude, if only to prevent economic disruption. And the French Government knows it holds a trump card: the presence, on French soil, of several hundred thousand Algerians whose savings help to keep alive over two million people in Algeria. One may deplore the fact that both on the French and on the F.L.N. side, such minorities should be used as pawns in the game of power politics. But such cold-bloodedness is preferable to the chaos which would follow the massive exodus of Europeans from Algeria to France and the systematic repatriation of Algerians to Algeria.

(2) *The F.L.N. on the Eve of Independence*

The "Battle of Algiers" and the subsequent French military "barrages" along first the Tunisian, then the Moroccan, borders ended all hopes that the F.L.N. might have entertained of achieving independence speedily and through a constant progression of "revolutionary forces" in the Algerian population as a whole. Leaders like Ramdane Abbane—who had put their faith in a "dynamic" revolution on the Vietminh pattern, in which all classes of society would gradually play their part, and in which the "National Army of Liberation" would grow naturally from a minority guerilla force into a nation-wide army, saw their

[1] Club Jean Moulin—*Les Garanties de la Minorité en Algérie* (February 1961).

dreams shattered: not one of the F.L.N.'s leaders, in 1956 and early 1957, could have predicted that France would sustain its military effort and keep half a million men engaged in "pacification"; it had under-estimated both the economic capacity of France to do so and the favourable weight of French public opinion.

France's unexpected military effort in Algeria began bearing fruit in the middle of 1958: for the F.L.N., the May 13 "revolution", including reports of "fraternisation", mattered less than the continuous military operations which, by the end of 1958, had resulted in serious defeats in the field: the scattering and disorganisation of guerilla troops, and the interruption in the chain of command, through the C.C.E. and the "Wilayas", which had been so painstakingly set up in 1956. The year 1958 was a bad one all round for the F.L.N.: its leaders were aware that in Algeria itself, morale had seriously dropped as a result of F.L.N. failures. At first, F.L.N. leaders in Tunis under-estimated the efficiency of the "Morice Line". Along the Tunisian border confusion reigned among the F.L.N. units settling into a period of enforced inactivity, and several minor mutinies broke out.

As time went on, and as it became increasingly apparent that independence would only come after a long-drawn-out struggle, the crumbling of F.L.N. organisation inside Algeria was to a certain extent compensated by the establishment, in Tunis, of a well-organised, indeed bureaucratic, administrative system: as a reply to the May 13 "revolution", the F.L.N.'s executive committee decided to set itself up as a full-blown government, and in September 1958 the "Gouvernement Provisoire de la Republique Algérienne" (G.P.R.A.) was created which superseded the "Comité de Coordination et d'Exécution". It was immediately recognised by Tunisia, Communist China, Pakistan, Morocco, the United Arab Republic, the Sudan and Iraq, and later by Guinea, Ghana, Liberia, Ethiopia and Mali (ex-French Sudan). The Soviet Union and Yugoslavia, without formally recognising the G.P.R.A., announced their "de facto" recognition in 1959 and 1960.

The "ministries" and services of the G.P.R.A. in 1958, were

unobtrusively scattered throughout Tunis and bore the stamp of the F.L.N.'s revolutionary, clandestine character. By the end of 1960, however, this was no longer the case: the F.L.N. had accredited ambassadors in all the countries which had recognised it as Algeria's valid government, and maintained unofficial "representatives" in several capitals which had not done so; it had also moved into impressive ministry buildings, of which unquestionably the most important was the ministry dealing with communications and armaments, headed by Abdul Hafid Boussouf. This ministry building—a solid three-storey affair in the centre of the residential quarter of Tunis, the Belvedere, had become, by 1960, the nerve-centre of the F.L.N. It was the only building over which armed F.L.N. security men mounted permanent guard; it housed some of the F.L.N.'s most costly radio equipment, and its officials bore the stamp of their chief—an austere, dedicated revolutionary leader with remarkable organising talent and a ruthless devotion to the F.L.N. cause. The story of the growth of the F.L.N. "government" between 1958 and 1960 was largely the story of Boussouf's own rise to power.

Boussouf, who proudly claims to have been an Algerian nationalist since the age of fifteen, was given the command of the Oranais "Wilaya" in 1956, and by 1957 had become communications chief in the C.C.E. His first public appearance was at a conference in Tangiers attended by the Moroccan Istiq-lal, the Tunisian Neo-Destour and the Algerian F.L.N. parties to decide on common policy. He first struck those journalists who met him there as a self-assured, ruthless and violently anti-French revolutionary leader, openly boasting of his military successes in the Oranais and of the fact that he was going to return to the maquis to kill more Frenchmen. Boussouf did not return to the "maquis" but moved to Tunis, and—for a spell—to Cairo. An ambitious man, Boussouf had realised, from the first, the importance of good communications in the kind of guerilla warfare the F.L.N. was waging. Gradually, as communications improved (thanks to costly long-range German-made radio equipment), Boussouf began acting, not merely as a channel of communication between the "forces of the interior" and the G.P.R.A., but as a selective and efficient policymaker. Gradually, it became Boussouf's prerogative to distribute, to the various ministries and services, all reports emanating from the F.L.N.'s emissaries abroad and from the guerilla army of the interior, withholding some and censoring others. He thus controlled not only communications, but information, and was able to shape it to his own taste. Simultaneously, he was put in charge of intelligence, and ran an effective counter-espionage organisation, whose main task was that of seeking out French intelligence agents (and there were many) who sought to infiltrate into the F.L.N. in Tunis. The same people who looked after counter-intelligence also kept a firm but discreet eye on the Algerians employed in various "ministries" and reported back on their loyalty. By 1960 Boussouf had devoted subordinates in a number of key posts in every single "G.P.R.A." organisation.

By 1960, besides communications and intelligence, Boussouf had become the leading military "co-ordinator": it was decided, in 1960, to establish a top-level military "triumvirate" within the G.P.R.A., and Boussouf became a member along with Lakhdar Ben Tobbal, the F.L.N.'s "Interior Minister", and Belkacem Krim, the F.L.N.'s "Foreign Minister". Since Krim spent most of his time in Cairo, and Ben Tobbal and Boussouf were close friends and men of the same type, Boussouf had no difficulty in achieving a predominant position within the "triumvirate", all the more so since Krim's deputy, Commandant Kassi (who held the rank of F.L.N. "Ambassador" in Tunis), was also a close friend and follower of Boussouf's as well as his brother-in-law. Finally, Boussouf also acquired, in 1959, overall responsibility for armaments and supplies. The commander-in-chief of the "Army of Liberation", with headquarters on the Tunisian-Algerian border, was also, from 1959 onwards, a "Boussouf" man—Boumeddiene, who had been Boussouf's second-in-command in the Oranais "Wilaya".

In Boussouf's hands, the F.L.N. "apparatus" gradually acquired other subjects of preoccupation than the actual waging of guerilla warfare in Algeria itself: it became apparent, to any observers in early 1961, that the well-armed, almost over-trained F.L.N. army (about 15,000 men) at the Algerian border but on the Tunisian side of the Morice Line was being kept in reserve, not for a big breakthrough, but as a disciplined force to enforce the F.L.N.'s authority once conditions had made it possible for the F.L.N. "government" to move back to Algiers. The F.L.N. leaders in Tunis in early 1961 had twin preoccupations. They wanted to retain their "governmental" status, and thus keep the by now isolated guerilla forces of the interior and the mass of pro-nationalist Algerians within Algeria under firm control. But they also sought to convene an Algerian "constituent assembly" which would supersede the wartime "Conseil National de la Révolution Algérienne" (C.N.R.A.) and grant Algeria both a constitution and a government. That this government would be an F.L.N. government the "G.P.R.A." had no doubt. But individually, its members, and the exiled members of the F.L.N. as a whole, recognised that the future of such a constituent assembly would reveal profound differences. The question of the European minority apart, there was plenty of scope for later divisions: most of the F.L.N. were former "M.T.L.D." men, whereas only a minority stemmed from Abbas's former "U.D.M.A."; there was the dormant rivalry between Kabyles and non-Kabyles; there was the realisation that in an independent Algeria, political and class differences might lead to serious clashes. The war-time "Front" managed to sink all apparent differences in a clearly established goal: in the ranks of the F.L.N. were to be found prosperous middle-class merchants, members of prominent land-owning families as well as socialists and openly marxist elements. For as long as the war continued, it became the principle of the G.P.R.A. never to think too far ahead: the G.P.R.A.'s "Finance Minister", Ahmed Francis, never produced a long-term economic blueprint of Algeria, and justified the absence of long-term planning on the grounds that a government-in-exile could not pretend to draft any such plans with the certainty of being able to put them into practice. "We will start thinking about Algeria's economy," one F.L.N. spokesman told me, "once we are back on Algerian soil." The only fundamental economic principle on which all the F.L.N. seemed agreed was the need for agrarian reform. In a newspaper interview in 1958, Boussouf had said: "We want to use the Algerian revolution to make Algeria a country with completely new structures. The big estates will be broken up... I have a cousin who owns several thousand hectares. He will not be allowed to keep them... Agrarian reform will be the principal objective of the new Algeria. We respect President Bourguiba for the help he has given us. But his methods are not ours. Circumstances are different." As another member of the G.P.R.A. put it to me, in 1961: "the rebellion had its roots in the under-privileged, exploited 'fellahin', and the 'fellah' was the backbone of the 'Army of Liberation'. It is inconceivable that the large estates—the very symbol of colonialism—should remain intact." But it seemed certain, right up to the start of formal negotiations with French government representatives, that the "G.P.R.A." had no clear notion of what it meant by "agrarian reform" beyond a vague inclination to do away with the huge estates held by a tiny minority of Frenchmen and large Moslem landowners.

Nor did the F.L.N., in Tunis, conceal the fact that its hold over the Algerians "of the interior" was tenuous: the nationalist riots in December 1960 proved that the F.L.N.—and particularly Ferhat Abbas—remained the symbol of hope for a vast majority of Algerians. But beyond this the F.L.N. leaders knew little about the evolution of eight million Algerians from 1957 onwards: sometimes their eagerness to learn of the state of Moslem public opinion inside Algeria was almost pathetic. Algerians from inside Algeria corresponded, through intermediaries in France, Italy and West Germany, with F.L.N. members in Tunisia. But detailed "intelligence reports" were rare and often inaccurate. There was a natural tendency, for every exiled Algerian F.L.N. member in Tunisia, to project his own image of a wartime Algeria rather than face facts. It was difficult, for example, to convey to F.L.N. leaders in Tunisia the extent of Algeria's economic transformation from 1957 onwards, or to make them realise that this transformation had affected the mentality of a large number of Algerians and made them—among other things—less receptive to revolutionary doctrines. It was difficult, too, to convey to Algerians engaged in a struggle for independence, but exiled for many years, the atmosphere of Algeria as it was after 1958: there was a tendency, among the members of the F.L.N. in Tunis, to think of Algeria in black-and-white, "image d'Epinal" terms: from 1958 onwards, Algerian nationalism inside Algeria had become tempered by a wily kind of resignation. No country is so fortunate as to possess a majority of heroes. It was one of the F.L.N.'s weaknesses, during the period immediately preceding the Évian negotiations, that it believed, and tried to get others to believe, that its struggle was a wholly idealistic, wholly pure struggle: one was reminded, reading the F.L.N.'s official weekly, "*El Moujahid*" (the Freedom Fighter) and being subjected to F.L.N. propaganda, of a Soviet-made film of the Stalin era. Not only did the F.L.N. ignore the many compromises which nearly all Algerians living in Algeria were forced to make during the rebellion, but it ignored, too, the passivity of the Algerian masses and their growing distrust of all forms of propaganda if and when the F.L.N. does become Algeria's first legal independent government, the gulf between the idealised image of exiled revolutionaries and reality will suddenly become apparent, and this too may be a source of discord among Algerians, whether as members of a "constituent assembly" or of a future government: difficulties of a similar kind confronted France on the eve of victory in the Second World War: then General de Gaulle's Free French forces, the communist and anti-communist "maquis" of the interior, the "*résistants de la dernière heure*" and the "*attentistes*" all threatened French unity and stability. Stability of a kind was achieved, partly because the French communists agreed to cooperate with General de Gaulle, partly because General de Gaulle himself was a figure around which the immense majority of Frenchmen, whatever their previous attitudes, could rally, partly because France possessed a strong national tradition. Algeria lacks these advantages. It remains to be seen whether it can achieve its "reconversion" from revolution to independence while disappointing those Frenchmen who claim that independence will mean not only economic but political chaos.

(3) *Algerian Nationalism and Communism*

Foremost in the preoccupations both of Frenchmen and of the outside world has been the question: to what extent was the Algerian rebellion fostered, encouraged and secretly directed by the communist bloc, and to what extent are its leaders under the influence of communist doctrine?

The answer is not easy. For the protagonists of "revolutionary warfare", for nationalist politicians like Messrs. Soustelle, Bidault and Duchet, the answer is devastatingly simple: the F.L.N. leaders *are* communists, or if not openly party members, at least communism's effective and secret agents. If one is to believe a pamphlet put out by M. Soustelle's lobby, the *"Centre d'Information pour les problèmes de l'Algèrie et du Sahara"* (Number 13, special "referendum" issue, dated December 29, 1960) "The rebellion of November 1, 1954, was entirely planned and prepared in Cairo, with the support of international communism." Such bold, bald statements are apt to fall a little flat, even when their purpose is to aim at the lowest "common denominator" in French public opinion. Most Frenchmen by now have some dim awareness that Cairo is not Moscow, that Gamal Abdel Nasser is not Stalin, and that Egypt's feud with General Kassem's Iraq is partly based on Egyptian fears that Iraq may be leaning too heavily on the Soviet Union.

The reasons which finally caused Algerian discontent to spark off an armed rebellion, it may be recalled, stemmed from a variety of grievances, not the least being disillusion at French "immobilisme" and the feeling that traditional political action was doomed to failure. Far from being under Moscow's, or under Nasser's, thumbs the original F.L.N. leaders operated in total, demoralising isolation. It is certain that they would have welcomed advice and material support, whatever its origin, in the earliest days of their struggle. It is equally certain that beyond some bombastic Egyptian broadcasts and a favourable Middle Eastern press they received no immediate effective backing from any outside power. It is common enough to discredit an opponent by accusing him of communism; French accusations directed at Algerian nationalists lose some of their force when it is remembered that exactly the same charges were made against the Tunisian Neo-Destour and Moroccan Istiq-lal leaders before Tunisian and Moroccan independence. Then, the clandestine structure of Istiq-lal and Neo-Destour "cells" was compared to the structure of communist parties, while it was only too obvious that the reason for such a structure lay in French intransigence which, by denying Tunisian and Moroccan nationalist movements any legal status, forced them into an underground mould.

All this could be true and the allegation yet retain some validity, for much has happened in the space of seven years. What started as an authentic Algerian nationalist movement could, over the course of time, have compromised itself hopelessly with communism. In the case of the F.L.N., such allegations deserve serious consideration. After all, F.L.N. leaders have made two trips to Communist China in the last two years, and their "provisional Government-in-exile" is recognised by nearly all members of the communist bloc; one of the chief reasons for General de Gaulle's reluctance in dealing with F.L.N. leaders directly to end the war stemmed from the feeling ("amounting," said one of de Gaulle's close aides, "almost to an obsession") that F.L.N. leaders were, by 1961, already so hopelessly compromised.

To trace the extent of communist influence behind the rebellion, one should recall that, prior to the rebellion, a small but well-organised Algerian Communist Party (some of whose leaders were Moslem, but most of whose rank and file were European) had a legal if troubled existence of its own. The suburbs of Bab el Oued and Belcourt, in Algiers, were, immediately after the Second World War, unmistakably "red"; the large Spanish element in Algiers and Oran had unquestioned sympathy for the Spanish republicans, and provided the core of European communist membership. At one stage of its chequered history, Messali Hadj's "Etoile Nord Africaine" became linked with the Communist Party and Messali Hadj himself had received part of his political training in the tough communist trade union cadres school in France.

But the pre-rebellion Algerian Communist Party, like the Algerian branch of the communist-led "Confédération Générale du Travail" (C.G.T.), itself suffered from the uneasy co-existence of Europeans and Moslems. Moslems found that even within a C.G.T. trade union branch, even with the Algerian Communist Party itself, relations between the two communities were not devoid of "racism". When the rebellion began, and when, through urban terrorism, it began to be noticeable in the towns, Algeria's communist membership dropped staggeringly. A few European communists, like Henri Alleg, the imprisoned former editor of the banned communist paper "*Alger Républicain*", threw themselves heart and soul into the struggle, losing their identity as Frenchmen, Europeans and communists in common cause with the F.L.N. But they provided only a minority: far more European communists living in Belcourt and Bab el Oued became, almost overnight, the fervent and vociferous allies of their more wealthy "Algérie Française" fellow-settlers. In France, the central committee of the French Communist Party adopted an ambiguous attitude towards the rebellion. As usual, the aims of the French Communist Party looked beyond the immediate Algerian conflict to long-term world policy: as far as Moscow was concerned, it was far more important to detach France from the Atlantic Alliance and loosen her ties with West Germany than it was to provide Algerian nationalists with moral or material support. Nor could communist leaders remain insensitive to the nationalist wave which, sweeping over France in 1956 and 1957, did not spare the rank and file of the Communist Party. Though there were some communist-fomented demonstrations in some barracks when the French Government first decided to send conscripts to Algeria, these never threatened to interfere seriously with France's "war effort" in Algeria; and a paratrooper colonel openly boasted to me, in 1957, that "on arrival in my regiment, nearly half my conscripts were communists". (Skilful French army indoctrination, the sense of belonging to an élite corps, the thrill of adventure all contributed to turn communist conscripts into enthusiastic paratroopers.) Only on one occasion did French communists in uniform directly and openly aid the rebel cause, and the circumstances of this aid are in themselves revealing.

In April 1956, a young French communist, Henri Maillot, called up in the French army with the rank of "aspirant" (second lieutenant) managed to steal an army truckload of 145 sub-machine-guns, which he intended to hand over to a communist "maquis" operating somewhere in Bainem forest near Algiers. Another French "aspirant", Lucien Guerrab, also deserted to join this "maquis" which was led by an Algerian schoolteacher from Tlemcen, Abdelkader Guerroudj. But the weapons, intended by Maillot to arm the communist "maquis", were instead diverted to the F.L.N. All the communist "maquis" received were twenty-four weapons in a bad state of repair. After three months of waiting, followed by a minor skirmish, the "red maquis" was pinned down by French troops and almost entirely wiped out. The few survivors were to join F.L.N. guerilla units as individual sympathisers, without being given the opportunity of indoctrinating the men they were with. There is no doubt that the F.L.N. treated Maillot and the "red maquis" members shabbily, taking advantage of the weapons Maillot had stolen and giving nothing in return. (Some French army intelligence officers believe that the F.L.N. deliberately betrayed the "red maquis" to the authorities.) But the behaviour of the F.L.N. was consistent with its policy, laid down before the rebellion actually broke out, of accepting the help of individual communists while denying them any political role or separate organisation. In the same way, the F.L.N. was to benefit from the small network of European communists in Algeria who agreed to take part in the "battle of Algiers" in 1957, but looked askance—and may even have contributed to the capture of a number of known communist terrorists—when the latter began indulging in urban terrorism of their own.

significant that a little-known Algerian communist, Larbi Bouali, has been kept "in reserve" in Moscow by Soviet authorities. Questions of ideology apart, most F.L.N. leaders regard Bouali much as de Gaulle's active resistance members may have regarded a French political figure kept "in reserve" in New York during the Second World War—with suspicion and contempt.

However much the F.L.N. may have safeguarded itself from communist infiltration at the lower echelons of its organisation, fears that its leadership might become hopelessly compromised increased—with a certain amount of reason—from 1958 onwards. It was in 1958 that the F.L.N. intensified its diplomatic offensive, turning not only to Middle East nations but to the communist bloc as well. From 1958 onwards, a few members of the F.L.N.'s "Government in exile" became identified with communism and part of the large F.L.N. "exterior organisation" budget comes from funds provided not only by Middle Eastern countries but by the communist bloc. It became the fashion to separate the "hard" (i.e. pro-communist) G.P.R.A. members from the "soft" (i.e. basically pro-Western) members "as though", one F.L.N. leader once told me, "we were some kind of toffee". Such distinctions stemmed from a natural desire for simplification, but were largely devoid of meaning. No outsider has yet breached the secrecy of G.P.R.A. "cabinet" meetings, and to attribute pro-communist feelings to one or other of the G.P.R.A. "ministers" is to fail to take into consideration the various pressures to which they have been subjected in the last five years.

Since all G.P.R.A. decisions are arrived at in common, and the "collegial" rule scrupulously observed, the extent of communist influence should be reflected in the course of F.L.N. policy in the last few years. And seen in this light, the F.L.N. appears to act at most times as a free agent. Substantial communist aid was first seriously offered in 1959. After the failure of the Melun talks with General de Gaulle's emissaries, in June 1960, the F.L.N. went a considerable stage further in accepting such aid, and Ferhat Abbas took off on a trip to Peking where he was given the treatment normally reserved for a friendly and important chief of state; aid agreements—including arrangements for the despatch of up-to-date ground equipment, mostly recoilless artillery and rockets—were completed; the Communist Chinese Government even wished to furnish the F.L.N. with the embryo of an air force, and offered to train and equip Algerian flyers; some arms consignments (from the communist bloc but not from China) started arriving in Morocco in the latter half of 1960; and the G.P.R.A. was faced with the alternative of accepting Chinese aid—with all the consequences of an aggravation in the cold war which such a decision would entail—or of witnessing the constant depletion in their guerilla forces in Algeria itself. (With the electrification of the Morice Line on the Tunisian frontier and the construction of an effective barrage along the Moroccan border few arms got through to the rebels inside Algeria in 1960, and French Intelligence authorities estimated the total arms strength of the F.L.N. in Algeria at 8,000 rifles and automatics.)

That the G.P.R.A. held out successfully against tempting offers of large-scale Chinese aid was due primarily to Tunisia's President Habib Bourguiba. Despite the failure of Melun, Bourguiba believed that General de Gaulle's genuine desire to put an end to the Algerian war would, sooner or later, overcome his unwillingness to deal directly with the Algerian rebels, but that direct negotiations would be hopelessly compromised if Algeria became an effective battleground in the cold war. Several times G.P.R.A. leaders called on Bourguiba to announce their decision to take up communist aid offers. Each time, Bourguiba asked them: "Do you really need this aid, here and now, in order to survive?" On each occasion, the F.L.N. leaders admitted that while such aid would be precious, it could be postponed. From postponement to postponement, the disappointments of Melun gradually lost their sting, and—with de Gaulle's specific reference to a future "Algerian republic"—F.L.N. leaders gradually reversed their earlier decision to turn their backs once and for all on direct negotiations and seek, instead, the arbitrage of the United Nations. Bourguiba's position was a delicate one: he could not openly oppose any F.L.N. decision to take advantage of communist aid:

despite his enormous personal prestige in Tunisia, he would be
cutting clear across Tunisian public opinion, which identified the
F.L.N. struggle with its own, and in any case he lacked the troops
to counter such a move if the F.L.N. decided to secure such aid
by force. On the other hand, he realised that should Algeria
become a new pawn in the cold war, his own small country
would almost certainly go under. These preoccupations led him
to become intensely suspicious of Soviet motives in Algeria, and
to denounce, to the F.L.N. leaders, any Soviet attempts to meddle
in Algerian affairs. When, as a preliminary to the February 1961
de Gaulle–Bourguiba meeting, Bourguiba's information minister,
Mohammed Masmoudi, came to Paris to meet de Gaulle and
other political personalities, he called on Soviet Ambassador
Sergei Vinogradov and bluntly asked him: "Will you try to
sabotage our attempts to arrange for direct negotiations between
the F.L.N. and France?" The Soviet Ambassador denied that the
Soviet Union had any such intentions, but in Rabat, where Soviet
diplomatic activity was less restrained, a Soviet-inspired "whisper-
ing campaign" against direct negotiations had got under way.
To a large extent, F.L.N. suspicions of Soviet and Chinese motives
were inculcated by Bourguiba, who pointed out that Soviet
support of de Gaulle immediately after the latter had returned to
power had stemmed not from a sentimental respect of the man
himself, but from the hope that he would put into practice the
isolationist, "anti-European" policy he had advocated at the time
of the negotiations and failure of the European Defence Community Treaty.

Paradoxically, the F.L.N.'s closest links with communism may
well stem from the activities of the one F.L.N. organisation which
is avowedly non-communist, the F.L.N.'s "Union Générale des
Travailleurs Algériens" (U.G.T.A.), a trade union which is a
member of the anti-communist I.C.F.T.U.[1] The U.G.T.A., which
had acquired a solid following in Algiers and Oran in the first few
months of the rebellion, was banned by French authorities in
1956. Its leader, Aïssat Idir, arrested and ill-treated by French

---

[1] International Confederation of Free Trade Unions.

paratroopers, then released by a military court which could find
no grounds for sentencing him, then promptly rearrested under
the Algerian emergency regulations, eventually died in an Algiers
Military Hospital of burns (which, French authorities maintained,
were self-inflicted). U.G.T.A. headquarters, established in a small
shabby office in Tunis, had clandestine links with Algerian workers
in Algeria and in France. But by far its most important function is
the operation of a kind of employment and education agency for
Algerians in exile. From the tens of thousands of young able-
bodied Algerian refugees in Tunisia the U.G.T.A. selected
several hundred for theoretical and practical trade union training.
From the beginning of the "battle of Algiers" until 1958 the
U.G.T.A. leaders attempted to place their candidates for training
courses in Western countries outside France with the help of
Western non-communist unions. Alone of West European
countries, West German trade unions accepted a few Algerians,
but mostly those unions approached responded with a blank
refusal. From May 1958 onwards the U.G.T.A. started approaching communist bloc countries, and the response was understandably enthusiastic. By 1962 it is estimated that at least one
thousand Algerians will have received some kind of professional
and trade union organisation training, mostly in East Germany,
Hungary, Czechoslovakia and other satellite countries, though
none have actually been sent to the Soviet Union or China. The
U.G.T.A. offices in Tunis are decorated with the familiar emblems
of Soviet and Chinese achievements—Russian model sputniks
and luniks and Chinese "souvenirs" from factory tours. The
U.G.T.A. leaders are almost pathetically anxious to convince
visitors that their choice of communist bloc countries was dictated by necessity, and the refusal of almost all western unions to
take the slightest interest in them.

To what extent the beneficiaries of scholarships and courses in
satellite countries will be marked by political indoctrination
depends, to a large extent, on the duration of the Algerian war:
for those who graduate from such courses do not return to Tunis
(where the U.G.T.A. fears they might be called up to serve

in the F.L.N.) or France or Algeria (where they would face arrest), but stay on in the country in which they received their training. Hundreds of Algerians, having gone through a technical and trade union organisation course, are working in satellite countries in factories, post offices, hospitals, public transport systems and the like. The U.G.T.A. aim is to train as many Algerians as possible to step into essential jobs should Europeans leave Algeria in large numbers. The training received may be rough-and-ready (no course lasts for more than six months) but experience is gained after schooling ends in the kind of job for which the candidate has been trained. U.G.T.A. leaders claim that Algerians behind the Iron Curtain avoid the systematic communist indoctrination with which they are forcibly provided, but it is obvious that the longer they remain in a satellite country, the greater they run the danger of being deeply marked by communist influence. The prospect is a frightening one, for it is from the ranks of the U.G.T.A. that Algeria's future leaders will almost certainly be drawn. Surprisingly, it is this aspect of a possible communist threat which French authorities know or care least about. Perhaps—once the "Algerian Republic" is a reality—the trend could to a certain extent be reversed by opening up western technical and training centres to suitably qualified Algerian candidates, and by sponsoring scholarships and training courses in which the communist bloc countries now enjoy a virtual monopoly. Even if relations between France and a future independent Algeria are good, the need for technically trained Algerians in industry and agriculture will remain great. The alternative—a communist-trained youthful élite reaching positions of key political responsibility in·about ten years' time—will almost inevitably result in the sovietisation of Algeria long after the war has ended and been forgotten.

(4) *"Atrocities", "Excesses", "Reprisals"*

France's allies and neighbours, as well as the French Government itself, watched uneasily as the lengthening rebellion threatened to turn Algeria into a pawn in the cold war. From 1959 onwards the free world acquired another anxiety: that France, in her attempt to win the war in Algeria, would forfeit her claim as a truly civilised nation. Stories gradually spread, of the most grue-some kind, telling of widespread and wanton destruction of villages, of the use of napalm, of torture as a routine method of interrogation. As in all wars, no one side could claim total inno-cence, and French newspapers meanwhile carried daily reports of Algerian Moslems butchered by other Moslems, of summary executions of recalcitrant villagers by guerilla leaders, of indis-criminate terrorism. In France alone some 15,000 Algerian Moslems were killed over the course of the rebellion in various "règlements de comptes", mostly gang warfare of F.L.N. versus the minority M.N.A. movement (more powerful in France than in Algeria). The F.L.N.'s "tax-gathering" system lent itself to racketeering: in Paris Corsican racketeers who had long con-trolled prostitution in Montmartre found their preserve invaded by Algerian gangs and were forced to beat a hasty retreat to less lucrative Montparnasse; in Nanterre, in certain parts of the 18th, 19th and 20th "arrondissements" of Paris itself, crime statistics shot up as a result of Algerian violence.

That all "civilised" armed forces—including the French armed forces—were capable of savage and occasionally revolting be-haviour had been proved long before the Algerian rebellion began: on my first North African assignment, in Tunisia in 1952, I followed the progress of a Foreign Legion unit through the Cape Bon area with fascinated horror: from village to village it left a trail of smashed and wantonly wrecked shops and houses, and all the evidence of a successful "ratissage": men summarily executed or severely injured, raped women, a population left in a dazed, hysterical condition. These scenes had been witnessed again in Morocco, particularly in the "bidonvilles" of Port Lyautey and Casablanca. But in Tunisia and Morocco the beatings and the brutalities of police officials and military personnel were sporadic and usually, in the long run, denounced. It was not until the Algerian rebellion spread that police and army brutality became a

permanent and quietly efficient instrument, a weapon of war of
the same calibre as the grenade or the mortar-bomb.

One of the first accounts of indiscriminate army brutality came
in a semi-autobiographical novel, *"Lieutenant en Algérie"*, by the
editor of *l'Express*, Jean-Jacques Servan-Shreiber. Called up for a
six-month spell in Algeria, Servan-Shreiber served as a lieutenant
in an air force commando unit. Published in 1956, the book caused
a fearful scandal. Yet Servan-Shreiber did not use his experience
to denounce individual sadism so much as to draw attention to
the needless brutality caused by vast military operations which
struck blindly at innocent and guilty alike. No serving officer in
Algeria could deny that *"Lieutenant en Algérie"* was an accurate
description of the French army in Algeria in 1956. Military anger
at Servan-Shreiber stemmed from the fact that the shortcomings
of the French army had been exposed by a member of their own
class and caste (Servan-Shreiber, before turning to journalism,
had been a pupil of France's famed "École Polytechnique" which
forms the cream of France's engineers and army officers), one who
had, in addition, been given the "croix de la Valeur Militaire"
for bravery in the field. Servan-Shreiber's book came at a time
when French nationalism was at its height. Few of those who
attacked it so bitterly appeared to have read it carefully. Looking
back on *"Lieutenant en Algérie"* years later, one is struck by its
extreme moderation: little mention is made of torture, and it was
torture—rather than lives lost in indiscriminately conducted
military operations—which was, years later, to stun the French public and contribute towards a change in opinion, making a peaceful
settlement possible. Torture was part of the "vicious circle"
denounced by Germaine Tillon[1] and from 1956 onwards, it
became, in French army units—and especially in paratroop and
Foreign Legion battalions—a recognised instrument. The "battle
of Algiers" could not have been won by General Massu without
the use of torture; in the field, information divulged by prisoners
and suspects was also mostly acquired through torture. What
befell the communist leader Henri Alleg (described in his book

[1] See Chapter Nine.

"*La Question*") happened to tens of thousands of less articulate Algerian Moslems and to some Europeans as well; in the field, the "*gégêne*"—French army slang for the army field telephone which could be adapted to send violent shocks through a suspect's genitals—became a standard item of interrogating equipment. So widespread was its use, and so frequent the "accidents" which resulted from its too-extensive practice, that a number of French army officers sought, from their superiors, some kind of codified procedure so as to apply torture without endangering the life of the captive subjected to it, and General Massu—whose personal bravery has never been called into question—even had himself subjected to the "*gégêne*" to see what it was like, ignoring, of course, the key factor in torture: that apart from the pain and humiliation involved, its most frightful aspect lies in the uncertainty of its duration. General Massu knew that his sampling of the "*gégêne*" was a mere experiment, sandwiched in between a crowded daily programme, like an appointment with one's dentist. For those Algerians subjected to it in real life, the circumstances were entirely different: "*gégêne*" sessions could go on for hours, be interrupted for hours or days at a time, and be resumed at any moment.

Every army in the world has had its moment of shame: terrorism, as Laurence Durrell wrote in "*Bitter Lemons*", his account of the Cyprus emergency, "poisons the very air we breathe". In France a highly civilised tradition has existed for years side by side with a taste, almost a ritual, of violence: the beating-up, the "passage à tabac", of French suspects by the French police force has long been an almost hallowed tradition in France, and one which, seemingly, not even General de Gaulle can put a stop to. Nor of course have such moments of shame been confined to France: I remember, as a young subaltern, the questionable conduct of a number of otherwise perfectly respectable, hearty and terribly "English" officers and men of a well-known county regiment in the months following the end of the Second World War in Indonesia, where a nationalist movement, backed by guerilla warfare and terrorism, was momentarily checked by British and Indian troops. There are other examples, perhaps more relevant to the North African situation: the brutal behaviour of Tunisian police and troops towards dissident "Youssefist" opponents of Habib Bourguiba, in 1955 (during which time scores were shot out of hand and hundreds brutalised), the equally brutal repression of the dissident Riff tribesmen by the Moroccan army after independence. But it was in Algeria that torture was made to exist as a routine affair, helped by the establishment, in 1957, of various military "special police" units, such as the "Détachements Operationnels de Protection" (D.O.P.). The ranks of the D.O.P. were mostly filled by Arabic-speaking European settlers, mostly reservists, by paratroopers no longer fit for parachute duty, by former police officials, some of whom had spent all their lives in the Tunisian and Moroccan ex-protectorates, and by Moslems who had changed sides after taking part in the rebellion. The result on the Algerian population can be imagined: operating without the control of local military commanders, responsible only to a department of General Headquarters in Algiers, and used solely to seek out information otherwise not obtainable, they were responsible for an appalling amount of needless excesses. The emergency powers enabled them to operate with almost complete freedom. It was not until the very end of the rebellion, in 1961, that General de Gaulle—through his cabinet and by government decree—put a stop to arbitrary arrests and made civilian authorities responsible for judicial procedure in all but a few areas of Algeria.

It is easy to moralise from a comfortable position of neutrality: once terrorism reached its peak in Algeria, the questionable processes used by the French army became almost inevitable. And there must be some sympathy for those French officers confronted with a moral problem for which they were totally unprepared, and about which they received no guidance for so long: M. Lacoste, the Algerian Minister who ordered the paratroopers to put an end to terrorism "by any means", like Pontius Pilate preferred to ignore the consequences of his decision. The stock answer, given by General Massu to eminent Frenchmen who

visited Algiers and enquired into French excesses, consisted in
confronting them with the following problem: "There are twenty
high explosive bombs about to explode in the crowded streets of
Algiers. It is your task to prevent them from exploding and you
know that unless you can lay your hands on the bombs in the
next few hours the explosions will occur, with immense loss of
innocent European and Moslem lives. You know that a suspect,
presently in custody, knows where these bombs are stored. What
do you do? Do you allow a routine police enquiry to take place,
during which time the bombs will almost certainly explode, or
do you use limited and momentary violence on the prisoner to
get him to divulge the necessary information?" Such a problem
did, in fact, confront Massu's paratroopers more than once. But
this example could not be used to justify the systematic brutality
to which nearly all suspects were subjected. It comfortably ignored
the fact that for one genuine suspect, hundreds of innocents
suffered. It was used to justify torture on nationalists who had no
part in actual terrorism (the charge against Alleg was not that he
had taken part in terrorism but that he had hidden "wanted"
F.L.N. leaders). It also ignored the fact that in a few areas in
Algeria, a small number of senior French local commanders—and
by no means the least successful in the French army's fight against
the rebellion—managed to do their job without indulging in
torture at all. Neither did it explain the "disappearances" which
unaccountably followed, in a number of cases, close on earlier
arrests. Most direct mentions of questionable French army
methods, made by British or American correspondents, resulted
in an angry reference to America's treatment of the Indians in the
19th century and to British excesses against the Mau Mau in
Kenya. In most cases it was impossible to get a French army officer
to admit that such counter-charges were irrelevant, or that
British excesses in Kenya, by a few individual officers, had been
publicly and severely punished. If French military justice resulted
in convictions against the worst, most gratuitous offenders in the
ranks of the French army, such justice was secret and remarkably
lenient; it is impossible not to have the feeling that throughout

the rebellion, the French army protected those officers and men who indulged in gratuitous torture, and concealed them from the arm of the law. There can be little point in dwelling on an aspect of the rebellion (which had best be forgotten if relations between France and Algeria are ever to be restored on a normal friendly basis), and I would not have done so unless it had become, with the F.L.N., an important propaganda theme and in France an important moral issue. It enabled F.L.N. spokesmen in Tunis to charge that the French army was waging a "war of extermination on the Algerian people". It was used to justify a number of F.L.N. excesses and summary executions, as well as the continuance of indiscriminate terrorism. Finally, through various appeals—and particularly the "Manifeste des 121", an open letter signed by 121 French intellectuals stating that in the "unjust" Algerian war, French conscripts had the right to evade military service—widespread attention was given to the behaviour of certain French army units in Algeria. But by 1960 the harm had been done. The excesses of the "black and tans" in Ireland may have been forgotten, but their memory lingers on in the shape of certain emotional Irish attitudes towards Britain and all things English; in the same way there is the fear that Algerian memories will be conditioned for years to come, long after the rebellion has ended. Few guerilla wars have lasted as long, or cost as much in human lives, and a whole generation of Algerian youth has grown out of adolescence into manhood with no knowledge of France other than as an occupying power wielding its instruments of destruction.

Should any French polemist still maintain that French army excesses are a myth carefully entertained by communists and sentimental leftists, I would advise him to hire a small plane and fly at low altitude from Tizi Ouzou in Kabylia to the foot of the Djurdjura mountains, or from Djidjelli to El Milia: unless he is totally blind, he will find evidence enough to convince him that the "scorched earth" policy in Algeria, introduced by Marshal Bugeaud some 130 years ago, found some highly successful imitators from 1956 to 1960. I would ask him to count the number of totally destroyed villages on his course, in an area with a population density comparable to that of Belgium; any number of witnesses will testify to the constant activity of rocket—and occasionally napalm—carrying French Air Force planes between 1956 and 1960. As any French publisher will confirm, the Algerian rebellion has led to a spate of manuscripts written by ex-conscripts, mostly of doubtful literary value but all obviously seeking some kind of release in self-expression.

But, a French polemist will probably remark, why this emphasis on the French army's destructive capacity: what about the schools, the S.A.S. officers, the roads, the free medical care? No one seeks to deny that "pacification" had a positive side to it, and did not merely mean an endless succession of "ratissages" and rocket-strafing. I well remember accompanying, in 1959, a French Foreign Legion patrol into a Kabyle village which had, until recently, been an F.L.N. stronghold: a medical team was at work in a small hut, and free milk was being distributed to children. The inhabitants, one by one, were being screened and details of their families were being set down in a large register. A French captain in charge of "psychological warfare" was having his section stick up posters urging the villagers to "talk to save lives". Suddenly the clerk in charge of the register gave a cry of surprise, and said: "Did you know, there is a French woman living in this village." The excited psychological warfare officer rushed off, muttering, "We must make use of her, we must put her in charge, we must make her into a 'harkette'" (feminine of "harki", meaning Moslem military auxiliary). A disgruntled sergeant who had been in the village some days stopped him. "I've seen her," he said. "She's the worst of the lot. She is 100 per cent F.L.N. You'll be wasting your time." The French woman had married a Kabyle worker some twenty years previously, and returned with him from Northern France to his native village. This village, typical of certain parts of Kabylia, had no male population between the ages of eighteen and sixty. From the register which the clerk had been compiling, it was possible to estimate where most of the men had got to. One-third were in France, mostly working in factories in Marseilles, Lyons or Paris; one-third were in the F.L.N.; and one-third were dead, or, as the register euphemistically had it, "disparu". The French woman's husband was in the last category. Naturally, the remaining villagers did not spurn either the free milk for their children or the free medical aid provided by the Legion. Nor did the children stay away from French army school-teachers' classes. But it would take more than free milk, schooling and medical aid to erase the memories of the last few years. In some areas, where the systematic rationing of villages by French army officers had not taken place, particularly in the Oran area, something akin to peace and mutual friendship sprang up between certain Moslem villages and certain army units. But in Kabylia, as in the Aurès-Nementcha mountains and the frontier areas, the bitterness was bound to remain, even once the military operations and "excesses" had diminished, as they did diminish from 1960 onwards.

There was another factor which caused suffering and ill-feeling between the rural Algerian population and the French army between 1957 and 1959: the French army's at first haphazard, then methodically organised policy of "regrouping" parts of the rural population so that they should no longer be in contact with the F.L.N.'s guerilla bands. Some "regroupments" were undoubtedly prompted by some individual villages, whose leaders begged for army protection against the famished "maquisards" who came most nights to eat up the already meagre rations; but in most cases such "regroupments" were forced on the population, with occasionally hideous results: in south-western Algeria the French army brought thousands of semi-nomadic Algerian Moslems together in large camps, and made separate compounds for them and their cattle. Used to sleeping with their cattle for warmth in winter, and placed in unheated camps with inadequate food, thousands of nomads died during the harsh winter of 1957; in other areas local army commanders under-estimated the numbers of Algerians living in villages in their military sectors, and flushed out thousands more than they could cope with. Overcrowding in temporary camps, and something akin to mass starvation occurred in certain regroupment centres in 1957 and 1958. In a few cases carefully prepared quarters, electric light, water and essential services (including an S.A.S. and medical team) actually meant a form of social progress for the Algerians forced to move out of their insanitary villages. Social promotion, it could be argued, outweighed the disadvantages of uprooting a population from its traditional surroundings. But more often than not the regroupment centres prepared by the army were hastily and inadequately equipped and staffed. Shocked by reports sent back by a team of investigators, General de Gaulle's first representative in Algeria, Paul Delouvrier, put a stop to the indiscriminate "regroupment" policy, and launched a plan to establish, in the place of the regroupment centres, a thousand new villages. Towards the end of 1960 it was estimated that over a million and a half Algerians were living in regroupment centres, and according to a French official who dealt with the problem of the regroupment centres full-time, one-third of the centres were adequate and provided the villagers so regrouped with better living conditions than before; one-third were "adequate" and one-third downright unsatisfactory.[1]

If the main reason for "regrouping" part of Algeria's rural population was to prevent the rebels from making contact with the population, and of being fed or hidden, a subsidiary reason stemmed from the French army's insistence on the need for "forbidden zones" where they could shoot at sight at anything that moved. The theory of the "zones interdites" seems to have been drawn up by some elderly officer of the French War School with a nostalgia for the kind of war fought in 1918. It certainly ran counter to the theory, held simultaneously by French strategists in Algeria, that, following Mao Tse-tung's maxim, "the army should be among the population like fish in the water". The "zones interdites" gradually came to cover, on French army war maps, more and more space, and this extension naturally went

[1] General de Gaulle ordered the progressive disbandment of many such camps at the time of the Évian Conference, and in consequence several hundred thousand villagers were able to return to their homes.

hand in hand with the "regroupment" policy. In theory the system was meant to safeguard innocent Algerians from indiscriminate fire of French planes or troops. But in practice, as many French officers themselves admitted, "il y avait des bavures".

One of the results of the twin policies of "regroupment" and "zones interdites" was that, in many cases, the villagers in newly established regroupment centres were cut off from both their cattle and their fields or olive groves. I personally witnessed a sight, in 1958, of almost Brechtian quality: in a Kabyle regroupment centre the French tricolour flag was hoisted every morning and the entire population of the regroupment centre—about two thousand Algerians, mostly women and children—were made to stand at attention while the "Marseillaise" was played. A few miles away, in a "zone interdite", lay a large olive grove which had been the "regrouped" village's most important means of support. The olives lay rotting on the ground: the inhabitants of the regroupment centre were, through bureaucratic stupidity or a deliberate desire to punish or frustrate, forbidden from harvesting them.

The passive resistance of many Algerians to the French army's "regroupment" policy was pathetic but not particularly effective. When the abandoned villages had not been totally destroyed, some families crept back there to live, hiding at the approach of planes or troops; hundreds of families hid in caves; finally, a number of Algerians obtained permits to travel through "forbidden zones" and never returned. That such a system was doomed to failure and liable to various abuses should have been obvious from the start. French Air Force planes could not tell the difference between Moslems travelling with valid permits through a "forbidden zone" and a rebel band; in the course of routine strafing of "forbidden zones" (later euphemistically referred to as "*zones de controle militaire renforcé*") many lives were needlessly lost.

In short, partly because of the nature of all guerilla movements based on surprise and terrorism, partly because of the lack of clear guidance on the limits of force which should not, under any circumstances have been overstepped, and partly through a well-meaning desire to win over the Algerian Moslems by kindness, French forces in Algeria behaved unpredictably, like the drunken man in Chaplin's "City Lights" who beats up the little man when he is sober and covers him with embarrassing signs of affection when drunk. A "good" local commander could be followed by one who destroyed all the local Moslems' patiently-instilled confidence in one day's savage and indiscriminate reprisals. Algerians could never be certain whether a French army unit was intent on destruction or on spreading goodwill: the murder of a soldier or a civilian, an indiscriminate act of terrorism, an ambush, could turn a well-meaning army unit into a group of heavily armed men seeking indiscriminate vengeance. And it must be remembered that from 1957 until early 1961 the merest French army corporal enjoyed, in practice, almost unlimited power: Algerians arrested on suspicion could be detained practically indefinitely; until General de Gaulle's representative, Paul Delouvrier, managed to put a stop to it, the official government-run detention centres were supplemented by a number of unofficial centres organised and run by individual units; arrest apart, a French army soldier could make life difficult for an Algerian Moslem in a number of ways: the withdrawal of the Algerian's identity card, for instance, was tantamount to a prison sentence or worse, since any Moslems devoid of identity papers were assumed to be rebels; and S.A.S. officers could—and did—withhold rations from shops and families and even "freeze" money orders from France in certain circumstances. That such aspects of the rebellion were rarely realised in France was proved when the French author-soldier Jules Roy published "*La Guerre d'Algérie*" in late 1960, a personal, day-to-day account of a recent visit to Algeria in which he described the various injustices and excesses to which the rebellion had led: in the first six months after publication, the book sold close on 100,000 copies. For Algeria and for France, it would have been a good thing if such interest had come earlier.

But even as the rebellion moved into its seventh year, there were signs that all was not irreparably lost. During the nationalist riots of December 1960, sparked off by earlier "ultra" demonstrations against General de Gaulle's visit to Algeria, I watched an Algiers Kasbah mob cheer a company of tough French "*Compagnies Républicaines de Sécurité*", the highly disciplined security units which had been used to put down the European riots and had behaved impartially and firmly in the face of immense provocations. I asked a young Algerian why the C.R.S. troops were being cheered. "Parce qu'ils sont courtois avec nous," he replied. Another Moslem bystander implied, with a smile, that it was because the C.R.S. troops had—for the first time—put down the European riots with a fine impartiality. One of the highly comforting aspects of the Algerian riots, in December 1960, was that, though anti-"pied-noir", they were seldom anti-French. Despite all the horrors of the last seven years, the basic cultural, economic and social links between France and Algeria may yet be preserved.

APPENDIX A

IF I have put on my uniform today to address you on television, it is in order to show that it is General de Gaulle who speaks, as well as the Chief of State.

In Algeria we are fighting against a rebellion which has lasted more than five years. France is valiantly continuing to exert the necessary efforts to put down that rebellion.

But she wants to arrive at a peace that is peace; to do what has to be done so that the tragedy does not begin all over again; to act in such a way as not—when all is said and done—to lose Algeria, which would be a disaster for us and for the West. The world, a prey to vast crises and movements which are well known, is watching this struggle which disturbs it and in which the various opposing camps seek to take a hand. It is obvious that the unity, progress and prestige of the French people are at stake, and that the future of this people is blocked as long as the Algerian problem remains unsolved.

Taking all this into consideration, I, in the name of France, made the following decision: the Algerians shall have free choice of their destiny. When, one way or another—through the conclusion of a cease-fire or through total defeat of the rebels—we shall have put an end to the fighting, when later, after a prolonged period of restored peace, the populations will have had a chance to understand what is at stake and, moreover, thanks to us, to achieve the necessary progress in the political, economic, social, educational and other fields—then, it will be the Algerians who will say what they want to be. This will not be dictated to them. For if their response were not really *their* response, then while for a time there might well be military victory, basically nothing would be settled. On the contrary, everything can be settled and, I believe, settled in France's favour, when the Algerians will have had an opportunity to make known their will in all freedom, dignity and security. In short, self-determination is the only policy that is worthy of France. It is the only possible outcome. It is the policy which has been defined by the President of the Republic, decided upon by the Government, approved by the Parliament and adopted by the French nation.

Now then, there are two categories of people who do not want any part of this free choice.

First, the rebel organization, which maintains that it will cease fire only if I negotiate with it beforehand, by special prerogative, on the political destiny of Algeria, which would be tantamount to building it up as the only valid representative and to elevating it in advance to being the Government of the country. That I will not do.

On the other hand, some persons of French descent demand that I renounce the idea of self-determination, that I say that everything has been done and that the fate of the Algerians has already been decided. That I will not do either. Self-determination is the only means by which the Moslems can themselves cast out the demon of secession. As to the terms of this or that French solution, I mean to have them worked out at leisure, when peace has been restored. After which, I reserve the right to commit myself—when the right time comes—for whatever I shall consider good. You may be sure that I will do this thoroughly.

It was then that, trying to force their pretended claims on the nation, on the State and on myself, certain people in Algiers started an insurrection; it was then that they fired on the forces of law and order and killed fine soldiers, and they are now rising up in arms against the authority of France. Aided in the beginning by the accommodating uncertainty of various military elements, and profiting from the fears and feverish passions stirred up by agitators, they have thus far obtained the support of part of the European population; they have instigated a forced strike, the halting of transportation and the closing of shops. Because of them, there is danger that a disruption of the national unity may occur, to the indignation of the French nation and in the very midst of the struggle being waged against the rebels. There is not a man with any common sense who does not see what the inevitable consequences would be if this dreadful secession carried the day.

In face of the foul blow that has thus been struck against France, I speak first of all to the community of French descent in Algeria. This community has known me for many years. It has seen me many times in its midst, especially during the war, when its sons, in great numbers, were serving in the ranks of the Army of Liberation, or else when, following the upheaval of May 1958, I once again assumed leadership of France in order to rebuild the unity of Frenchmen on both shores of the Mediterranean. Whatever any agitators are trying to make this community believe, there are, between it and myself, very special ties that are very dear to me and very much alive. I know perfectly well what services this community renders France through its century of toil in Algeria, what cruel trials it is undergoing, what moving sorrow it has for the victims it mourns. But I must speak to this community in plain and unmistakable words.

Frenchmen of Algeria, how can you listen to the liars and the conspirators who tell you that in granting a free choice to the Algerians, France and de Gaulle want to abandon you, to pull out of Algeria and hand it over to the rebellion? Is it abandoning you, is it wanting to lose Algeria, to send there and to maintain there an army of 500,000 men equipped with tremendous amounts of material; to consent to the sacrifice there of a good many of our children; to pay out there, this very year, civil and military expenditures amounting to a thousand billion [old francs], to undertake there a tremendous programme of development; to draw from the Sahara, with great difficulty and at great expense, oil and gas in order to bring them to the sea?

How can you doubt that if, some day, the Moslems freely and formally decide that the Algeria of tomorrow must be closely united to France—how can you doubt that nothing would bring greater joy to our country and to de Gaulle than to see them choose, between one solution or another, the one that would be the most French? How can you deny that all the work for the development of the Moslem populations, which was initiated eighteen months ago, and is now still being pursued and which, after pacification, will have to be expanded yet more—how can you deny that this work tends precisely to create new and manifold ties between France and the Algerians? Above all else, how can you fail to see that, in rising up against the State and against the nation, you are surely heading towards ruin and at the same time you are running the risk of causing France to lose Algeria at the very moment when the decline of the rebellion is becoming evident? I solemnly appeal to you to return to law and order.

Next, I speak to the army, which, thanks to its magnificent efforts, is in the process of winning the victory in Algeria; however, some of the elements of this army might be tempted to think that this war is their war, not France's war, and that they have a right to a policy which would not be France's policy. To all our soldiers I say: in your mission there is no room for any equivocation or interpretation, you must liquidate the rebel force, which is seeking to drive France out of Algeria and to impose upon that land its dictatorship of want and sterility. At the same time that you are conducting the battle, you must contribute to the material and spiritual transformation of the Moslem populations so as to win their hearts and minds to France. When the time comes for the people to vote, it will be your responsibility to guarantee the complete freedom and sincerity of this vote.

Yes, that is your mission, as France gives it to you, and it is France that you serve. What would the French army become but an anarchic and absurd conglomeration of military feudalisms, if it should happen that certain elements made their loyalty conditional? As you know, I have the supreme responsibility. It is I who bear the country's destiny. I must therefore be obeyed by every French soldier. I believe that I shall be obeyed, because I know you, because I have a high regard for you, because I feel affection for you, because I have confidence in General Challe whom I have placed at your head, soldiers of Algeria, and finally, because I have need of you for France.

This having been said, listen to me carefully. In the presence of the insurrection in Algiers and in the midst of the agitation—bordering on a paroxism—the Delegate-General, M. Paul Delouvrier, who is France in Algeria, and the commander-in-chief may, on their own responsibility, not have wanted to give the signal themselves for a pitched battle, but no soldier, under penalty of being guilty of a serious fault, may associate himself at any time, even passively, with the insurrection. In the last analysis, law and order must be re-established. The methods to be employed so that law and order will prevail may be of various sorts. But your duty is to bring this about. I have given, and am giving, this order.

Finally, I speak to France. Well, my dear country, my old country, here we are together, once again, facing a harsh test. By virtue of the mandate that the people have given me and of the national legitimacy that I have embodied for twenty years, I ask all men and women to support me, no matter what happens.

And while the guilty ones, who dream of being usurpers, take as a pretext the decision that I have made concerning Algeria, let it be' known everywhere, let it be clearly understood, that I do not intend to go back on that decision. To yield on this point and under these conditions would be to destroy the trump cards that we still hold in Algeria, but it would also be to make the state bow before the outrage that is being inflicted on it and the threat that is aimed at it. Thus France would become but a poor broken toy adrift on the sea of hazards.

Once again, I call upon all Frenchmen, wherever they may be, whoever they may be, to reunite themselves to France.

Long live the Republic.

Long live France.

APPENDIX B

EXTRACTS FROM A SPEECH BY GENERAL DE GAULLE TO FRENCH OFFICERS AT BLIDA, ON DECEMBER 9, 1960

"THE work of France in Algeria must go on, and it is only too evident that it cannot go on under the conditions of yesterday. One may regret this, and you well realise that a man of my age and background may have his regrets at that which probably could have been done earlier and which was left undone . . .

"But when one assumes national responsibilities one must take the problem as a whole, as it is—and such as it is, it cannot be dealt with as in days gone by . . .

"From the fact of the insurrection itself, the population of this Algeria which is in the great majority Moslem, has acquired an awareness which it did not previously have. Nothing can stop this. It is also true that the insurrection, and all that is connected with it, is taking place in a new world, in a world which is not at all like the world I knew myself when I was young. There is—you are all aware of this— the whole context of emancipation which is sweeping the world from one end to another, which has swept over our Black Africa, which has swept, without exception, over all those which once were empires, and which cannot but have considerable consequences here . . ."

BIBLIOGRAPHY

ALLEG, Henri: La Question (Paris, Ed. de Minuit, 1958).

ANSKY, Michel: Les Juifs d'Algérie du Décret Crémieux à la Libération (Paris, Editions du Centre, 1950).

ARON, Raymond: La Tragédie Algérienne (Paris, Plon, 1957).
L'Algérie et la Rébellion (Paris, Plon, 1958).

BROMBERGER, Serge: Les Rébelles Algériens (Paris, Plon, 1958).

BROMBERGER, Serge et Merry: Les 13 Complots du 13 Mai (Paris, Fayard, 1958).

BROMBERGER, Serge et Merry, Georgette ELGEY et Jean-François CHAUVEL: Barricades et Colonels (Paris, Fayard, 1960).

BUGEAUD, Thomas-Robert: La Guerre d'Algérie (Paris, 1839).
Réflexions et Souvenirs Militaires (Paris, 1845.)

DÉON, Michel: L'Armée d'Algérie et la Pacification (Paris, Plon, 1959).

DUQUESNE, Jacques: L'Algérie ou la Guerre des Mythes (Paris, Ed. de Brouwer, 1958).

DUVIVIER, Franciade-Fleurus: Solution de la Question d'Afrique (Paris, 1845).

ESQUER, Gabriel: Histoire de l'Algérie (Paris, Presses Universitaires de France, 1951).

FAVROD, Charles-Henri: La Révolution Algérienne (Paris, Plon, 1958).

GIRARDET, Raoul: La Société Militaire dans la France Contemporaine (Paris, Plon, 1953).

JEANSON, Colette et Francis: L'Algérie hors la loi (Paris, Ed. du Seuil, 1955).

JULIEN, Charles-André: L'Afrique du Nord en Marche (Paris, Julliard, 1952).

LUETHY, Herbert: France against Herself (New York, Meridian Books, 1957).

MAZÉ, Pierre et Roger GENEBRIER: Les Grandes Journées du Procès de Riom (Paris, La Jeune Parque, 1945).

MITTERAND, François: Présence Française et Abandon (Paris, Plon, 1957).

MONTEIL, Vincent: Les Officiers (Paris, Ed. du Seuil, 1958).

NORA, Pierre: Les Français d'Algérie (Paris, Juilliard, 1961).

PLANCHAIS, Jean: Le Malaise de l'Armée (Paris, Plon, 1958).

ROY, Jules: La Guerre d'Algérie (Paris, Julliard, 1960).

SAINT-ARNAUD, Louis-Adolphe: Lettres du Maréchal de Saint-Arnaud (Paris, 1855).

SAVARY, Alain: Nationalisme Algérien et Grandeur Française (Paris, Plon, 1960).

SECRÉTARIAT SOCIAL D'ALGER: L'Algérie et sa Jeunesse (Ed. du Sec. Soc. d'Alger, Alger, 1958).

L' Algérie Surpeuplée.

DE SERIGNY, Alain: La Révolution du 13 Mai (Paris, Plon, 1958).

SERVAN-SCHREIBER, Jean-Jacques: Lieutenant en Algérie (Paris, Julliard, 1957).

SIMON, Pierre-Henri: Contre la Torture (Paris, Ed. du Seuil, 1957).

SOUSTELLE, Jacques: Aimée et Souffrante Algérie (Paris, Plon, 1956).

Le Drame Algérien et la Décadence Française (Paris, Plon, 1957).

TILLON, Germaine: L'Algérie en 1957 (Paris, Ed. de Minuit, 1957).

Les Ennemis Complémentaires (Paris, Ed. de Minuit, 1960).

TOURNOUX, J.-R.: Carnets Secrets de la Politique (Paris, Plon, 1958).

WAHL, Nicolas: The Fifth Republic, France's New Political System (New York, Random House, 1959).

PERIODICALS

Esprit, La Nef and *Les Temps Modernes* have consistently published valuable material about Algeria since 1954. *Foreign Affairs* (January 1961 issue) contains an excellent article by Jean-Marie Domenach.

The press and information division of the "Délégation Générale du Gouvernement en Algérie" has published detailed studies of Algeria's population growth, economic development and future needs. The annual reports of the "Constantine Plan" for Algerian industrialisation represent the most detailed and up-to-date examination made so far of Algeria's economic and social problems. The *Club Jean Moulin* has issued two controversial studies on the subject of Algeria's European minority.